SYNCHRONICITY

MIND AND NATURE by Gregory Bateson
THE MIND'S I by Douglas R. Hofstadter and Daniel C. Dennett
THE NEW STORY OF SCIENCE by Robert M. Augros and
    George N. Stanciu
ON HUMAN NATURE by Edward O. Wilson
ORDER OUT OF CHAOS by Ilya Prigogine and Isabelle Stengers
ORIGINS: A SKEPTIC'S GUIDE TO THE CREATION OF LIFE ON EARTH
    by Robert Shapiro
PERFECT SYMMETRY by Heinz R. Pagels
PROSPERING WOMAN by Ruth Ross
SHAMBHALA: THE SACRED PATH OF THE WARRIOR
    by Chogyam Trungpa
SPACE-TIME AND BEYOND (The New Edition) by Bob Toben and
    Fred Alan Wolf
SYNCHRONICITY: THE BRIDGE BETWEEN MATTER AND MIND
    by F. David Peat
SUPERMIND by Barbara B. Brown
SYMPATHETIC VIBRATIONS: REFLECTIONS ON PHYSICS AS A WAY OF
    LIFE by K. C. Cole
THE TAO OF LEADERSHIP by John Heider
THE TAO OF PHYSICS, Revised Edition, by Fritjof Capra
TO HAVE OR TO BE? by Eric Fromm
THE TURNING POINT by Fritjof Capra
THE WAY OF THE SHAMAN: A GUIDE TO POWER AND HEALING by
    Michael Harner
ZEN AND THE ART OF MOTORCYCLE MAINTENANCE by
    Robert M. Pirsig

SYNCHR

ONICITY

THE BRIDGE BETWEEN MATTER AND MIND

F. DAVID PEAT

BANTAM BOOKS

TORONTO · NEW YORK · LONDON · SYDNEY · AUCKLAND

SYNCHRONICITY: THE BRIDGE BETWEEN MATTER AND MIND

A Bantam Book / June 1987

New Age and the accompanying figure design as well as the statement "the search for meaning, growth, and change" are trademarks of Bantam Books, Inc.

Library of Congress Cataloging-in-Publication Data

Peat, F. David, 1938–
  Synchronicity : the bridge between matter and mind.

  "Bantam new age books"—P.
  Includes bibliographies.
  1. Coincidence.   I. Title.
BD595.P42   1987   116   86-47890
ISBN 0-553-34321-1

Published simultaneously in the United States and Canada

Bantam Books are published by Bantam Books, Inc. Its trademark, consisting of the words "Bantam Books" and the portrayal of a rooster, is Registered in U.S. Patent and Trademark Office and in other countries. Marca Registrada. Bantam Books, Inc., 666 Fifth Avenue, New York, New York 10103.

CONTENTS

Acknowledgments   ix

1. The Physicist and the Psychologist   1

2. The Mechanical Universe   35

3. The Living Universe   59

4. Patterns of Mind and Matter   85

5. Patterns in the Bone   113

6. Mind, Matter, and Information   148

7. The Creative Source   185

8. Time and Transformation   214

Index   242

ACKNOWLEDGMENTS

In a sense the origin of this book lies in a radio documentary for four voices, which I wrote back in 1974. For this I must thank the insight and creativity of the producer, Paul Buckley. As a result of this program, and the essay I wrote following it, I received further encouragement to pursue the notion of synchronicity from Arthur Koestler, Arnold Mindel, and M-L von Franz.

Over ten years later, during the writing of this book, I had a number of interesting discussions with Eduardo Casas, Sean Kelly, and Anthony Storr. I am also indebted to David Bohm for many conversations on the nature of reality and mind.

In researching the relationship between Jung and Pauli I was greatly assisted by several of Pauli's friends, colleagues, and biographers. They were particularly patient and helpful in replying to all my queries and letters.

Finally, in reaching this version of the manuscript I thank my agent, Adele Leone, and my editor, Tobi Sanders.

1 THE PHYSICIST AND THE PSYCHOLOGIST

Synchronicity: *Meaningful coincidence, significantly related patterns of chance.*[1]

Each of us is faced with a mystery. We are born into this universe, we grow up, work, play, fall in love, and at the ends of our lives, face death. Yet in the midst of all this activity we are constantly confronted by a series of overwhelming questions: What is the nature of the universe and what is our position in it? What does the universe mean? What is its purpose? Who are we and what is the meaning of our lives?

Science attempts to offer answers to these questions, for it has always been the province of the scientist to discover how the universe is constituted, how matter was first created, and how life began. Theories about the natural world can be particularly powerful in their predictive abilities and beautiful in their internal, abstract structuring. But nevertheless, scientific theories can never come to life of themselves, they must always remain what they are—theories, objective accounts of the world that must be set beside the immediacy of our personal experience and those rare flashes of insight that suggest a deeper reality lying beyond the world of appearances. Science may have uncovered the internal structure of the atom, studied the geometry of the DNA molecule, and probed the mysteries of the black hole, but what can it make of T. E. Lawrence's experience on traveling one early morning in the desert?

We started off on one of those clear dawns that wake up the senses with the sun. For an hour or so, on such a morning, the sounds, scents and colors of the world struck man individually and directly, not filtered through or made typical by thought.[2]

And can it shed light on Wordsworth's recollections of his childhood?

> There was a time when meadow, grove, and stream,
> The earth, and every common sight,
> To me did seem
> Appareled in celestial light,
> The glory and the freshness of a dream.[3]

On the one hand we have the immediacy and flavor of our lives, of poetry, music, art, and mysticism, and on the other the objective discoveries and explanations of science. On the one there is excitement, beauty, and wonder, and on the other the possibility that consciousness is an epiphenomenon of certain complex electrochemical reactions, that life is the product of random molecular processes, and the universe is an accident. There appears, therefore, to be an unbridgeable gap between the objective and the subjective approaches to the question of the universe and our role within it. There seems, at first sight, to be no way in which the theories of science can be spiced with the flavor of human experience or that a poetic insight can be transformed into the rigor of scientific objectivity. These two worlds appear to be simply too far apart.

It is, however, the argument of this book that a bridge can indeed be built between interior and exterior worlds and that synchronicity provides us with a starting point, for it represents a tiny flaw in the fabric of all that we have hitherto taken for reality. Synchronicities give us a glimpse beyond our conventional notions of time and causality into the immense patterns of nature, the underlying dance which connects all things and the mirror which is suspended between inner and outer universes. With synchronicity as our starting point, it becomes possible to begin the construction of a bridge that spans the worlds of mind and matter, physics and psyche.

THE REALITIES OF NATURE

To view the world in terms of patterns and interconnections of individual events would not have appeared strange to the inhabitants of the Middle Ages or, for that matter, ancient China. The Bayeux Tapestry, which relates the Norman Conquest of England in 1066, heralds this dramatic invasion with the appearance of a new comet in the sky. And so the crowning of kings, outbreaks of war or disease, and the birth of famous men was always accompanied by a variety of natural portents. According to such a worldview there are affinities between apparently different things and sympathies that act between body, soul, and the outer world. Indeed all of nature was considered to be a single, giant organism in which each person had his or her own place. To become part of this harmony of the universe was the key to right action and bred a form of knowledge which was never separate from subjective values and beliefs.

With the rise of science, however, the universe was found to be describable in other ways. Heavenly and earthly matter were no longer of different orders, for both could be subsumed under Newton's law of universal gravitation. In place of mysterious affinities and sympathies was the scientific concept of force which could be accurately quantified and mathematically related to changes in motion. Anatomy and an understanding of the circulation of the blood replaced humors and astrological correspondences and eventually led to such medical insights as the germ theory of disease, vaccination, and a host of modern drugs. Science, assisted by mathematics, was able to describe the universe in quantative terms that had impressive predictive power. Using the scientific approach, any phenomenon could be isolated and analyzed under repeatable conditions until even the most complex of processes were reduced to a collection of known elementary units acting predictably as a result of the forces between them.

At its height, toward the end of the nineteenth century, Newtonian mechanics had become the model for all other sciences, and the great Lord Kelvin, addressing the Royal

Society of England, argued that physics was nearing its end, an end in which all phenomena would be explicable in terms of a handful of physical laws, with the more complex fields of biology and chemistry reduced in principle to the certainty of physics. For Lord Kelvin, the universe had been transformed from a living organism into something that was much closer to a machine, a machine albeit of immense ingenuity in its construction and operation but nonetheless mechanical, in that its behavior could be reduced to the operation of parts in motion, each obeying a few basic laws. Within such a machine, however, there is little room for values and meaning or for the inner facts of experience and revelation. And even human nature could be apparently reduced to the functioning of the instincts and repressions, which, in turn, had their origins as flows of energy arising in electrochemical reactions of the nervous system.

Quantum theory and relativity had a revolutionary effect upon this Newtonian approach, not only in transforming the formalism of physics but also in changing the worldview that was associated with it. Neils Bohr, for example, stressed that quantum theory had revealed the essential indivisibility of nature while Heisenberg's uncertainty principle indicated the extent to which an observer intervenes in the system he observes. A contemporary physicist, John Wheeler, has expressed this new approach in particularly graphic terms:

> We had this old idea, that there was a universe out there, and here is man, the observer, safely protected from the universe by a six-inch slab of plate glass. Now we learn from the quantum world that even to observe so minuscule an object as an electron we have to shatter that plate glass; we have to reach in there. . . . So the old word *observer* simply has to be crossed off the books, and we must put in the new word *participator*. In this way we've come to realize that the universe is a participatory universe.[4]

This participatory universe of Bohr and Heisenberg, this relativity of space and time, this interconnectedness of things, points to a very different worldview than that of Newtonian mechanism. Yet despite the important revolutions that have taken place within physics, old ways of thinking continue to dominate our relationship to nature. Time, we believe, is external to our lives and carries us along in its flow; causality rules the actions of nature with its iron hand and our "consensus reality" is restricted to the surface of things and seems closer to the rule-bound functioning of a machine than to the subtle adaptability of an organism. Even scientists themselves, who accept the formalism and mathematics of what has been called the "new physics," retain many of the attitudes of nineteenth-century science. Most believe, for example, in some form of objective reality that is external and independent of themselves. They look for *ultimate* particles and *elementary* entities out of which all nature is supposed to be built. They believe that the more complex fields of chemistry and biology can be reduced, in principle, to the laws of physics, and they consider consciousness to be an epiphenomenon of the physical brain. Paradoxically, scientists have not yet caught up with the deeper implications of their own subject.

The worldview that we have all inherited from an outmoded physics still has a profound effect on our whole lives; it permeates our attitudes to society, government, and human relationships and suggests that every adverse situation can be analyzed into an isolated "problem" with a corresponding solution or means of control. It is for such reasons that synchronicity can have such a profound effect on us, for it reaches beyond our intellectual defenses and shatters our faith in the tangibility of surfaces and the linear orders of time and nature.

SYNCHRONICITY

Consider the following chain of circumstances.

A young woman is visiting friends when suddenly everyone in the house smells a burnt-out candle. Despite a thorough search of the rooms no source for this smell can be found and it is certain that no candle had been lit in the house that day. Everyone is particularly puzzled by the event and speculates on what it may mean. Later the same evening the woman receives a transatlantic telephone call saying that her father is, unexpectedly, about to undergo an operation. A few weeks later her father dies and the woman flies home to her parents' house. On the morning of the funeral the woman sees a large painting that had originally been given to her parents as a wedding present fall from its place on the wall.

That such events could have any significance within a mechanistic universe is clearly absurd, for everything that takes place in such a world does so in response to known forces, acting according to deterministic laws that unfold in a linear time and are unresponsive to human affairs. Chance events only produce patterns that are random, and to see meanings in such patterns is as pointless as looking for messages in that interference called "snow" that sometimes appears on a TV screen. To believe that certain chance events are a manifestation of some underlying pattern to nature, or are the result of an "acausal connecting principle," would therefore be utter nonsense.

But how then are the events of the burnt-out candle and the falling picture to be explained, for they were witnessed by several people? It is as if the young woman became a nexus into which events from the external world, past and future, flowed and out of which the synchronious phenomena emerged. The illness of her father and his eventual death, the pained reaction of her family, and her own feelings appear to have enfolded within her and emerged at the phenomenon of the burnt-out candle—*before the telephone call was received*. The events which took place in that room, focusing on the phenomenon of a burnt-out candle, represent in microcosm the unfolding drama of the father's death and the young woman's return to her parents' home.

One of the "classic" examples of synchronicity, told by Carl Jung himself, concerns a crisis that occurred during therapy. Jung's patient was a woman whose highly rational approach to life made any form of treatment particularly difficult. On one occasion the woman related a dream in which a golden scarab appeared. Jung knew that such a beetle was of great significance to the ancient Egyptians for it was taken as a symbol of rebirth.

As the woman was talking, the psychiatrist in his darkened office heard a tapping at the window behind him. He drew the curtain, opened the window, and in flew a gold-green scarab—called a rosechafer, or Cetonia Aureate. Jung showed the woman "her" scarab and from that moment the patient's excessive rationality was pierced and their sessions together became more profitable.

Despite our appeal to a "scientific" view of nature, such events do occur, and while it is true that any one of them can be dismissed as "coincidence," such an explanation makes little sense to the person who has experienced such a synchronicity. Indeed the whole point of such happenings is that they are *meaningful* and play a significant role in a person's life. Synchronicities are the jokers in nature's pack of cards for they refuse to play by the rules and offer a hint that, in our quest for certainty about the universe, we may have ignored some vital clues. Synchronicities challenge us to build a bridge with one foundation driven into the objectivity of hard science and the other into the subjectivity of personal values.

SERIALITY

One of the earliest researchers to inquire into the nature of life's coincidences was an Austrian biologist, Paul Kammerer, who, at the turn of the century, collected together examples of coincidences and unexplained clusterings of events. Over the years Kammerer recorded hundreds of coincidences; while on the train, sitting in the park, or walking to work he would classify passersby according to various parameters such as age, sex, clothing, and what they carried in their hands. Later this data was subject to careful statistical analysis in order to discover if certain of these parameters tended to cluster in time. Kammerer also collected a number of anecdotes such as the following. In 1916 Kammerer's wife was reading a novel in which a certain Mrs. Rohan appeared. That day while traveling on a streetcar, she saw a man who looked very like Prince Josef Rohan and overheard him speaking of the village of Weissenbach. Later that day a shop assistant asked her if she happened to know of Weissenbach as she had a delivery to make and did not know the correct postal address. That evening Prince Josef Rohan paid the Kammerers a visit.

It must be admitted that the above incident is not particularly staggering; we have all had that experience of reading a new word or name in a book and then meeting it over and over again. The conventional explanation is that such names have always been around but that once we notice them for the first time we then become sensitized to pick them out again and again. To Kammerer, however, his notebooks packed with examples, such things went beyond mere chance and pointed to a universal principle of *seriality*. Seriality was defined as "a lawful recurrence, or clustering, in time and space whereby individual members of the sequence—as far as can be ascertained by careful analysis—are not connected by the same active source."[5]

The type of coincidence that intrigued Kammerer is exemplified by the story of Monsieur de Fortgibu and the Christmas pudding. A certain Monsieur Deschamps, while a boy in Orléans, was given a piece of plum pudding by a certain Monsieur de Fortgibu. Ten years later he discovered another plum pudding in a Paris restaurant and asked if he could have a piece. He was told, however, that the pudding had already been ordered—by M. de Fortgibu. Many years afterward M. Deschamps was invited to partake of a plum pudding as a special rarity. While he was eating it he remarked to his friends that the only thing lacking was M. de Fortgibu. At that moment the door opened and an extremely old man, in the last stages of disintegration, walked in. It was M. de Fortgibu, who had got hold of the wrong address and had burst in on the party by mistake.

Just as asteroids drift together in space under the influence of gravity so, Kammerer hypothesized, random events also fall together into clusters. It was as if Kammerer was suggesting that one event exhibits an affinity for other causally unconnected happenings which share in some overall form or pattern. Seriality and its clusterings therefore take place under the influence of *acausal* connections rather than by means of the familiar causal pushes and pulls of physics. Kammerer had therefore produced an argument for the existence of an underlying harmony or mosaic to nature, a pattern that is "the umbilical cord that connects thought, feelings, science and art with the womb of the universe which gave birth to them."

Einstein referred to Kammerer's work as "original and by no means absurd," and Arthur Koestler felt that seriality is an expression of the overall "integrative tendency of the universe."[6] Nevertheless Kammerer's ideas on chance clusterings are not particularly well known today and have not excited the interest of the scientific community. The reason is not difficult to discover. While Kammerer began on an interesting track by suggesting that the underlying patterns of nature manifest themselves in patterns of chance, there is a major logical drawback in accepting his evidence that *serial* clusterings are somehow different from purely *random* ones. Consider the tossing of a coin. On the average there will be as many heads as there are tails but in any long sequence of tosses there may appear a run of heads; for example, three, four or even five heads in succession. It is not necessary to invoke some special and hitherto hidden law to explain this clustering of heads for, in any long, random sequence there will be many particular patterns and runs of heads or tails which, in the long run, average out. It is true that if a particular run of heads were to persist or to occur repeatedly, a skeptical gambler would suspect that the coin used was not true. A weighted coin could be checked by accurate measurements but if this were never done, one could not be certain if a persistent run of heads was due to an uneven balance of the coin or simply the result of chance clusterings. No matter how persistent a particular sequence is, on logical grounds there is always the possibility that it is a random occurrence.

Therefore in analyzing clusterings such as a sequence in a coin toss or the coincidence of several people wearing green hats on a bus, the problem is one of differentiating between a mysterious underlying affinity and the result of pure chance. In addition, when one leaves coin tossings and roulette wheels for the coincidence of names, places, and the way people are dressed, there is the additional difficulty of determining what is a *normal* probability and how much a given sequence deviates from it. Encountering several people with green hats on a bus may indeed be the result of an acausal affinity of the color green, it may be pure chance, or it may be St. Patrick's Day!

It is of the nature of Kammerer's results that clusterings, unless they are particularly exceptional, are remarkably difficult to differentiate from pure chance, and even when this is done, it is often possible to invent some plausible, causal explanation. His work has a particularly interesting slant in that it hints at a basic interconnectedness of things within the deeper patterns of the universe, but this principle of seriality will never convince the scientific skeptic when it is founded purely on a collection of coincidences and curious anecdotes. It was left to Carl Jung therefore to emphasize that what truly differentiates a synchronicity from a mere coincidence is its inherent *meaning*.

CARL JUNG

The true story of synchronicity begins with the collaboration of two remarkable thinkers, the psychologist Carl Jung and the physicist Wolfgang Pauli. Their concept of synchronicity originated in a marriage between the approaches of physics and psychology. The lives and works of these two men contain the embryo out of which synchronicity was to evolve, and since the curious story of the encounter between them has never been publicly told, it is well worth relating here. But first, let us look at the very different backgrounds of these two men and the paths that were eventually to bring them together.

Carl Jung was born in the Swiss village of Keswill in 1875, and after a solitary childhood filled with illness and an introverted tendency toward dreams and fantasies, he emerged into a robust, heavy-drinking, extroverted medical student. Jung chose psychiatry as his field of specialization, and while working at the famous Burghölzi Clinic, the young doctor began to correspond with Sigmund Freud, whose *Interpretation of Dreams* showed how the internal content of the unconscious mind can be pieced together. When Jung and Freud met in 1907, the

Swiss analyst had already made significant contributions to the field with his word-association test and his theory of complexes. Their discussions together were an unqualified success; Jung admitted to "a 'religious' crush with undeniable erotic overtones," and Freud, for his part, treated the younger man as his adopted son and wrote, "I could hope for no one better than yourself to continue and complete my work."[7]

Much to the chagrin of the Vienna Freudians, Jung's rise to power within the organization was meteoric; he organized the first international gathering in Salzburg in 1908 and was elected president of the Psycho-Analytic Congress. However, despite their closeness, Freud and Jung had a profoundly differing view to the unconscious. Even their methodology and approach to research was different, for while Freud was based in a rational, scientific tradition, Jung was more interested in spiritualism, fantasy, and the curious nature of images drawn and dreamed by his patients. While Freud argued that our unconscious life is dominated by the instincts and repressions over which the thin veneer of civilization is stretched, Jung considered that the unconscious mind has a hidden, creative dimension and is not solely powered by sexual drives.

As early as 1909, while still close friends, there was nevertheless an underlying tension to their relationship. One day Freud was chastising Jung over the latter's interest in spiritualism and warning him against being overwhelmed by "the black tide of the mud of occultism." Jung experienced a red-hot sensation in his diaphragm, and at the same time, the two men heard a loud crack from the direction of the bookcase. Jung suggested that this was an example of "catalytic exteriorization," to which Freud replied, "Sheer bosh." The younger man predicted that a second event would occur, and sure enough, another report was heard, the sound of which shook Freud considerably.

A year or two later Jung was carrying out his researches in a very different direction from that laid down by Freud. By 1912 a major rift was created when Freud pointed out a "Freudian slip" in one of Jung's letters. Jung replied:

You see, my dear Professor, as long as you hand out this stuff I don't give a damn for your symptomatic actions; they shrink to nothing in comparison with the formidable beam in my brother Freud's eyes.[8]

Jung resigned as president of the Psycho-Analytic Congress and Freud rejoiced, "So we are at last rid of the brutal, sanctimonious Jung."

The events that followed this break with Freud and his school are particularly significant in the development of the idea of synchronicity. At first, Jung felt free to explore his own ideas without the shadow of Freud looming over him. His work on psychological types argued that each person is the result of a balance between the forces of Intuition, Sensation, Thinking, and Feeling, and in addition, he also defined the nature of Introversion and Extroversion. Clearly Jung's approach

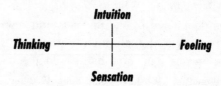

pointed to an inner structure within the unconscious mind rather than a disordered mass of repressions and drives.

In the midst of this activity, however, Jung experienced the first symptoms of what his biographers have referred to as a total mental breakdown, the details of which can be found in his autobiography, *Memories, Dreams and Reflections*.[9] Over the months that followed, Jung journeyed deeper and deeper into the hidden areas of his mind and, in one dream, symbolized his mind as a house with a hidden basement containing a trap door which led to an even more remote, prehistoric cavern. Jung was beginning to uncover a deep and universal area of the mind, which he was later to call the collective or objective unconscious. Within this realm, which Jung was to show is common to all humankind, he discovered a variety of symbols, which he termed mandalas, as well as a number of autonomous personalities. During his breakdown Jung conversed with these internal and apparently independent figures, including Philemon, the wise old man, and Anima, the young woman who had once served as a spiritual guide to Simon Magnus, Lao-tzu, and Klingsor. With regard to the former, Jung wrote:

> . . . at times he seemed to me quite real, as if he were a living personality. I went walking up and down the garden with him, and to me he was what the Indians call a guru. . . . He said things which I had not consciously thought. For I observed clearly that it was he who spoke, not I.[10]

These visitations reached their peak in 1916 when for several days the whole Jung home was haunted, and one Sunday morning, the doorbells rang with no one outside.

> The atmosphere was thick, believe me. Then I knew that something had to happen. The whole house was filled as if there were a crowd present, crammed full with spirits. They were packed deep right up to the door, and the air was so thick it was scarcely possible to breathe. As for myself, I was all a-quiver with the question: "For God's sake, what in the world is this?" Then they cried out in chorus, "We have come back from Jerusalem where we found not what we sought."[11]

Over the next three nights Jung wrote while possessed by these spirits the *Seven Sermons to the Dead (VII Sermones ad Mortuos)*, a work composed in prophetic style which presents a whole cosmology of the universe of matter and mind. Within the *Sermons* the world of created things, the *creatura*, emerges out of an undifferentiated background, the *pleroma*, and the book itself becomes a metaphor for the emergence of consciousness out of the collective unconscious and ultimately from the psychoid which is prior to the distinction between matter and mind. Just as modern physics has produced a myth for the creation of matter out of the undifferentiated vacuum state or the primordial big bang, so Jung had created an account for the origin of mind in the universe.

The *Sermons* are important for they contain in an enfolded, symbolic form much of what Jung was to make explicit within the researches and writings of the rest of his life. This program for research suggests that the human mind can be excavated far beyond the personal unconscious, and in its deepest levels, it possesses a rich structure of dynamic forces, symmetrical patterns, and autonomous centers of energy. As one probes even deeper, one encounters the common ground out of which matter and mind emerge, an echo of Kammerer's "umbilical cord that connects thought, feelings, science and art with the womb of the universe which gave birth to them."

But what exactly happened to Carl Jung during this period of breakdown? To say that he was mad explains nothing, for the whole point about his voyage into the unconscious is that it was by no means chaotic but exhibited its own interior order. The world that Jung discovered is not mad and senseless but highly structured so that the psychologist was able to return to the surface of "normal sanity" bringing profound insights and discoveries that formed the basis for all his later work. That this profound transformation of his inner being was accompanied by a number of synchronicities, such as the hauntings and doorbell ringings, suggests that considerable energies and internal repatternings were involved during this period.

From this point onward, Jung was to see confirmation of his visions through the symbolism of alchemy in the Middle Ages, Tantric texts and other writings from China, visits to Africa, and the dreams and fantasies of his patients.

WOLFGANG PAULI

Let us leave Jung as he unfolds the contents of the unconscious mind and turn to the physicist Pauli. Wolfgang Pauli was born in 1900 into a well-to-do Viennese family. His father was Professor of Biochemistry at the University of Vienna and his mother had artistic leanings. As a young child Pauli excelled at school but was frightened by fairy tales. At eighteen he enrolled at the University of Munich, where, two years later, Werner Heisenberg was to meet him.

I spotted a dark-haired student with a somewhat secretive face in the third row. Sommerfeld had introduced us during my first visit and had then told me that he considered the boy to be one of his most talented students, one from whom I could learn a great deal. His name was Wolfgang Pauli and for the rest of his life he was to be a good friend, though often a severe critic.[12]

Pauli could indeed be ruthless in his scientific criticism for he had a profound insight into physics and his intuition was quick to spot false trails, shaky arguments, and errors of assumption. For this reason the young man was nicknamed *Die Geissel Gottes* (the whip of God) and *Der fürchterlichi Pauli* (frightful Pauli). Even Einstein himself was not immune from critical attacks. However, when the young man produced a book-length review of the theory of relativity,[13] Einstein wrote:

> No one studying this mature, grandly conceived work could believe that the author is a man of 21. One wonders what to admire most, the psychological understanding for the development of ideas, the sureness of mathematical deduction, the profound physical insight, the capacity for lucid systematic presentation, the complete treatment of the subject matter, or the sureness of critical appraisal.[14]

But Pauli had also become interested in the atomic level of matter and in Neils Bohr's early attempt to arrive at a quantum theory. During their student years together Pauli and Heisenberg spent many hours criticizing the existing theory and exploring other approaches. Indeed, Heisenberg later wrote that his walks with Pauli "constituted the most important part of my studies."[15] When in 1925 Heisenberg finally created the new quantum mechanics, Pauli followed only months later with a theory of the hydrogen atom that "convinced most physicists that quantum mechanics is correct."[16] Indeed it is only relatively recently that the significant extent of Pauli's contributions to the birth of this new theory have been realized.[17]

Of all Pauli's contributions to physics the best known is his exclusion principle, an addition to Heisenberg's quantum mechanics which makes an interesting resonance to the general notion of synchronicity. Synchronicity, we will suggest in this book, arises out of the underlying patterns of the universe rather than through a causality of pushes and pulls that we normally associate with events in nature. For this reason synchronicity has been called by Jung an "acausal connecting principle." But an acausal connection is exactly what was proposed by Pauli in his exclusion principle.

The Pauli principle may be clear enough to the physicist when expressed in mathematical terms but conceptually it is rather abstract. Possibly the best way to understand it is to rely on a simple image. Pauli argued that, at the quantum level, all of nature engages in an abstract dance. Moreover all the elementary particles and quanta of energy can be divided into two groups depending on the type of dance they execute. Electrons, protons, neutrons, and neutrinos, along with other particles, form one group (and engage in an *antisymmetric* dance) while the other group includes mesons and photons of light (and forms a *symmetric* dance). It turns out that, in the former case, the nature of this abstract movement or dance has the effect of keeping particles with the same energy always apart from each other. However, this *exclusion* of particles from each other's energy space is not the result of any force which operates between them nor indeed is an act of causality in the normal sense, rather it arises out of the *antigymmetry of abstract movement* of the particles as a whole. Hence the underlying pattern of the *whole dance* has a profound effect on the behavior of each individual particle. For example, it is the exclusion principle which causes electrons in an atom to stack up in a series of energy levels and makes one atom chemically distinguishable from another. It is the Pauli principle which gives rise to the rich chemistry of nature, and without it, the whole universe would seem more or less featureless. It is the symmetric dance of the Pauli principle which is at work behind the intense coherent light of the laser as well as superfluids and superconduction. The antigymmetric dance of the Pauli principle is in constant battle against the force of gravity and the various stages of this battle result in the collapse of a star through the white dwarf, neutron star, and black hole stages.

So Wolfgang Pauli's most famous contribution to physics involved the discovery of an abstract pattern that lies hidden beneath the surface of atomic matter and determines its behavior in a noncausal way. It is in this sense that the Pauli principle forms a parallel to the principle of synchronicity which is to be developed in this book.

THE DREAM OF THE WORLD CLOCK

Despite his interest in inner symmetries, Pauli's own life was falling into greater and greater disorder. In 1928 he was appointed to the chair of theoretical physics in Zurich, where his lectures were confusing and ill-prepared. In addition, his critical tongue was becoming more sarcastic and biting. Within a year of attaining his professorship, Pauli's mother had poisoned herself and the twenty-nine-year-old professor had married a small-time cabaret singer who walked out on him a few weeks later. By now Pauli was drinking heavily and on one occasion was thrown out of a bar for fighting. Close to a breakdown he sought professional help and visited the office of Carl Jung.

While Jung maintained the professional confidences of his patients, it is today possible to piece together what happened next. Jung found his patient to be:

. . . a university man, a very one-sided intellectual. His unconscious had become troubled and activated; so it projected itself onto other men who appeared to be his enemies, and he felt terribly lonely, because everyone seemed to be against him.[18]

Again:

. . . he had lived in a very one-sided intellectual way, and naturally had certain desires and needs also. But he had no chance with women at all, because he had no differentiation of feeling whatsoever. So he made a fool of himself with women at once and of course they had no patience with him.[19]

Jung discovered that Pauli was "chock full of archaic material" and, not wishing to influence his dreams and images, handed him over to one of his (Jung's) students, who worked with the physicist over the next five months.

In his study of psychological types, Jung had argued that each person is the result of an equilibrium or balance between polarities.

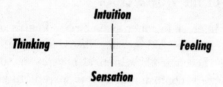

In a healthy psyche Thinking is in harmony with Feeling so that logic and reason can work in a constructive way with the emotional side of an individual. However, in Pauli's case, thought had dominated Feeling so that the emotions were relegated to what Jung termed the Shadow side of the Ego. In other words, Pauli's emotional and Feeling nature had never fully developed but existed in a raw and highly energized form which tended to break through in the form of irrational behavior, dreams, and neuroses. Thought, sensing what it felt to be primitive forces at work, put the lid on even tighter so that Feeling found itself in the position of a red-hot pressure cooker with the valve jammed. The result was Pauli's absurd marriage, his increasingly sarcastic attacks on colleagues, and his bouts of drunkenness.

According to Jung, the cure lay in bringing Feeling out of the Shadow and into the light, where it could perform its proper function and restore harmony to Pauli's whole personality. The method for Pauli was to come to terms with the content of his unconscious through dreams and waking fantasies. Over the next months Pauli produced "over a thousand dreams and visual impressions," which were later analyzed by Jung and formed the basis of one of his major writings—*Individual Dream Symbolism in Relation to Alchemy*.[20] The psychologist had discovered that the symbolism within Pauli's dreams was

The World Clock. An impression generated by W. Byers-Brown based on accounts of Pauli's dream.

remarkably similar to that of the medieval alchemists. The culmination of this series of dreams was Pauli's vision of the world clock, an image of "the most sublime harmony" which left a deep impression on him and, in Jung's words was "what we would call—in the language of religion—a conversion."

The *world clock* or *great vision*, as it is described in Jung's essay, is replete with geometrical and numerical symbols of wholeness:

> There is a vertical and a horizontal circle, having a common center. This is the world clock. It is supported by the black bird.
> The vertical circle is a blue disk with a white border divided into 4 × 8 = 32 partitions. A pointer rotates upon it.
> The horizontal circle consists of four colors. On it stand four little men with pendulums, and round about is laid the ring that was once dark and is now golden (formerly carried by the children).

The *"clock has three rhythms or pulses:*
1. The small pulse:
> *The pointer on the blue vertical disk advances by*
> *1/32.*
2. The middle pulse:
> *One complete revolution of the pointer. At the same*
> *time the horizontal circle advances by 1/32.*
3. The great pulse:
> *32 middle pulses are equal to one revolution of the*
> *golden ring.*[21]

The illustration of the world clock was created by W. Byers-Brown on the basis of Pauli's dream. It is taken from a particularly interesting lecture, "Wolfgang Pauli—Physicist and Dreamer," which Byers-Brown gave in London, on April 13, 1980, to The Scientific and Medical Network.

In interpreting the dream, Jung identified the point of rotation of the disks with the mystical *speculum*, for it both partakes of the rhythmic movement yet stands outside it. The two disks belong to the two universes of the conscious and the unconscious, which intersect in this speculum. The whole figure together with its elaborate internal movement is therefore a mandala of the Self, which is at one and the same time the center and the periphery of the world clock. In addition, the dream could also stand as a model of the universe itself and the nature of space-time. Jung himself noted that the construction of the clock and the numerical divisions it contained bore a striking resemblance to the systems of the Quabala. But it should also be pointed out that Pauli, as a physicist, was also seeking to discover an inner unity between the elementary particles and their abstract symmetries. The vision of the world clock is therefore capable of many levels of interpretation, and it is indeed a particularly rich image in its resonances of meaning.

Pauli's rebirth as "a perfectly normal and reasonable person . . . completely adapted" was therefore the result of sensing a deep inner symmetry to his own mind, a dynamic pattern that had been illustrated in symbolic times by the early Gnostics, the alchemists of the Middle Ages, and the Taoists of ancient China. According to Jung, Pauli's very heavy drinking was also "cured," a diagnosis not supported by the physicist's friends. In his autobiography, H. B. G. Casimir describes a harrowing drive from Lucerne to Zurich after Pauli had consumed many drinks. *"Ich fahre ziemlich gut,"* Pauli cried as he swerved from side to side on the road.[22] Clearly Jung had overdramatized the extent of Pauli's "conversion"; however, he was certainly on the right lines in describing Pauli's new interest in inner harmony and symmetry. The notion of symmetries in nature and in the psyche continued to preoccupy the physicist for the rest of his life. The results confirmed Jung's findings on what he called the *archetypes,* dynamic forces and mosaics of energy within the collective unconscious which are revealed to us symbolically through dreams, fantasies, works of art, and myths. In the chapters that follow we will learn more about these archetypes and the role they may play in synchronicity.

With the encouragement of Pauli, Jung was now able to explore the question of a hidden symmetry within the universe from the perspectives both of physics and of psychology. It was also as a result of Pauli's promptings that Jung was eventually to publish his meditations on synchronicity. For, following Pauli's analysis, the two men became colleagues in their search for nature's inner patterns. Pauli attended meetings of the Zurich group of psychologists and, in turn, introduced Jung to many of the leading physicists of the day, who often proved sympathetic to his approaches.

But before we leave Pauli, it is worthwhile exploring the "Pauli effect," a phenomenon which has gone down into the mythology of science. While many theoreticians are deeply allergic to experimental work and laboratory apparatus, in Pauli's case this reached such absurd proportions that it was said that Pauli had only to walk into a laboratory for a vacuum vessel to implode or a sensitive gauge to fracture. Many examples of this "Pauli effect" are still recounted by physicists, and a particularly curious anecdote comes from Professor J. Franck. On one occasion a complicated piece of apparatus collapsed in his Gottingen laboratory. Franck wrote to Pauli pointing out that, since the theoretician was living in Zurich, the Pauli effect could hardly be to blame in this case. Pauli, however, replied that he had in fact been traveling to Copenhagen and that his train had stopped in the Gottingen station at the time of the mishap!

One of the most curious of these stories about Pauli concerns the number 137. One of the great unsolved mysteries of modern physics is the value of the fine structure constant, for while the other fundamental constants of nature are all immensely small or enormously large, this fine structure constant $\frac{1}{137}$ turns out to be a human-sized number. This number 137 and its place in the scale of the universe particularly puzzled Pauli and continues to challenge physicists today. It was a mystery that Pauli was to take to his death, for on being admitted into the hospital, the physicist was told that he was being put into room 137. According to one version of this story, on learning of his room number, Pauli said, "I will never get out of here." The physicist died shortly after.

SYNCHRONICITY

At first there were only a few tantalizing hints as to Jung's thoughts on synchronicity. In 1929, while lecturing to a group of students, Jung said, "Synchronicism is the prejudice of the East, causality is the modern prejudice of the West." A year later, during a memorial address on the death of Richard Wilhelm, the noted student of Chinese thought, Jung expanded a little on his original remark. "The science of the *I Ching*, indeed, is not based on the causality principle, but on a principle (hitherto unnamed because not met with us) which I have tentatively called the synchronistic principle."[23] During a lecture at London's Tavistock Clinic five years later, Jung appears to have used the term "synchronicity" for the first time. "Tao can be anything, I use another word to designate it, but it is poor enough. I call it *synchronicity*."[24]

Now, thanks to Pauli, Jung was able to crystallize his ideas further, and in 1952, the two men published together *The Interpretation and Nature of the Psyche*, a book containing two essays, one by Pauli on the influence of archetypes in Kepler's theory of planetary motion, and the other by Jung on the nature of synchronicity.[25] Although the latter essay bears only Jung's name, it is clear that it is the result of long discussions with Pauli. It is not so much a definitive explanation of synchronicity but rather a starting point (indeed it forms the starting point of this present book), for as Jung writes in the introduction:

> In writing this paper I have, so to speak, made good a promise which for many years I lacked the courage to fulfil. The difficulties of the problem and its representation seemed to me too great. . . . If I have now conquered my hesitation and at last come to grips with the theme it is chiefly because my experiences of the phenomenon of synchronicity have multiplied themselves over the decades. . . .[26]

Within this essay, and certain of Jung's other writings, synchronicity is variously referred to as:

- "the coincidence in time of two or more causally unrelated events which have the same or similar meaning"
- "creative acts"
- "acausal parallelisms"

He also wrote that:

- "meaningful coincidences are unthinkable as pure chance— the more they multiply and the greater and more exact the correspondence is. . . . they can no longer be regarded as pure chance, but, for the lack of causal explanation, have to be thought of as meaningful arrangements."

In the chapters that follow we shall excavate the deeper meanings of these statements and claims and see how they reveal a universe that unfolds according to a hidden, dynamic order.

Jung also attempted to integrate his intuitions on synchronicity into the framework of modern physics. Just as he had suggested that the mind results from a dynamic equilibrium of dualities, so he produced a diagram showing how synchronicity balances causality in the dual patterns of nature.

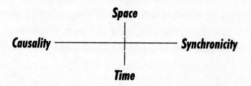

However, in his discussions with Pauli, the physicist suggested a modification of the diagram which emphasized both the differences and similarities of synchronicity to causality.

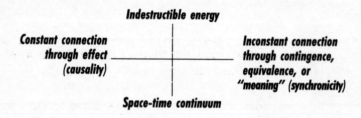

By introducing the value of "meaning" into this conception of nature, Pauli was suggesting a way in which the objective approach of physics (constant connection through effect) could be integrated with more subjective values (connection through contingence, equivalence, or meaning). This whole notion of meaning was clearly the vital clue as to the nature of synchronicity and represented a distinct step beyond Kammerer's seriality. For while random events may always throw out patterns by pure chance, the essence of a synchronicity is that the particular pattern has a meaning or value for the individual who experiences it. While the conventional laws of physics do not heed human desires or the need for meaning—apples fall whether we will them to or not—synchronicities act as mirrors to the inner processes of mind and take the form of outer manifestations of interior transformations. The cracking sound in Jung's bookcase and the ringing of his doorbells both took place in conjunction with violent, internal states. While

Kammerer's seriality generally comprises fairly neutral cluster-ings and coincidences, a synchronicity involves strong paral-lels between interior and exterior events that are emphatically endowed with meaning. To discover just how meaning can play a role in our objective, physical universe is one of the major challenges of this book.

Jung and Pauli presented their insights into what they be-lieved was a new principle of nature that would complement the approach of physics. Pauli believed that synchronicity made it possible to begin a dialogue between physics and psychology in such a way that the subjective would be intro-duced into physics and the objective into psychology. Rather than looking exclusively to physics or psychology alone for the solution to nature's secrets, Pauli felt that a complementary approach was called for in which subjective and objective aspects would reveal different features of the same underlying phenomena.

On Pauli's death, in 1958, Jung wrote:

> It is most unfortunate that Pauli died so early, as he was a physicist who had the ear of his time, more so than a psychologist like myself. There is a chance, however, that the future may develop a better understanding of the psychology of the uncon-scious and its far-reaching problems, and though it is even in its medieval pre-stages may become fertile ground for the problems raised by nuclear physics and the psychology of the unconscious.[27]

Several of Jung's colleagues and students have attempted to extend and clarify this ground-breaking work on synchronicity. Ira Progoff, for example, speculated that "if great sums of energy could be released by breaking the elementary unit of the atom, equivalent sums of energy might be brought forth if the depth of the psyche could be opened in a comparable way."[28] Barbara Hanna, friend and biographer of Jung, sug-gested that a form of "synchronistic thinking" exists which lies outside time and space,[29] and Marie-Louise von Franz, one of the most original of the Jungians, believed that synchronicity is a manifestation of a much wider principle of "acausal ordered-ness" which is also found in mathematics and quantum theory and represents "acts of creation in time."[30]

With the possible exception of Dr. von Franz, who has an intuitive sympathy to the inner structure of mathematics, the investigators who followed Jung all tended to approach synchronicity from one direction only, from the world of experience, dreams, fantasies, and the unconscious. But in order to obtain a deeper integration of physics and psychology, it is necessary to explore synchronicity from both sides and invoke some of the latest views of physics as well, building in a complementary fashion from both the objective and subjective perceptions of nature.

Right up to the end of his life, Pauli retained a deep conviction in the powers of symmetry. While struggling with a unified field theory he wrote to his life-long friend Heisenberg:[31]

> Division and reduction of symmetry, this then the kernel of the brute! The former is an ancient attribute of the devil. . . . If only the two divine contenders—Christ and the devil—could notice that they have grown so much more symmetrical.

On December 15, 1958, the day of Pauli's death, I was taking a university examination in Liverpool. By a curious synchronicity one of the questions on the paper before me concerned Pauli's exclusion principle and asked what would be the nature of the universe if this principle had never existed!

THE NATURAL HISTORY OF SYNCHRONICITIES

Jung's investigations into synchronicity were prompted by the various patterns and acausal clusterings that had occurred in his own life. A particular example, which is recorded in his essay on synchronicity, deals with the motif of the fish. In many European countries April 1 is referred to as April Fish Day. On that particular day Jung happened to be working on the symbolism of the fish and when his patient arrived Jung was shown a picture of a fish and a piece of embroidery with a fish on it. On the following day another patient told him of a dream of a large fish that had occurred the night before. While writing down these accounts Jung went for a walk beside the lake and saw a large fish.

Jung himself gives prominence to this pattern of fishy occurrences. But to many readers they will seem to be nothing more than simple coincidences. Their importance, for Jung, appeared to come from the strong sense of meaning they had for him. Possibly of more interest, however, were the events that occurred to his patients during therapy—such as the appearance of the golden scarab mentioned earlier. In such situations, in which the patient and psychiatrist are able to activate the deep forces of the unconscious together, the occurrence of synchronicities may be particularly favorable.

This observation has been confirmed by the research of a Swiss analyst, Arnold Mindel. Mindel began his professional training as a physicist but later switched to Jungian psychology, which he studied in Zurich. His interest in synchronicity and the possibility of resonances between physics and psychology led him to conduct a survey by means of a questionnaire sent out to a number of Jungians.[32]

When Mindel's work is taken in conjunction with Jung's, and with other commentators, it is possible to build up a profile for synchronistic happenings. As Jung had earlier pointed out, it is the nature of synchronicity to have meaning and, in particular, to be associated with a profound activation of energy deep within the psyche. It is as if the formation of patterns within the unconscious mind is accompanied by physical patterns in the outer world. In particular, as psychic patterns are on the point of reaching consciousness then synchronicities reach their peak; moreover, they generally disappear as the individual becomes consciously aware of a new alignment of forces within his or her personality.

Synchronicities are therefore often associated with periods of transformation; for example, births, deaths, falling in love, psychotherapy, intense creative work, and even a change of profession. It is as if this internal restructuring produces external resonances or as if a burst of "mental energy" is propagated outward into the physical world. The cracking sound from Jung's bookcase is a clear example of such an externalization. Arnold Mindel gives the example of a psychotic patient who declared that he was Jesus, the creator and destroyer of light. At that very moment the lighting fixture dropped from the ceiling, knocking the man out.

An extreme example of the release of such psychic energy occurs with what Jungians call "The Gambler," the person who must risk everything on the final turn of a metaphoric card. In many cases a patient is at the end of his or her tether with all resources exhausted and no hope remaining. In symbolic terms this is not unlike the person who has reached the final door in a castle, who has one magical wish left, who faces a dragon, or who is on the point of death. In such circumstances all the energies are focused and concentrated upon the final turn of a card and synchronicities are bound to occur.

Mindel tells of the psychiatrist who was at his wit's end trying to treat a woman patient. No matter what he did he seemed unable to communicate with her. One day, under extreme stress he dreamed that her husband was trying to pull her into the world beyond and was wakened by knocks on the office door—but no one was outside. He developed the intuition that the woman's husband was in some way responsible for this knocking and, during their next session together, told this story to his patient. To his surprise she admitted that her husband had in fact died several weeks earlier.

Faced with an apparently impossible task, the therapist had become involved in a synchronicity involving a knocking on the office door and the dream of a dead husband. From that time onward, communication improved between doctor and patient and led to an eventual cure.

The involvement of synchronicities between the dreaming and the waking state is not unusual, nor is it confined to these "last resort" situations. Anthony Storr, author of *The Essential Jung*, told me that his wife dreamed that she had been decapitated. On the same night, an Oxford don lay down on the railroad tracks and was decapitated by a train. G. H. Lewis, life-long companion of the writer George Eliot, tells the following story about Charles Dickens:

Dickens dreamt that he was in a room where everyone was dressed in scarlet. He stumbled against a lady standing with her back towards him. As he apologised she turned her head and said quite unprovoked "My name is Napier."

He knew no one of the name Napier and the face was unknown. Two days later before a reading a lady friend came into the waiting-room accompanied by an unknown lady in a scarlet opera-cloak, "who" said his friend "is very determined of being introduced." "Not Miss Napier?" he jokingly inquired. "Yes Miss Napier." Although the face of his dream-body was not the face of Miss Napier, the coincidence of the scarlet cloak and the name was striking."[33]

Synchronicities occur not only to the disturbed or hypersensitive but may even intrude into the life of the rational and skeptical. Indeed, Mindel noted how they sometimes have the effect of perturbing an otherwise ordered and overrigid worldview by appearing as the jokers in the pack of life.

Some synchronicities begin within the outer world and then move inward as their meaning is revealed. Such synchronicities depend on detecting a deeper meaning to the patterns and clusterings of the phenomena around us. They may involve our becoming linked with the environment in a special way, anticipating events or sensing some underlying pattern to the world. Jung's case of the fish motif is one example. But one could also point to the ways in which artists and writers seem to have sensed major events or social changes long before they happened. A curious coincidence is provided by the astronomers in Jonathan Swift's *Gulliver's Travels*, who know that Mars possesses two moons, and this long before real-life stargazers were in a position to make such observations. More ominous is M. F. Mansfield's 1898 novel of the fabulous Atlantic liner, *Titan*, the largest ever built, which sailed into the Atlantic along with its rich and famous passengers. Supplied with an inadequate number of lifeboats, the *Titan*, like the real-life *Titanic* some years later, struck an iceberg and sank.

Perhaps more interesting, however, are the films made in Germany of the 1920s that anticipate the psychological turmoil that exploded in the Nazi era. F. W. Murnau's *Nosferatu* involves a plague that sweeps across the land and shows how respectable townsfolk are stirred into the blood lust of a hunt. Robert Weine's *The Cabinet of Dr. Caligari* depicts a sonambulist who is used as the instrument of murder by a mad doctor. Within the doctor's asylum the patients appear rational and the staff insane.

A particularly telling synchronicity or acausal connection with the environment can be found in the sinologist Richard Wilhelm's story of the rainmaker since it contains the essence of a Chinese worldview of how man and nature form an individual whole. A certain Chinese village had been without rain for some weeks when they sent for the rainmaker. On the old man's arrival he went straight to a house provided for him and there he stayed without performing any ceremonies until the rains came. On being asked how he had caused the rain to fall the old man explained that causation had nothing to do with it. Upon arriving in the village the rainmaker had realized that a state of disharmony was present and consequently the normal processes of nature were not operating according to their proper design. The rainmaker himself was also affected so the old man retired to his hut to compose himself. When his internal harmony was restored and equilibrium established then the rain fell, as it is its natural pattern to do so.

This story contains elements of a moving inward and a moving outward, a dynamism between the physical and the mental aspects of the universe. But there are also synchronicities that appear to exist only inwardly and not have significant physical manifestations. These could, for example, involve acausal patterns of dreams, memories, thoughts, symbols, and perceptions and express themselves as coincidences or clusterings between different people. An obvious example of such synchronicities are the simultaneous discoveries made by scientists who are not in direct communication with each other. Scientists often speak of ideas as "being in the air," almost as if new concepts take the form of radio transmissions, complete in themselves but waiting for a competent receiver to pick them up. One of the most famous of such coincidental discoveries is that of the theory of evolution.

Charles Darwin, acting on the advice of his friend Sir Charles Lyell, had begun to write out his theory of the evolution of new species:

> . . . I got through about half the work on this scale. But my plans were overthrown, for early in the summer of 1858 Mr. Wallace, who was then in the Malay archipelago, sent me an essay *On the Tendency of Varieties to depart indefinitely from the Original Type*; and this essay contained exactly the same theory as mine.[34]

One of the most revolutionary theories in science had therefore been independently discovered by two men working quite unrelatedly to each other. Of equal importance was the independent discovery of calculus by both Newton and Leibnitz.

Even more striking synchronicities can be found when such parallel evolutions of thought take place in totally different fields. While it is possible that the theory of evolution was simply waiting to be discovered, how is one to explain the following examples of our increasing understanding of the nature of light? Around the middle of the sixteenth century, Vermeer and other painters working in Holland had become interested in the interior nature of light, in its effects on entering rooms through doors, windows, and tiny cracks and its transformation on passing through colored glass. At this same time, Isaac Newton was using a prism to explore the composition of light as it entered a small hole in the shutters of his Cambridge room.

Two hundred years later the painter Turner was portraying light as being a swirling vortex, an energetic power which dissolved form and could be equated with the surging movement of wind, rain, and waves. A little later the physicist Maxwell was to formulate his wave theory of the electromagnetic field in which light is produced by the mutual revolution (swirling motion) of electrical and magnetic waves around each other. By the turn of the century the impressionists were treating light as a pure force which produces and dissolves form and can be broken down into its component atoms of sensation; the logical extension of this work was pointillism, in which all of nature is reduced to dots or quanta of color. A few years later the same notion was being formulated in physics by Planck and Einstein as the quantum theory of light and matter.

Do such concepts and insights exist in some enfolded, symbolic form within the unconscious mind? Or are they approached within nature, not directly but in some hidden way which must then be unfolded within the languages of art, literature, music, or science? The many examples of coincidental movements of thought, feeling, and ideas between unconnected groups and across disciplines suggests that a deeper meaning lies beyond these coincidences and synchronicities.

On a less dramatic note, Arnold Mindel has noted the synchronious movement of couples in which one partner undergoes a dramatic experience while separated from the other. It is not unusual, for example, for a husband or a wife to experience some profound inner change while the partner is undergoing psychotherapy in another city or country. Such curious events may not be so much the result of a "psychic link" or mental communication but rather indicate that a mutual process is unfolding out of the same ground and that this ground must therefore lie beyond the individual consciousness that is located in space and time.

CONCLUSIONS

So far we have explored the notion of synchronicity on a phenomenological basis, by giving some examples and hinting that they may be evidence of some deeper, universal principle of hidden order. But as we approach this new principle of nature, it will first be necessary to look a little closer at the nature of synchronicities which we have characterized as being *acausal, meaningful, unique events* and involving some form of *pattern*. In order to do so, however, we must also consider the limitations of our current worldview with its notions of causality, the arrow of time, objectivity, the separation of mind and matter, and the emphasis upon reproducibility rather than on unique, single events.

In the next chapter we begin this exploration by focusing on ideas of causality and asking if it makes any sense to speak of an "acausal connecting principle" in our physical universe.

NOTES

1. Tom Chetwynd, *A Dictionary of Symbols* (New York: Granada Publishers, Paladin Books, 1982).
2. T. E. Lawrence, *Seven Pillars of Wisdom* (Harmondsworth, Eng.: Penguin, 1976).
3. W. Wordsworth, *"Ode: Intimations of Immortality."*
4. J. A. Wheeler in Paul Buckley and F. David Peat, *A Question of Physics* (London: Routledge and Kegan Paul, 1979).
5. Paul Kammerer, *Das Gestex der Serie* (Stuttgart-Berlin: Deutsche Verlags-Ansalt, 1919). Quoted in Arthur Koestler, *The Roots of Coincidence* (New York: Random House, 1972).
6. See also Arthur Koestler, *The Case of the Midwife Toad* (New York: Random House, 1973); and Alister Hardie, Robert Harvie, and Arthur Koestler, *The Challenge of Chance* (London: Hutchinson, 1973).
7. Sigmund Freud and C. G. Jung, *The Freud-Jung Letters: The Correspondence between Sigmund Freud and C. G. Jung,* trans. Ralph Manheim and R. F. Hull. Bollingen Series No. 94 (Princeton University Press, 1974).
8. Ibid.
9. London: Collins, The Fontana Library, 1971.
10. Ibid.
11. Ibid.
12. W. Heisenberg, *Physics and Beyond* (New York: Harper & Row, 1971).
13. This article has since been reprinted as W. Pauli, *Theory of Relativity* (New York: Dover, 1981).
14. Quoted by W. Byers-Brown in "Wolfgang Pauli—Physicist and Dreamer," lecture given to the Scientific and Medical Network, on April 13, 1980, in London.
15. Heisenberg, op. cit.
16. B. L. van der Waerden, ed., *Sources of Quantum Mechanics* (New York: Dover, 1968).
17. John Hendry, *The Creation of Quantum Mechanics and the Bohr-Pauli Dialogues* (Boston: D. Reidel, 1984).
18. C. G. Jung, *Analytical Psychology: Its Theory and Practice. The Tavistock Lectures* (New York: Random House, Vintage Books, 1968).
19. Ibid.
20. This paper, along with an account of Pauli's dreams and the deductions Jung made from them, can be found in C. G. Jung, *Psychology and Alchemy,* trans. R. F. C. Hull. Bollingen Series XX (Princeton University Press, 1968). The paper is also reprinted in C. G. Jung, *Dreams,* trans. R. F. C. Hull. Bollingen Series (Princeton University Press, 1974).

21. *Psychology and Alchemy, loc.* cit.
22. *Haphazard Reality* (New York: Harper & Row, 1983).
23. Quoted in R. Wilhelm, *The Secret of the Golden Flower* (London: Routledge & Kegan Paul, 1962).
24. *Analytical Psychology, loc.* cit.
25. C. G. Jung and W. Pauli, *The Interpretation and Nature of the Psyche*, trans. R. F. C. Hull and P. Silz. Bollingen Series LI (New York: Pantheon, 1955). Unfortunately this book is now out of print and Pauli's essay has therefore been lost to the general reader. Jung's essay, however, is reprinted in C. G. Jung, *Synchronicity*, trans. R. F. C. Hull. Bollingen Series (Princeton University Press, 1973).
26. Ibid.
27. C. G. Jung, *Letters Nineteen Fifty-one to Nineteen Sixty-one*, Vol. 2, eds. Gerhard Adler and Aniela Jaffe. Bollingen Series No. 95 (Books on Demand, University Microfilms International, n.d.).
28. Ira Progoff, *Jung, Synchronicity and Human Destiny* (New York: Julian Press, 1973).
29. Barbara Hanna, *Jung, His Life and Work* (New York: Putnam, 1976).
30. M-L von Franz, *On Divination and Synchronicity* (Toronto: Inner City Books, 1980).
31. Heisenberg, op. cit.
32. Arnold Mindel, *Synchronicity, An Investigation of the Unitary Background Patterning Synchronous Phenomena*. Dissertation Abstracts International 37:2 (1976).
33. Quoted in *The Canadian Illustrated News*, 1870–1880.
34. *The Autobiography of Charles Darwin 1809–1882*, ed. Nora Barlow (London: Collins, 1958).

2 THE MECHANICAL UNIVERSE

Carl Jung defined synchronicity as "the coincidence in time of two or more causally unrelated events which have the same meaning." His implication is clear—certain events in the universe cluster together into meaningful patterns without recourse to the normal pushes and pulls of causality. These synchronicities therefore must transcend the normal laws of science, for they are the expressions of much deeper movements that originate in the ground of the universe and involve, in an inseparable way, both matter and meaning.

However, an "acausal connecting principle" clearly flies in the face of a very compelling worldview that is based on a causally dominated universe in which nothing takes place that does not have an ultimate cause. If synchronicities really have a deeper meaning and are not simply random coincidences or projections of the imagination, then science is faced with the problem of finding a place for them somewhere within its universe. Yet when everything is determined by causality, how can a pattern of events occur which does not conform to this most ubiquitous of laws? In other words, what possible meaning can there be to this paradoxical "acausal connecting principle"?

Causality is defined as "a chain of cause and effect." This suggests a chain or series of links, in which each one is firmly locked into its two neighbors so that the whole chain is able to stretch out indefinitely in both directions. In this way every event in the universe is causally linked to an event that comes before it, and to one that comes afterward. A more dynamic image is that of a railway line along which an engine is shunting a number of railcars. As the engine reaches the first of the uncoupled cars, it bangs into it, causing an impulse of motion that travels from car to car on down the line. An intuitive sense of what is meant by causality is not unlike this impulse that passes from car to car along the line, so that whenever a car is seen to move, it must have been involved in an impact somewhere back along the line.

In a similar way whenever a change or some new form of motion is seen within the universe, it is natural to assume that somewhere back along the "railway line of time," a cause has been operating and that sometime in the future the effect will, in turn, be passed on. Nothing happens in this world of causality that does not originate in some cause. So the idea of an "acausal connection" seems to be ruled out right from the start—there is simply no room for it in a universe of causality. This also seems to mean that the quest for synchronicity must end in contradiction.

The causal universe had a particularly elegant description in terms of the classical physics of the eighteenth and nineteenth centuries; a worldview that continues to influence the ways in which most of us continue to perceive and deal with reality. Isaac Newton, for example, placed causality on a rigorous basis with his laws of motion and the various mathematical equations that followed from them. According to his system of mechanics, if the initial conditions of a body are known (specifically its initial velocity, position, mass, and the nature of the forces that act on it), then it is possible to predict its exact path and, in addition, all the collisions that it will encounter. Indeed this approach can describe an entire system of particles so that when a number of bodies are found clustering together in a particular pattern, there is no need to invoke seriality or synchronicity. It is simply a matter of solving the equations of motion for each body and noting the inevitability with which their paths and collisions have caused them to congregate together into a particular pattern in space. Within this Newtonian worldview, therefore, there seems to be no room for synchronicity.

This Newtonian description can be extended to even larger and more complex systems without limit. Indeed if Newton had stood next to God on day one of creation, he would have asked Him for the positions, masses, and velocities of the bodies He had created and in this way could have predicted every subsequent event that was to occur in the entire universe. Implicit in such an arrogant vision of the power of science is the image of a scientist who stands outside the system as an impartial observer, able to predict all events according to deterministic laws, and without disturbing events in any way. If such an eighteenth-century scientist were to build a large enough computer, it could then be possible to make a giant simulation of the universe that would forever run parallel with reality. This simulation would contain every event that has happened since time began, and that will happen until the end of time. How then could there be room in this simulation for free will, creativity, and synchronicity?

The scientist today is no longer an impartial observer who stands outside the universe and watches its various events. In John Wheeler's words, the term "spectator" must be struck from the record and the new word "participator" must replace it. By virtue of the quantum theory, it is clear that any observation or attempt to determine initial conditions, has an irreducible effect on the rest of the universe. Physics and physicist are no longer separable but are one indivisible whole.

Will an appeal to the quantum theory therefore provide a loophole for escaping from the dilemma of absolute causality? For example, while a particular isotope decays with a well-defined half-life, there is no way of predicting which one of its particular atoms will disintegrate next. One atom may decay in less than a minute; another will last for a week, or several months. Quantum theory will not allow the individual event to be pinned down in any exact way. Moreover, the theory asserts that this breakdown in predictability has nothing to do with an ignorance about the fine details of the system, which could be filled in with some more detailed theory (as is the case with life insurance which is averaged over a large population of different individuals); rather it is a fundamental and absolute indeterminism. With such indeterminism lying at the most basic level of nature, it appears that the entire Newtonian appeal to absolute causality and determinism is now invalid and a loophole has been discovered for synchronicity. This is indeed true, in one sense, but it is still not possible to get off the hook so easily, for most of the fluctuating, unpredictable effects of atomic indeterminism vanish in the face of what has been called the law of large numbers.

The law of large numbers argues that in any very large ensemble of probabilistic events, things will always average out to the point where individual deviations and happenings can be ignored. Suppose, for example, that a large number of quarters are tossed and all the heads put in one sack, and the tails in the other. After thousands and tens of thousands of tossings, the two sacks will weigh the same. True enough, any one event is indeterministic, and on the fine scale, there will be occasional runs on heads or on tails, but in the long term the law of large numbers acts to hide the effects of individual fluctuations within the overall average. Now what is true for a few thousand coins is even more the case for the atoms comprised in an everyday object, say a pool ball. The number of atoms involved in this case is very large indeed, around 10^{23}, about the same as the number of stars in the universe. In such a large ensemble the individual quantum deviations will be well averaged away by the time things reach the human scale. Therefore, while indeterminism rules the microworld, as far as most phenomena are concerned its effects are lost when averaged out over the law of large numbers that applies in the everyday world. Newtonian determinism still appears to rule and it has closed the doors to synchronicity and firmly locked them with the chain of cause and effect.

THE GROUND OF CAUSALITY

The linear chain of causality and the predictive power of mathematical equations have dominated science for so many generations that it is now difficult to see what room there can be in the universe for freedom, novelty, and creativity. Scientists are able to argue that their causal explanations will account for all phenomena, not only of the mechanical universe, but also of life and behavior itself. According to *reductionism*, even such a complex phenomenon as consciousness will eventually be explained in terms of the mechanisms of a biological system, such as the operation of action potentials within neurons, the flow of neurotransmitters, and the growth of neural networks. While these accounts are all biological in nature, they can be reduced to concepts in chemistry such as ion potentials, pathways for chemical synthesis, osmosis, and so on. In turn, each of these chemical phenomena is explicable using the laws of physics as they apply to the properties of solutions and the interactions of atoms and molecules. In this way, reductionism argues that even the most complex phenomena of society, consciousness and life, can be reduced to the behavior of matter and the laws of physics. While it is true that many thoughtful scientists do not accept reductionism in its full form, nevertheless it does continue to have a very strong influence within the sciences so that, on meeting new phenomena, the natural scientific instinct is to reduce it to its most basic elements. Reductionism, when combined with causality, threatens to cause the complete evaporation of synchronicity into the movement of atoms and the operations of fields of force. However, as this book progresses, it will become clear that a pluralistic approach is being suggested in which reductionism and causality have a more limited usefulness.

Causality has been pictured in terms of an engine that shunts railcars along the line of time. Another mechanistic image was particularly appealing to physicists of the late nineteenth century. This was the game of pool, or of billiards, in which the initial impact of the cue gives rise to all the subsequent movements and patterns of balls on the table. Following any shot, the paths of the various balls and their intercollisions may appear quite complex, yet each trajectory is a direct consequence of its initial position and the impact it received from the cue ball.

The dynamics of pool and billiards are so elegant that they

provided the material for many of the problems that Professor Sommerfeld of Munich University set his two young students, Pauli and Heisenberg, to work on. However, the real world is not a game of pool, and when it is explored in much greater depth, it turns out that many of its phenomena appear to emerge and unfold in much more complex and subtle ways. Indeed it is as the notion of causality is pushed to its limit, in an effort to explain such systems, that its usefulness begins to break down. In the following chapters a number of examples will be given in which causality does not seem to be appropriate as a formal description, because nature acts in ways that are much closer to those of an organism than a machine. In these chapters the new laws of emergence and organic dynamics will be unfolded, such as Prigogine's dissipative structures, Bohm's implicate order, and Sheldrake's formative fields. With the help of these new descriptions it will be possible to explore the inner operations of synchronicity.

But before nature can be viewed as an organism, it is first necessary to break the hypnotic hold of causality on our vision. In this respect it is well worth recalling that, for philosophers, the notion of causality is by no means clear or well founded. In the eighteenth century, David Hume made a very careful examination of the whole issue and concluded that causality cannot be placed on a strictly logical footing. Just because it has been observed on many occasions in the past that B follows A, it does not logically follow that this succession will occur in the future. The belief in causality is therefore based on a habit of mind through repeated historical precedent and is far from being a logical proof of inevitability. Indeed, as Hume wrote, "We have no other notion of cause and effect, but that of certain objects, which have been *always conjoined* together. . . . We cannot penetrate into the reason of the conjunction."[1]

Causality is inferred from the past behavior of the universe but it is never possible to get inside the phenomena of nature, in any logical or philosophical sense, and directly apprehend what is taking place. However, Hume despaired from ever making any dent in the firm common sense belief of cause and effect, "by dint of solid proof and reasoning I can never hope

. . . to overcome the inveterate prejudices of mankind. Before we are reconciled to this doctrine, how often must we repeat to ourselves, *that* the simple view of any two objects or actions, however related, can never give us any idea of power, or of a connection betwixt them."[2]

The chain of linear causality, therefore, is a mixture of habit, belief, and common sense. But this common sense is based on a number of assumptions, namely:

- That two events are unambiguously separated from each other and have their own independent existence, as, for example, two bodies with well-defined boundaries.
- That some contact, force, or influence flows from one body or event to the other.
- That there is a clear flow of time with the cause occurring in the past and the effect in the present.

Clearly, shunting railcars and colliding pool balls fulfill all these criteria. First, pool balls have hard edges and do not merge together or have a sporadic existence. The collision between two pool balls is very different from the meeting of, for example, two smoke rings or the intersection of two high-energy protons in a particle accelerator. Second, the causal flow is clear-cut in a pool game; it can be seen in the physical contact of the balls as they collide. Again, this is very different from the "action at a distance" of the moon on the earth's tides, the influence of a large rock on the vortices within a river, or the lunar cycle on the breeding habits of certain fish. Finally, there is no argument to the passage of time during a game of pool; it can be measured by the clock on the wall and by the player's own heartbeats. Time, however, is not so clear-cut when we come to mental and atomic events or to the early seconds of the universe, in which no independent clocks existed. In addition, some systems could be said to have their own internal time in which certain time scales are coupled or, alternatively, are independent of each other, while systems in total equilibrium may lack any real sense of time.

As long as objects and events are clear-cut and distinguishable, forces are well defined, and time flows on, collectively and unperturbed, then the notion of causality does not present problems. But as science probes deeper into a universe of internal flows and dynamic unfoldings, of subtle influences and intersecting time scales, then causal chains can no longer be analyzed and reduced to linear connections of individual events so that the very concept of causality begins to lose its power.

Synchronicities represent a bridge between matter and mind, and the concept of causality is clearly not appropriate to the world of mental events. While it is true that some of our more primitive behaviors may be causally "conditioned," it is clear that thoughts are not distinct, individual objects but are closer to smoke rings in the way they appear to enfold each other and merge. While there may sometimes exist a "train of thought," which implies a linear progression in time, this "train" does not have the form of a series of causal links, for the mechanism that triggers one thought may be very different from that which triggers another. Some thoughts flow by association, one from the other, while others emerge out of a common ground or even appear to be quite unconnected. In short, psychological time is profoundly different from that shown on the clock in the pool hall. When you play a game of pool, part of your thought is locked into the game itself while other aspects involve memories, anticipations, and even waking fantasies. Part of the mind may therefore be involved in a sort of timeless awareness while other aspects pursue a linear "train of thought." In general, therefore, our inner world does not fulfill the three criteria on which causality is based:

- Events are not clearly distinguished nor are they independent.
- There is no clear flowing of influence from one event to the next.
- Time is not linear and unambiguous.

The movements of the mind therefore require a more general description than is possible with linear chains of causality, and which evolves naturally out of events that flow and merge out of each other as expressions of a timeless order within some deeper ground. In building the bridge between mind and matter, the notion of causality must be bypassed in favor of transformations and unfoldings. In the chapters that follow, some of these new descriptions, which follow from an organic universe of unfolding patterns, will be explored.

THE GAMES CAUSALITY PLAYS

Causality, however, still holds us in its hypnotic grip and it is only by pushing the concept to the extreme that its limitations are realized. Take, for example, the game of tennis. Nothing could be clearer, in causal terms, than a game played with a well-defined, distinct tennis ball. Each time the ball is hit back across the net the very reality of the causal impulse can be felt right down the muscles of the arm. This palpable impact also provides the initial conditions of velocity and position that determine the path of the ball as it speeds toward the net.

However, other forces are also operating, notably gravity, which attempts to pull the ball down to the surface of the court. But gravity does not act like an initial impact, rather, it operates over the *whole path* of the ball. It is a truly holistic force that arises out of the total distribution of matter that surrounds the tennis court. While, for Newton, gravity was a mysterious "action at a distance," for Einstein it arose through the curving of space-time that is brought about by matter and energy. For all practical purposes, the effects of gravity on the tennis ball are all due to the earth's mass. But if causality is to be pushed to its logical limit then the miniscule effects of nearby mountains, the passage of the moon overhead, the more distant stars and planets, and even the masses of the players who run across the court must be taken into account. Each one acts to curve the fabric of space-time, which, in turn, governs the ball's trajectory across the net.

Another major influence on the ball's path is the effect of air resistance, which acts to reduce its velocity. Like gravity, air resistance acts over the *whole path*, but unlike gravity, its force strictly depends on how fast the ball is going. The faster the tennis ball travels, the greater are the effects of air resistance, and indeed, when the ball is moving slowly, this force is negligible. Air resistance can be calculated in a causal way, knowing the density of air in the tennis court and the characteristics of the ball and its flight. However, there will also be subtle variations in this resistance for the air may not be uniform in density; for example, its temperature may change over various segments of the court and the effect of an evaporating puddle will be to lower air temperature and increase humidity. All these effects in air resistance add up to very subtle causal correlations that arise from the whole situation of the court, the weather, the temperature, surrounding vegetation, and so on.

Finally, there are the effects of currents of air which act to deviate the ball as it travels across the net. When players are dealing with a steady wind they compensate each of their shots. However, it is more difficult to deal with sudden gusts of wind or changes in direction. To trace the origin of the gusts that blow across the tennis court is a particularly tall order for the world of causal chains. Their ultimate origin lies in the earth's daily rotation, which produces what are known as Coriolis forces, which give rise to the great swirls of weather in the northern and southern hemispheres. In addition to these global currents of air there are also the varying effects of the moon's pulling on the earth's atmosphere, temperature changes from region to region, and the complications induced by masses of air flowing across oceans, deserts, and mountain chains. Within any given region more and more perturbations must be taken into account, not all of them being small. As air rises up a gentle slope, for example, it is cooled, producing density fluctuations and local gusting. Wind passing across a lake will take up moisture, and as it approaches a city, it will be heated and perturbed by tall buildings. By the time it reaches the tennis court the behavior of any one gust will be the result of such a multitude of complex causes that it lies far beyond the predictive power of even the largest and fastest modern computer. Indeed, Edward Lorenz, a pioneer in researching the dynamics of weather, has spoken of the "butter-fly effect." Since the nonlinear equations involved in describing weather are so extremely sensitive to the slightest change in initial conditions, tomorrow's weather, he suggests, may be drastically changed by something as slight, but as critical, as the beating of a butterfly's wings today.

While Newton's laws make it possible to calculate the initial trajectory of a tennis ball, so many other effects contribute to its final motion that it will never be possible to pin down the ball's exact path to an arbitrarily fine accuracy. This *chain* of causality that gives rise to the ball's motion is in fact a complex *network* of causation. And the more the limits of this network are extended, the more it is seen to stretch out over the entire earth and ultimately the universe itself. Indeed if any phenomenon is examined in fine-enough detail it will turn out that "everything causes everything else."

It is of course possible to raise the objection that, while extending the chain of causality into an ever more complex network may be logically valid, it has no practical signifi-cance. To talk of planetary influences on a game of tennis is obviously far-fetched. In one sense this objection is true, but the analysis does show what can be expected when causality is pushed to its limit. Moreover, when more complex and subtle systems than tennis games are investigated then the very fine-tuned effects may turn out to be more and more important and quite novel forms of behavior may begin to emerge.

Not too long ago I attended a conference where one of the speakers, Dr. R. H. Peters, a biologist from McGill University in Montreal, was explaining the complex effects of phosphorus on a Canadian lake. (Phosphorus is normally present in lake water but also enters as a pollutant and in the rain runoff from fertilized fields.) The question that Peters had posed himself in his research was: What is the effect of various phosphorus concentrations on a lake's ecology as measured, for example, by its chlorophyll levels? To start, he explored a number of theoretical models of how lakes are supposed to behave and how phosphorus is taken up by plankton which then enter the food chain of the lake.

Using a model with only a few input parameters, Peters found that the predictions were totally inadequate. So in order to extend the model, more terms had to be added and additional effects included. However, as the model became more and more complex, the "small corrections" were sometimes found to produce large effects, and as more causal links were added, yet more were found to be hiding around the corner. As Peters put it:

> By causal mechanism, I believe we imply a direct link or series of links between a linear sequence of causes and effects. Ball 1 hits ball 2, ball 2 moves, etc. This view simply does not apply in ecology. . . . In consequence, the search for deeper and more ultimate causes, can lead reductionists into an infinite regress of cause after cause. Worse, alternative chains of similar length exist. As a result the search for ultimate causes can lead us along divergent paths further and further from our original goal of research. . . . Infinite regression, interpolation and expansion remove any possibility of mechanistic explanation. In compensation, they provide a richly textured, highly complex abstraction which can keep us measuring and experimenting forever.[3]

In short when causality and determinism are used in something as complex as an ecological system, the networks involved become evermore complex to the point where theories and mathematical models are in danger of breaking down. While some small corrections may produce negligible corrections, others may "blow up" and totally change the nature of the solutions. What was hair-splitting in the game of tennis becomes of overwhelming importance in the behavior of more complex and subtle systems. Any attempt to reduce all the facets of nature to a causal chain will simply fail. Moreover, while the example of the lake includes living systems, this high degree of subtlety is also found in inanimate matter such as weather systems, the dynamics of fluids, plasmas, and shock waves.

BOUNDARY CONDITIONS

By probing causality to its limit, it has been discovered that "everything causes everything else" and that each event emerges out of an infinite web or network of causal relationships. But could this prove to be a backward step in which the rigor of physics is exchanged for some more mystical approach to nature? How will it be possible to retain the framework of science while, at the same time, acknowledging the limits of causality and determinism?

The rise of science was accompanied by attempts to reveal pattern and order in the complex web of interconnections that exists in nature. Science, therefore, exposes the abstract relationships and regularities that exist within different individual phenomena of nature. Galileo, for example, made careful observations of how balls roll down a slope and along a flat table. In every case the balls came to rest, as a result of friction and air resistance, but Galileo's leap of insight was to realize that if these effects were totally eliminated then the balls would roll on forever. One of Galileo's major contributions to physics was his realization that uniform motion in a straight line, or rest, was the natural motion of all objects when they are not being acted on by an external force. Even more important than this deduction was the method Galileo used to arrive at it. It is clear that air resistance and friction can never be eliminated *in practice;* however, they can be eliminated in *thought experiments* and in the abstract world of mathematical physics. Galileo, therefore, taught that in order to uncover the laws, regularities, and patterns of nature, it is necessary first to *abstract* phenomena from the real world and consider laws in isolation from the contingencies of everyday life. Causality, in physics, is therefore an idealization, a reality that exists only within the world of equations and computer simulations. It must never be confused with the varied, complex, and subtle individual events of reality. In a universe in which "everything causes everything else," it is only by performing thought experiments and abstracting out the contingencies of nature that single underlying patterns can be inferred.

Galileo's observation became Newton's first law of motion. His approach was expanded into a general method of describing nature mathematically. Newton, however, took things even further. While claiming that straight line motion, or rest, is the natural condition of all bodies, he had to face the problem of the moon's closed orbit around the earth. How was this caused; what mysterious force acted in the depths of space to constantly pull the moon away from a straight line path?

Newton knew that the force of gravity acted to cause apples to fall from a tree. But the earth's attraction for apples and cannonballs had never been truly codified into a law of nature. Neither had anyone the insight to project this force out into empty space and identify it with the mysterious pull exerted on the moon's path. It was Newton who first formulated the insight that the fall of an apple is, in terms of theoretical physics, identical to the fall of the moon. According to his theory of universal gravitation a host of different phenomena—such as the flight of cannonballs, the earth's tides, and the motion of the moon and the planets—all arise through the action of the same law of attraction.

Thanks to Newton, a universal and abstract pattern was used to unite many of nature's different events and processes of change. What to the primitive mind had looked like the animating power of individual spirits was, within the physicist's imagination, the working of a handful of physical laws. With the help of this handful of laws, reality can, in principle, be explained.

The emphasis in the above statement should, however, be placed on the phrase "in principle." Scientific laws are always of the nature of abstractions, which apply *exactly* only in the domain of idealized "thought experiments." In the real world, contingencies and individual events tend to impose their own unique characteristics on physical law so that tendencies can be revealed only by averaging over repeated, controlled experiments. At one and the same time, therefore, laws of nature both rule the universe and are concealed within the fluctuations of individual phenomena. An example may serve to focus the force of this point.

Because of Newton, we now know that the force of gravity acts on the apple as it falls from the tree and causes it to accelerate at 32 feet per second per second. (That is, each second the apple's speed is increased by an additional 32 feet per second.) Now 32 feet/second/second is only an approximate value; how can the acceleration due to gravity be determined to an arbitrary accuracy? With a tape measure and stopwatch? Neither of these is particularly accurate. Moreover, the effects of air resistance and other forces perturbing the apple's motion must be eliminated. Laws of nature work exactly only in the imagined laboratories of physicists' minds.

Very accurate experiments, to determine the acceleration due to gravity using a falling body, have from time to time been carried out. But to eliminate all contingencies and extraneous causes requires the resources of a major standards laboratory. Several decades ago an experiment, using a falling metal bar, was designed at the National Research Council of Canada. I had the opportunity to talk to the various scientists and technicians about their experiments.

In order to insulate the experiment and the particular effect— the acceleration due to gravity—from the rest of the universe, many hundreds of person-hours were spent in designing and constructing apparatus which extended into several rooms. To begin with, the tube down which the bar would fall had to be evacuated to remove the effects of air resistance. In addition, the drop had to be carefully shielded to eliminate all electrical and magnetic forces on the bar. The whole apparatus had to be precisely temperature controlled to eliminate changes in length due to expansion and contraction. Timing was done using an atomic clock, and any earth tremors, which would perturb the local gravitational force and, moreover, act to vibrate the apparatus, were monitored. Even the way in which the bar was released had to be carefully designed, for if one edge were to be released a fraction of a second before the other, this would start the bar vibrating and oscillating.

With all the resources of a major research institute, an attempt was made to eliminate the effects of the universe from this experiment and to create ideal, insulated, and repeatable conditions in which to measure the acceleration due to gravity. But even with all this effort, each experiment differed slightly in its result. The final value was therefore obtained by averaging, but even after all the experimental errors and deviations had been taken into account, the averages over two separate series of measurements were still different by a significant degree. So even during something as straightforward as the fall of a metal bar, nature conspires to introduce fluctuations into each individual event.

And what about that game of tennis in which, in principle at least, the movement of the moon has an effect on the path of the ball? The illustration appeared far-fetched, if logically correct. But if the example is changed, then the results become particularly surprising. In place of tennis consider a game of pool in which a player tried to pot the black ball indirectly by means of the red ball. To achieve a clean shot, the player must carefully aim the cue ball at the red. But suppose there is a slight fluctuation in initial conditions, a slight tremor of the hand, for example. This tremor results in a very slight deflection in the way the cue ball travels down the table toward the red. Since the tremor in the cue is slight, then the error in the "initial conditions" of the cue ball will not be large, just sufficient to divert its path by a millimeter or so by the time it reaches the red. After this collision, the red moves toward the black, but now the error has been compounded and the red's path is several millimeters out. It still strikes the black but not at the right angle so that instead of going into the side pocket the ball bounces back off its cushion. A very slight error in initial conditions, therefore, results in the failure to pot a ball.

Now jump from pool to the molecules in a gas, all 10^{23} of them. According to Newton, once their initial conditions have been specified, the future behavior of each molecule, and every collision it experiences, can be predicted. But suppose that there is a microscopically small fluctuation in the initial conditions of only one of these molecules. This may be small enough to carry the molecule correctly through the first few of its collisions, but sooner or later, it will miss one of its

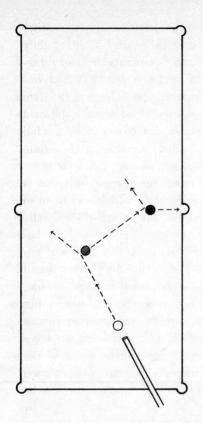

In this trick shot the white cue ball strikes the red, which then nudges the black into the side pocket. A slight error in the motion of the cue will still cause the cue ball to hit the red, but an accumulation of errors will result in the black ball missing the pocket.

destined targets and, having done so, the initial order inherent in the gas will have been lost. If, for example, all the molecules in the gas were simultaneously reversed, they would never get back to their original state for one vital collision would be missing. Any information inherent in the system would, therefore, have been irreplaceably lost.

Since there are such an enormous number of molecules in a gas, and an even larger number of collisions take place in a fraction of a second, it is clear that only the very smallest perturbation of the system is required to confuse the initial order. Are the gravitational effects of motion of the moon moving above the earth large enough? Calculations show that this is a far larger effect than needed! In fact, something as slight as the act of lifting a pool ball on the star Alpha Centuri is sufficient to totally disrupt with a fraction of a second any ordered motion of a gas here on earth!

Faced with the fact that the universe is in a constant state of flux and that each volume of space is being bathed in a fluctuating bath of radiation, incoming particles and gravity, it is clear that there is no possibility of absolute isolation in nature, no special region in which all effects can be shielded out and removed. Causality therefore remains an idealization that can never be put into absolute practice. In claiming that "everything causes everything else," the suggestion is that the various phenomena of the universe arise out of the flux of the whole, and are best described by a "law of the whole." While linear causality may work well enough for restricted, mechanical, and well-isolated systems, in general something more subtle and complex is needed to describe the full richness of nature. Pool and tennis may not be much affected by small fluctuations, but in the next chapter, we will examine systems that are so finely balanced that even the smallest perturbations may result in totally new ranges of behavior being produced. As such descriptions are probed, they will be found to have elements of what could be called a "synchronistic nature," which will open the door onto meaningful coincidences within the universe.

VARIATION PRINCIPLES AND THE LAW OF THE WHOLE

The limitations inherent in Newtonian causality have been discussed in the above paragraphs. But it should also be stressed that the Newtonian theory has proved to be enormously successful. Not only has it been used to predict eclipses, planetary movements, and the trajectories of space rockets, but it also explains how tides arise from the moon's gravitational attraction and it forms the foundation for several other branches of physics. Moreover, Newtonian causality has a unifying effect on the whole of science for it demonstrates how a wealth of phenomena can be explained on the basis of a handful of laws and assumptions. But while this Newtonian approach still tends to dominate science to some extent—it is most successful when describing what could usefully be called mechanistic systems—there are a host of other phenomena in the natural world which call for a totally different approach. In discovering the basis for synchronicity, therefore, an alternative path from that of causality, mechanism, and determinism needs to be followed.

It is interesting to note that Newton's was not the only theory that could explain the behavior of objects on our everyday scale. While Newton's mechanics was founded on the notion of forces which act piecewise on each element of a body's path through space, this alternative approach began with the idea of the *whole path*. Rather than analyzing motion into causative elements, the variation principle, as it is called, considers that motion emerges out of the *whole action* and is, in consequence, closer to the ideas we are exploring in this book.

Variation principles, which attempt to describe motions by recourse to their whole action or gesture, have a distinguished history and, in fact, predate Newton's own approach to mechanics. Indeed, a little reflection on Newton's laws shows that there is something rather odd about his first law. It derives from Galileo's observation that the natural state of a body that is not acted on by external forces is either rest or uniform straight line motion. While the second law relates force to the rate of change of motion and is applied piecewise to each segment of a particle's path through space, the first law applies to the entire path and suggests that there is some natural or ideal state of motion in the universe. This first law, therefore, is in some senses not unlike a variation principle. Its origins can be traced back to Aristotle's argument that planets move in circles because such motion is the swiftest and the "minimum." Likewise, Hero of Alexandria showed that a ray of light always takes the shortest possible path.

In the Renaissance, Leonardo argued that a falling body takes the shortest path, and Copernicus, Kepler, and Galileo were preoccupied with similar notions. Clearly these early thinkers were groping toward some universal principle in which observed motion arises as the universe expends the minimum amount of effort and achieves its ends in the simplest possible way. Motion and change, according to this picture, are not strictly analyzable into more elementary units but emerge out of the universe as a whole, or as Nicholas Malebranch suggested, there is an "economy in nature."

It was not until the seventeenth and eighteenth centuries that scientists such as Fermat, Maupertius, Euler, and Lagrange were able to provide a mathematical basis for these earlier intuitions and showed that motion and change were always achieved in a way that minimizes the "action" of nature. (This *action* is a measure of the momentum and velocity associated with a moving particle and can be generalized in the case of more complex systems. *Action* also plays an important role in the quantum theory.) It was as if a falling apple, a speeding rocket, a flowing river, or an orbiting moon all have a sense of the possible paths open to them and chose that which offers nature the greatest economy of *action*. Nature, therefore, is somewhat like a ballet dancer, the meaning of whose gestures are contained in the *whole movement*. While it is possible to analyze the motion of a dancer's body by means of photographs, it is clear that each element has its origin in the entire gesture and any static element is therefore incomplete. In a similar way, variation principles suggest that the movements of nature are similarly complete and can be understood only in a whole sense—as opposed to being built out of smaller elements.

Max Planck, the discoverer of the quantum of energy, was so impressed by the power of variation principles that he believed they were truly universal and should apply not only to the paths of moving bodies but to all types of behavior within the universe. Indeed, since Planck's time it has been possible to show how the theory of relativity and quantum theory both follow from variation principles. In a sense, therefore, Aristotle was correct when he speculated that the orbits of the planets are in some sense a "minimum," for in the curved space-time of Einstein's relativity, they indeed follow what are called "geodesic paths" that obey a variation principle.

Newtonian mechanics, however, is fairly simple to understand. A large range of problems can be solved with nothing more than a little high school physics, and for this reason it tended during the last century to overshadow the variation approach. However, with the flow of fluids and the behavior of electromagnetic fields, these phenomena arise out of the properties of the *whole field* and the *whole flow* so that the variation principle is essential to an understanding of the system. Clearly for the field theories of nature, it is more natural to think in terms of events unfolding out of a continuous background rather than built up in a piecewise fashion out of distinct elements. In addition, when things are no longer distinguished and flow one into the other, chains of causality are no longer appropriate. Electrical fields and flowing rivers are continuous things that defy analysis and vary smoothly from place to place. Since the variation principle applies both to fields as well as to material distinguishable particles it was inevitable that, at some point, a theory should be created that would embrace both aspects of nature.

One of the most intellectually impressive developments of the variation principle was created early in the second half of the nineteenth century by an Irishman, William Hamilton, and Karl Gustav Jacobi, a mathematician from Potsdam. Their combined work, known as the Hamilton-Jacobi theory, provides a uniform framework for treating everything from moving particles to the nature of light. Truly, this new form of dynamics shows that all motion and change emerges out of a "law of the whole" and that the patterns and events of nature are the expression of an underlying unity of form.

The Hamilton-Jacobi theory can therefore stand as a metaphor for patterns and gestures that emerge out of a background, rather than through the interaction of elements one with another. When the first violins and cellos in an orchestra sweep their bows across the strings of their instruments all at the same time, it is not because of some interaction or force that passes between them. Rather the origin for that movement is to be found in the musical score. The gestures made by orchestra players and the movements of ballet dancers on the stage all flow out of the same ground—the music itself—and are truly meaningful conjunctions of external events. Even within the "mechanical universe" of moving particles it is possible to describe events and happenings as the result of unfoldings from an underlying ground.

The Hamilton-Jacobi theory, in its purest form, treated the world as composed of interacting waves, so that motion emerges out of the whole complex movement of these waves, rather than through the action of a force acting on infinitesimal elements of a trajectory. Movement is a little like a boat being tossed and moved around by the ocean. The appearance of any given wave in one location is not so much a "mechanical" phenomenon as the overall expression of wavelets coming from all over the ocean. The movement of the boat at any one moment is, therefore, an expression of the total motion of the ocean as it is folded into that particular region.

The Hamilton-Jacobi theory provides a natural framework not only for discussing field phenomena such as light and the behavior of fluids, but it also suggests a metaphor for the structures and movements of matter in which material objects are pictured as concentrations or packets of wavelets that undergo coherent motion together. The collision of two billiard balls, according to this picture, represents the coincidence in a particular region of space of two concentrations of wavelets that come together and then move apart. While, at one level, these wavelengths can be interpreted as "colliding" and interacting with each other according to Newtonian laws, an alternative account is that the phenomena arise out of the general global conditions of the entire system. In this latter sense, the collision between the balls is "acausal." It does not involve a causal exchange between independent objects but emerges out of the whole wave field. In the next chapter, a similar image arises out of the way particlelike "solitons" emerge from the nonlinear background.

The richness of this whole approach can now be seen, for on the one hand, it is possible to abstract causal regularities and forces which act piecewise on the trajectories of bodies. But on the other hand, these simply arise out of the "law of the whole." Hence the mechanistic and organic accounts of nature are in no sense opposed to each other, but rather, they give a complementary account of the unfolding of phenomena. It is in this way that the dualities present in the diagram of Jung and Pauli can be understood. Causality and synchronicity are not contradictory but are dual perceptions of the same underlying reality.

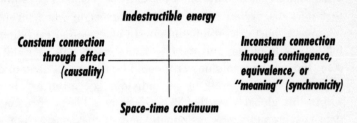

Indestructible energy

Constant connection through effect (causality) — *Inconstant connection through contingence, equivalence, or "meaning" (synchronicity)*

Space-time continuum

In this way it becomes possible to retain a subjective experience of nature and a sense of the meaning and interconnectedness of things without needing to reject the scientific approach. Science, after all, is an attempt to understand nature by asking questions and trying to face the facts of things, no matter where they may lead. It is an objective approach in which nothing is taken for granted and reason and experiment go hand in hand. By setting this approach within the context of a direct perception of the wholeness of things and the unity of nature it will be possible to combine subjective experience with the rigor of mathematical description and experimental method. In this way it may be possible to combine the subjective and the objective and build a bridge between mind and matter.

In the chapters that follow, new patterns and conjugations will be investigated as they flow from this global approach to nature. Within them will be found the seeds of synchronicity that will eventually flower into a unity of consciousness and the universe. Indeed it will be discovered that the deeper things are probed the more marvelous and meaningful they will become.

CONCLUSIONS

The major question that was posed in this chapter is, how can synchronicities exist in a world that is dominated by causality? At first sight the Newtonian vision of nature determines all events in the universe and therefore leaves no room for meaningful patterns of coincidence. While quantum theory has successfully challenged the exclusive nature of this worldview, the loophole it offers is simply not wide enough to admit synchronicity. It is only when causality is pushed to the limit that it is discovered that the actual context in which events take place must extend indefinitely. In other words, everything that happens in our universe is in fact caused by everything else. Indeed the whole universe could be thought of as unfolding or expressing itself in its individual occurrences. It is within this global view that it becomes possible to accommodate synchronicities as meaningful events that emerge out of the heart of nature.

NOTES

1. David Hume, *Treatise of Human Nature*. There are a number of editions of this work, for example, one edited by L. A. Selby-Bigge and P. H. Nidditch (Oxford University Press, 1978).
2. Ibid.
3. R. H. Peters, *Prediction and Understanding: Alternative Goals in Science*, talk delivered at the symposium "Reductionism versus Holism," University of Ottawa, January 1985.

3 THE LIVING UNIVERSE

The previous chapter used the examples of tennis and pool to show that beneath their simple exteriors was concealed all the subtlety of a holistic universe. This chapter goes to the other extreme. It illustrates and explores the full implications of complexity within living and nonliving matter and shows how new forms emerge out of a general background and how meaningful patterns are born out of chaos and change. As these processes of unfoldment are understood, it becomes possible to come a little closer to uncovering some of the mysteries of synchronicity.

THE ORGANIZATION OF LIFE

Suppose that you were to observe the growth of a human cell from the moment of conception through its development into a fully functioning baby. A fraction of a second after fertilization the membrane of this first cell undergoes a rapid change which makes it impenetrable to other sperm. Inside, the pooling of genetic material from father and mother begins, and within twenty-four hours, this cell divides and the process of geometric growth accelerates toward its final goal.

During the first days, the ovum maintains its initial size as cells inside continue to divide and multiply, each one identical to its neighbors. However, once the ovum is safely implanted on the uterus wall, new forms of growth begin which involve the complex processes of morphogenesis.

It is a giant step from an undifferentiated colony of cells to an autonomous being, for cells must migrate, collect together, change their rate of growth and division, die, fuse, split, bend, and fold, all in a coordinated fashion until the first organs appear. Some cells are destined to grow into the spine, arms, heart, or hair while others become the brain, spleen, blood, skin, or eyes. In this process of morphogenesis, or the making of form, two neighboring cells may begin the complicated processes of differentiation that will cause them to develop into quite different organs, possibly even located in very different parts of the body. This stage of growth involves staggering geometrical and topological transformations. The cells of the optic nerve, for example, grow from the retina of the eye and move toward the brain, where a million individual nerve fibers find their way to precise locations within the geniculate cortex.

The process of morphogenesis presents some of the most challenging and exciting questions in biology today. How are individual cells able to differentiate and cooperate so that each knows its precise function in such an infallible way? How are different organs of the body able to grow in such a coordinated fashion, each developing at precisely the correct time, accelerating and slowing down their rate of growth when needed and making exact connections to other organs?

While most molecular biologists feel that the complete answer to these questions lies in the way that genetic instructions in each cell's DNA are expressed through various chemical triggers, a few have argued that more subtle mechanisms must be called into play. For example, to ask how the optic nerve completes its path from eye to brain is to demand a very different order of explanation from that which can normally be given by reductionism. It may be true that a part of this answer can be provided by a detailed analysis of individual events at the molecular level. But the global story may in fact require an additional order of explanation that takes into account the living, evolving nature of organisms and the possibility of the creative emergence of new forms and novel states of behavior. The more analytical types of explanation would then play an important role, but within the general context of a more global description.

It is possible that such an approach could evolve from what was termed, in the previous chapter, "the law of the whole" and some of its implications will be unfolded in this and later chapters. In exploring this field it will be possible to take an additional step along the line that separates causality from synchronicity in Jung and Pauli's diagram.

The final stage of morphogenesis and growth is the complete living being, autonomous, purposeful, capable of reacting to the environment and of anticipating the future. While, on the one hand, this individual is a mass of cells, the elementary units of its body, it is certainly not a machine that is built out of independent, interacting elements. Rather these cells cooperatively form organs which integrate and function together, each one depending on the whole body for its correct functioning. Brain, heart, blood, liver, kidneys, spleen, and intestines work in an internal harmony together. The heart supplies the body with blood and, in turn, owes its life to the continuing supply of freshly oxygenated blood from the lungs. The lungs serve the heart and, for their part, rely on it for their blood supply. Each organ in the body could, therefore, be thought of as a member of a highly complex ecosystem that relies on the correct functioning of the whole. Clearly reductionism is only of limited applicability for such a system.

From the perspective of the body, the mutual coordination of functions, the organization of flows, and the harmonization of structures appear almost as synchronicities. Indeed, they *are* the synchronicities of living organisms for they involve *meaningful coincidences* in which the *meaning* lies within the context of the body's ordered functioning and the *coincidence* involves the precise synchronization (or coincidence) of events occurring in remote parts of the body. While at one level it is possible to analyze these organic synchronicities in terms of the release of hormones, blood sugars, neurotransmitters, and so on, at another level these patterns are a function of the body as a whole and an expression of its *meaning*.

This can be clearly seen in the operation of the immune

system, which is a complex pattern-recognition system distributed over the entire body. The immune system, with its 10^{12} lymphocytes and 10^{20} antibody molecules can be compared only to the brain in its degree of subtlety. Indeed, the way in which it recognizes the pattern of an invading virus or foreign organism bears a striking resemblance to the pattern recognition properties of the brain. Recent research, using a technique called patch clamping, has demonstrated that, at the cell level, lymphocytes employ similar mechanisms to those of nerve cells and may even contain receptor sites for brain transmitter molecules.

The immune system therefore acts as a pattern recognition system which communicates information across the body and stores it as a memory. During invasions by viruses the immune system may even be able to communicate in some direct way with the nervous system and hence the brain itself. The immune system could therefore be said to depend on *meaning* for its activities, on the meaning of the molecular structure of an invading virus, the meaning of the pattern of a disease, the meaning of the normal functioning of the body. It even appears that, during periods of excessive stress, the immune system's failure to fight off disease may be related to the whole organism's internal lack, or confusion, of meaning. Indeed, if the meaning of the body is taken to be its intelligent, coordinated activity in health, then disease is a degeneration or breakdown in meaning.

From within the perspective of a living being, synchronicity, or the meaningful coordination of events, may be a more appropriate description than causality alone. The organism is concerned with its internal meaning, with *the way things happen together* and with the integration of events that support its dynamic form and so maintain its meaning in the world.

But the developing cell and the functioning adult are worlds apart from the games of pool and tennis that were discussed in the previous chapter. Can the same descriptive metaphors serve the universe of both matter and human life? Suppose that mechanism and organism are treated not as contradictory descriptions of nature but rather as complementary ones, dual aspects of the same reality. Many of the insights into the processes of life and the evolution of novel forms also then apply to the inanimate, so that the deeper the world of physics is penetrated, the closer it approaches a synchronistic order.

Beyond Reductionism

There is an obvious advantage in being able to explain complex things in terms of simpler ones, or large systems in terms of smaller. Therefore analysis, with its reduction from complexity to simplicity, is traditionally a useful way of doing science. However, its drawbacks become apparent when analysis adopts the position of "nothing but." When chemistry is "nothing but the physics of molecules," an organism is "nothing but its constituent chemistry," and mind "nothing but nerve cells and neurochemicals in action," then a narrowness of perspective results.

By contrast, in this book, mind and matter must be understood through dualistic, even pluralistic, descriptions, each one being complementary to the other. Qualified reductionism therefore has its place, but when it pretends to offer an exhaustive account of nature, then misrepresentation and confusion result.

As previously pointed out, the human body is composed of cells which depend upon the whole organism. So at one level the operations of the body can be explained in terms of its constituents, yet at another, these constituent parts must be defined in terms of the goals, operations, and meaning of the whole. In such systems, it becomes clear that at each new level of organization and each new scale of size and complexity, different meanings are present and new and possibly unexpected behaviors and structures manifest themselves. Each level of structure therefore requires its own level of description which contains concepts and relationships that were not present in what went before. But in turn, this level of description is conditioned by what lies above and below in the scale of size and complexity. Living systems, therefore, depend upon a series of levels of descriptions, with none being more fundamental than the other.

But can this analogy of the interweaving of descriptive levels be extended to the nonliving? Nobel laureate Ilya Prigogine argues forcefully that there is no true "fundamental level" in nature but rather each level involves its own unique description and is conditioned by the levels around it. The implication is clear—absolute reductionism will never work, for whenever one level is chosen as a foundation it will, ultimately, be found to depend on all other levels for the definition of its concepts and the context of its meanings.

It is generally assumed that quantum theory and the elementary particles, or some yet-to-be-discovered subquantum entity, constitute the most basic level of nature and that all descriptions can ultimately be reduced to this quantum level. However, as soon as this proposal is examined, it is discovered to be false. To say that everything can be analyzed in terms of elementary particles implies that all levels of description can be reduced to the lowest—the quantum level. But what exactly is this quantum level and what are the basic entities that it comprises? Any attempt to measure or determine the properties of a quantum state meets with Heisenberg's fundamental limitation, that the observer is irreducibly linked to the quantum system and that any act of observation disturbs this system in a finite way. To measure a quantum state and determine its properties therefore requires the presence of a macroscopic observer who will disturb the state. So while the macrolevel can be analyzed in terms of the quantum level, this quantum level, in turn, is conditioned by the macrolevel. The notion of reality becomes somewhat like a scene viewed in two parallel mirrors in which each image enfolds the next and almost appears to become self-sustaining with no final limit.

Reductionism and analysis are limited in their power, for any level can be used *provisionally* as the basis for an explanation. Nature, therefore, requires pluralistic descriptions and we anticipate that this pluralism must contain both causal and synchronistic aspects.

By exploring the implications of the mechanistic and organistic

approaches to nature, it becomes possible to move closer to a model of reality which accommodates mind in a natural way. As the subtleties of nature unfold, they are found to be further and further removed from simple mechanisms so that mind no longer appears to be alien to the universe. Likewise the synchronicities that form a bridge between matter and mind can not be reduced to a single level of description. Rather, complementary descriptions, approaches, and metaphors are necessary so that synchronicity appears as through the facets of a rotating crystal, constantly displaying new forms and colors that are the reflection of an underlying ground.

The Clustering in Human Affairs

During a synchronicity, different objects and events congregate together to form an overall pattern in space and time. According to the writer Arthur Koestler, these conjunctions indicate how different objects in the universe show an affinity for each other.[1] Koestler's idea echoes a philosophy that was prevalent during the Middle Ages and was based on the correspondences between objects. According to this belief, planets, animals, minerals, and the dispositions of the body have various sympathies to each other so that apparently disconnected events tend to happen together. Rather than these conjunctions taking place through Newtonian forces of attraction they are brought about because, in Koestler's words, "certain things like to happen together."

Such conjunctions of events were crucial to the ancient Chinese concept of history. According to our Western approach, a war, treaty, strike, or social movement can be traced back along causal lines to its roots in, say, social unrest, changes in legislation, or new balances of trade. The Chinese, however, preferred not to view history in terms of causal networks but rather were concerned with *how things happen together in time*. Therefore omens, domestic details, and changes in the weather were listed alongside a military expedition or a powerful marriage. According to Hellmut Wilhelm, son of the famous translator of the *I Ching:*

The interplay of forces that determine a historical moment sounds as a single chime. . . . only by concentrating on this sound and yielding to it may we recognize its essence and its effect. The mode and effect of these immanent powers can only be understood through their manifestations. In other words, only absorption in the historical moment can lead us to the meaning of events.[2]

So, to other thinkers in different times, the universe and human history present an integrated face in which events are not so much the end result of causal links but are aspects of an overall pattern that results from certain "immanent powers." But how can this notion of events that cluster together in time have any connection with our current scientific view of the universe? At first sight these two approaches to nature are remote, yet as the ideas of collective motion and the emergence of order out of chaos are explored, significant resonances will be discovered between modern science and the "synchronistic thinking" of ancient China and the Middle Ages.

ELECTRONS AND SLIME MOLDS

The prime image of this chapter is not the game of pool or tennis but the slime mold. Nature has produced some five hundred different varieties of slime mold that live on rotting vegetation. The singular property of these microscopic organisms is that, like the wave/particle duality of the subatomic world, they can exist in two entirely different forms. In its normal state, a slime mold colony consists of a large number of independent individuals, amoebalike cells that take nourishment from vegetation on the forest floor. These cells multiply by simple division and so spread out, eating everything in their path until the colony exhausts the food supply around it. At this *critical point* chemical signals move between cells, like expanding ripples, and trigger an entirely new form of behavior. Individual cells now begin to congregate together and the separate elements of the colony transform themselves into members of a single, multicellular organism.

The cooperative colony has a slug-like appearance and be-

gins to move across the forest floor. When the slug reaches a suitable new location it rears up and develops a head on top of a long stalk. Within this head, spores form and mature until they are shot out across the forest in an explosive burst. As each spore comes to rest it produces an individual slime mold cell that begins its life of eating, dividing, and ultimately producing a new colony of cells. In the future, progeny of this primal cell will again reach the critical point where their food runs out, they will congregate together into a new slug, and so begin the process of migration and dispersal yet again.

A slime mold has a dual nature and provides a striking metaphor for the dual or multiple descriptions of nature. On the one hand, since the colony is composed of independent individuals, its description should be close to a causal, reductionist one. On the other, it is a single, cohesive body which demands a holistic, global description. The slime mold therefore shows how collectivity and individuality, holistic and reductionist aspects can exist within the same system.

What is particularly interesting about the slime mold is the way in which collective or holistic behavior is enfolded within the individual, and likewise, individual behavior is unfolded across the whole. The individual and the global elements are both contained one within the other—an approach that clearly requires a new mathematical approach to nature, one in which each element is both interior and exterior to every other. Such a formal approach will be explored in Chapter 6, where it will be shown to give important insights in the way that quantum theory can be interpreted. As with the slime mold so with the universe it will be shown that within each element of matter and space-time is enfolded the entire universe.

The collective order that is contained within an individual slime mold cell can also be found in the world of ants, bees, wasps, and termites. While the single insect seems to be living an independent existence it also carries within it, in some hidden or enfolded fashion, the behavior of the hive or the colony.

Closer to home is the simultaneous existence of individual and collective behavior in a football crowd. Each member of

the crowd is an individual with memories, goals, drives, and needs, and most important, a sense of his or her own free will. Yet the crowd has its own dynamics that swing between joy and violence. A crowd, therefore, can behave in ways that appear alien or even repulsive to the individual. Nevertheless the individual is enfolded within the crowd and the crowd within the individual, each appears both interior and exterior to the other.

The image of the slime mold is a powerful one, but does it have any relevance for the world of inanimate objects or do hidden and cooperative orders emerge only at the level of life and society? The answer turns out to be that this dualistic nature of things is universal and many examples can be found of how material systems are governed by similar very subtle orders.

Consider, as a first example, the electrons in a metal; any metal—the blade of a knife, the chassis of an automobile. Many of these electrons are bound to individual atoms that make up the metal's lattice structure, but in every metal, some of them are relatively free to move about and can be pictured as forming a "gas" of electrons that occupies the space between the lattice of atoms. Just as air consists of molecules freely moving about, so a metal contains a free-moving gas of electrons.

These electrons, of course, interact with each other since each one has a negative electrical charge. However, to a good approximation, physicists can treat them as being free, or at least quasi-independent. Their movement is, therefore, not unlike that of a random swarm of bees around the hive. Electrons fly past each other, some are deflected, others collide; the gas is a buzzing confusion of an astronomically large number of chance movements.

When a little energy is added to the metal, it is shared with the electron gas and electrons move faster so that confusion and chaos seem more pronounced. However, when this energy reaches a critical point, electronic chaos is transformed into a totally new kind of behavior, for the gas begins to oscillate *as a whole* with what are called plasma vibrations. At first sight the

electron gas behaves in an analogous fashion to the slime mold, for at a certain critical point, it exchanges its individualistic behavior for a collective one, but in fact, the situation is far more subtle. In the case of the slime mold, the first period of its life is lived as an independent individual, in the second, as the member of a collective organism. In the electron gas, however, the plasma vibrations are superposed upon the "random" background motions of the electrons. Therefore within the chance, to and fro motion of each electron is hidden its simultaneous participation in the electron gas as a whole. The formal, mathematical treatment of the electron gas shows that each electron is, in a sense, simultaneously both a quasi-independent entity and a dependent component of global vibrations that involve an astronomical number of identical electrons. In other words, within random chaotic motion is contained a global order, so that chance and order become intimately related. The electron gas therefore has something in common with a crowd, or society, for it exhibits both individual and collective behavior. Enfolded with each electron's movement is the plasma and in turn the plasma unfolds out of the individual electrons.

This ability to enfold both cooperative and individual behaviors is also found in some metals at the other end of the energy scale. As an electron gas moves within a regular atomic lattice its individual electrons are like the balls in a pinball machine, always moving and colliding with the atom pins. When an electrical current passes through this metal, it produces a large scale drift in the electron gas, or to put it another way, the passage of current *is* this drift. During the current flow, however, electrons are constantly being scattered from vibrating atoms in the lattice and this has the effect of retarding the drift of the gas. In this way the phenomenon of electrical resistance is produced out of the random scattering of electrons from vibrating atoms.

Now suppose that the metal is cooled. This has the effect of reducing the strength of atomic vibrations and therefore of lowering the resistance. But even at absolute zero important quantum effects still keep the atomic lattice vibrating so that resistance is still present. In certain metals, however, as a critical temperature is reached, the behavior changes dramatically and all electrical resistance vanishes. The metal is suddenly transformed into a superconductor. Within this superconductor all electrical resistance vanishes and a current, once established in a superconducting ring, will continue to flow for hundreds of thousands of years.

This phenomenon of superconductivity arises from a form of cooperative and collective order. At the critical temperature the vibrating atoms no longer act to perturb the electron flow but work in a subtle way to allow the cohesive movement of electrical current. Close to absolute zero, this combination of quantum fluctuations of the atoms and random electron motion no longer gives rise to resistance, but rather, it is welded into a novel behavior in which the entire system *acts as a whole*.

In the previous chapter it was argued that the law of larger numbers will average out all quantum effects so that they vanish in the everyday scale of things. But where cooperative effects such as superconductivity are concerned, each infinitesimal electron motion becomes part of the whole. The result is a cohesive quantum state, a superconducting wave function that is measured in meters rather than atomic distances. What was previously the random scattering of electrons off a vibrating lattice has been transformed into the subtle, cooperative motion of the whole.

Global, cooperative behavior is also found in the laser and the superfluid. In the latter, all resistance to flow vanishes as randomly moving helium molecules suddenly act as a single quantum entity. The critical temperature transition, from the normal to the superfluid state, could be compared to that between a single slime mold cell and the moving slug.

The examples above suggest that extremely subtle behavior can be discovered not only in living organisms and society but also within the electron gas, the laser, and the superfluid. In each case this collective order is hidden within chaotic and random motion so that radically new forms of behavior emerge at critical points, not so much from the interactions of many individuals, but through the cooperative action of the whole.

THE WORLD OF NONLINEARITY

The examples considered in this chapter all revolve around the duality of describing a system in terms of its parts, and the parts in terms of the overall system. Such complementariness has its counterpart in the mathematics of linear and nonlinear differential equations that play such a vital role in engineering, physics, chemistry, biology, and economics. These equations span the whole range of behaviors from the animate to inanimate and give an understanding of the abstract principles that lie beneath many different orders of behavior.

Linear differential equations, and the systems they describe, have been studied since Newton invented the calculus and are so well understood that today well-defined and relatively simple procedures exist for their solution. These linear systems are predictable in their behavior; they can normally be broken down into simpler parts, and to understand one class of solution helps the mathematician to write down others. Linear systems are gradual and gentle; their smooth and regular behavior is met in slowly flowing streams, electrical circuits that operate under normal conditions, slowly reacting chemicals, small vibrations, engines working at low power, quiet sounds, and structures under low stress.

But once the power or violence of a system is increased, it leaves the familiar linear region and enters the more complex world of nonlinear effects: rivers become turbulent, amplifiers overload and distort, chemicals explode, machines go into uncontrollable oscillations, plates buckle, metals fracture, and structures collapse. However, in some cases these nonlinear effects may not be destructive but can involve novel forms of behavior and the emergence of new forms of structure.

A metal bar that is loaded with weights responds at first linearly. Each time a small weight is added, the bar bends by a correspondingly small amount; small loads produce small effects and a graph of bending versus loading is smooth and predictable. But suppose that this loading reaches a critical point; suddenly the bending is no longer simply related to the load and the bar deforms or fractures. At this nonlinear stage, or "the straw that broke the camel's back," a small cause produces a drastic effect and the graph of bending versus loading has a sudden, unexpected discontinuity.

Pressing the gas pedal on a car results in a smooth increase of speed. At first this increase lies in the linear region and everything is regular and predictable. However, as the car approaches a certain, critical power output, nonlinear effects become important. A small additional pressure on the gas pedal may cause the car to vibrate violently or the engine to overheat and seize up. Likewise, a small turn of the volume knob of a stereo will produce a linear response from the speakers, but if the volume is turned too far, nonlinearities in the electrical circuitry produce a marked distortion.

Nature is rich in examples of nonlinear behavior. In fact, it turns out that nonlinearity is the rule rather than the exception; the world must be described mathematically by equations that exhibit critical points and novel orders of behavior and cannot always be analyzed or decomposed into simpler forms. Why then have the concepts of linearity and predictability held such a prominent position in science? The answer is simple; until the advent of high-speed computers and the development of new mathematical techniques, nonlinear differential equations were something of a closed book. Their linear cousins, however, could be solved in a straightforward fashion. They corresponded to simple physical laws and the analysis of complex systems into simpler interacting elements. For this reason, until a decade or so ago, most scientists tended to concentrate on systems in their linear range and, to some extent, ignore other behavior. In studying the flow of water down a narrow pipe or the passage of air across an airplane, the nonlinear region was referred to as "turbulence" and only a few special cases treated in detail. But today, thanks to the most advanced computers, it is possible to make simulations of the various forms of turbulence and use new forms of mathematics to classify the different orders of solution. The richness of the nonlinear world is, therefore, a comparatively recent discovery that is only now being opened up to mathematical explorers.

Linearity, however, encourages an attitude of mind in which a complex system is analyzed into simpler systems. This is so because a linear system can always be broken down into a collection of coupled linear differential equations that correspond to interacting elements. For example, the conduction of heat and sound in a metal can be described in terms of interacting abstractions called phonons. In the linear region, therefore, a metal behaves *as if it were composed* of elementary phonons—just as atoms act as if they are composed of elementary particles!

But as the temperature of the metal is raised, or it is perturbed more violently in other ways, nonlinear behavior dominates and it is no longer possible to explain its properties in terms of interacting phonons. The behavior of the metal now emerges out of *the system as a whole* and new and unexpected effects may suddenly appear. One obvious form of novelty, unexpected from a set of interacting phonons, is the breakdown of the atomic lattice that occurs at the metal's melting point when it is transformed from solid to liquid.

This consideration provides a reason for the tradition of seeing nature in terms of analysis and the causal interaction of elementary entities. Provided that attention is always restricted to systems that operate within a limited, linear range, this approximation is valid. But in more general cases of chaos, turbulence, changes of state, transition, and evolution, nature displays far more subtle mechanisms in which new and emergent properties manifest themselves and descriptions must take into account *the whole system* and not just its parts.

This nonlinear nature is much closer in its operation to an organism than to a machine. Its understanding therefore requires new attitudes that lie closer to synchronicity than they do to linear causality, in which patterns and orders unfold out of the general background of change. Within such an approach, mind may no longer appear as an alien stuff in a mechanical universe; rather, the operation of mind will have resonances to the transformations of matter, and indeed, the two will be found to emerge from a deeper ground.

In Chapter 2 an image of the movement and collision of material bodies was given in terms of waves in the ocean. But

now, thanks to a deeper understanding of the nonlinear interactions involved, the complex and apparently random motions
of the ocean itself have been found to conceal a particularly
subtle form of order. H. C. Yuan and B. M. Lake, two
physicists who have made a study of nonlinear wave interactions, suggest that the surface of the ocean is in fact "highly
modulated," or ordered, so that it in fact contains a "memory"
of all its earlier configurations![3]

SOLITONS

One of the most striking properties of a certain class of nonlinear
equations is the soliton, which dramatically demonstrates how
the part can emerge as an expression of the whole. Using the
image of the soliton, it also becomes possible to see how
meaningful localized patterns can unfold out of a general
background.

Although the soliton came under close mathematical study
only within the last decade, it was first observed in 1834 by a
Mr. J. Scott Russell, who, while riding beside a narrow channel of water, observed a curious wave that:

> . . . rolled forward with great velocity, assuming the form of a
> large solitary elevation, a rounded, smooth and well defined heap
> of water, which continued its course along the channel apparently
> without change of form or dimunition of speed.[4]

Russell chased the wave on horseback for a mile or two until
he "lost it in the windings of the channel." Instead of rapidly
dissipating like any normal wave, this "solitary wave," as he
called it, persisted for a great distance as a well-defined
shape, complete in itself and moving at high speed. The
solitary wave, or *soliton* as it is now called, has since been
discovered in a wide variety of nonlinear systems such as
electrical circuits, nerve impulses, and the vibrations of atoms.
It has even been suggested that elementary particles are not, in
fact, the fundamental building blocks of matter but are the
solitons of an underlying nonlinear quantum field.

Solitons are distinct and localized; they can move along trajectories just as tennis balls do, and when two solitons meet, they interact and deflect together. In other words, solitons have all the appearances of elementary entities or independent units of the world. However, by virtue of their very existence, solitons are totally subsistent on the ground that gave them birth. For solitons are local phenomena that are constantly sustained through a global activity; they are born, persist as patterns in space and time, and then die back into their ground. These nonlinear manifestations of nature have been discovered in such diverse systems as atmospheric pressure waves, tidal bores, the Great Red Spot of Jupiter, heat conduction in solids, superfluidity, and superconductivity.[5]

This example makes it possible to discover a significant role for analysis and reduction within the "law of the whole." In the previous chapter reductionism and linear orders of causality were rejected as being overrestrictive and unable to capture the essential richness of nature. But in the case of solitons it has been possible to analyze a system into relatively independent parts, *within the context of the whole*. Hence analysis has an important place within the overall activity of wholeness, for it enables thought to take things apart, explore relationships, and observe the patterns of internal structures. It is only when analysis and reduction become absolute and the "solitons" are taken for truly independent elements of reality that confusion sets in.

An example of the complementary global and analytic approaches can be found in the way a pianist approaches a new composition. At first the musician must develop a "feel" for the music, its overall sense, and impact. But this also involves a detailed analysis that reveals the way the piece is put together, why certain things work the way they do, and the various internal relationships that exist within the work. Through study of the score and by "trying out" various passages at the piano, the musician begins to understand the inner working of the music. But this is always carried out with reference to the overall form of the music and the effect which is to be produced in the concert hall. The final performance therefore emerges out of both the holistic or global approach and the local or analytical exploration.

Something similar can happen in the way a scientist approaches nature, although in many cases the more global considerations tend to be lost in details. Thus, the theoretical physicist devises thought experiments and mathematically dissects the system's behavior. In turn the experimental physicist probes and explores the internal structures of the physical phenomenon. When this takes place within the global context of the whole, a deeper understanding of a system will be revealed. However, there is always a danger that what is taken apart in theory, or inferred through experiment, will be confused with reality. The fragmentation and confusion of science comes about when a system is taken to be a collection of units that belong apart and are not internally related in a deeper sense. Equally erroneous is the treatment of a system as essentially indivisible when in fact it contains relatively independent parts. In some cases, for example, a nonlinear system is best treated as composed of interacting solitons, in others as a single whole system.

But to return to solitons. Toward the end of his life, Albert Einstein believed that it would eventually be possible to generalize the nonlinear differential equations of general relativity in such a way that matter and energy emerge as the humps and hillocks of curving space-time. Without knowing about such things at the time, Einstein had anticipated the soliton and argued that what is taken as the very essence of things, a stone for example, is in fact the complex focusing of geometry which provides the ground of all matter. For example, a knot in space-time may remain stable over very long periods, and just like a particle, it can move about and collide with other knots. In Einstein's vision, the universe is like an organism in which each part is the manifestation of the whole. What appear to be separate and independent are in fact the excitations of a nonlinear field, excitations that are sustained for a time and then are merged back into the ground that gave them birth.

Einstein was unable to achieve this final unification of matter, energy, and space-time. However, a different kind of unification is now taking place in the world of elementary particles. It is interesting to note that some physicists are pursuing the idea that elementary matter is nothing more than the manifestation of solitons and excitations in some unified quantum field.

The image suggested by nonlinear mathematics is one in which the universe appears as a single, undivided whole whose patterns and forms emerge out of a ground, are sustained for a time, and then die back into the field. Clearly such an image has something in common with synchronicity. Moreover the approach may eventually be able to accommodate mind, for consciousness too can be considered to arise out of a deeper ground that is common to both matter and mind. In this sense, therefore, the unfolding patterns of matter and mind, which are observed within a synchronicity, in fact emerge out of a single activity.

DISSIPATIVE STRUCTURES

The writer C. P. Snow once said that ignorance of the second law of thermodynamics is equivalent to not having read a work by Shakespeare. So, to spare everyone's possible embarrassment, recall that the second law deals with the direction of change in the universe and dictates that natural processes are always accompanied by an increase in entropy. Since entropy is a measure of the disorder, randomness, and lack of correlation in things, the second law indicates that, left to itself, a system will always run down, fall apart, and decay into disorder and chaos. Indeed this is generally the case—seal a grandfather clock in a large box and eventually its ticking pendulum will come to rest, for the clock will run down. Wait long enough and the very material out of which the clock was built will fall apart or rust—the march of entropy cannot be halted.

But if systems always run down and, without constant maintenance, structures fall apart, then how can it be that the plasma and the slime mold spontaneously develop higher forms of order? How can new patterns and structures appear and mature, and how are stabilities created in nonlinear systems? Are these examples nothing more than isolated freaks of nature or must the second law be modified in some way? The answer to this question is popularly associated with the name of Nobel Prize winner Ilya Prigogine (author of such books as *From Being to Becoming* and, with I. Stengers, *Order Out of Chaos*). During his professional life Prigogine has developed an extension or reinterpretation of thermodynamics which shows that the second law can also point to the emergence of novel structures and indicates the ways in which order is born out of chaos. Since synchronicities can be thought of as patterns that spontaneously emerge out of the contingencies and chaos of nature, the metaphors that are found in Prigogine's work provide interesting insights into the nature of meaningful conjugations.

By revealing the full implications of the second law, Prigogine is able to show that where flows of matter and energy sustain a system away from its equilibrium point, then it is possible for new forms and orders of structures to grow. One of his favorite examples is called the Bernard instability. It occurs when a pan of water is heated on a stove or when hot air in the desert lifts tiny particles of sand into the night air. If the pan of water is heated slowly, heat at first moves upward into the cooler water by conduction. Since no part of the liquid is far from thermal equilibrium, the surface is smooth and undisturbed. However, as the water at the bottom becomes hotter, and therefore less dense, it tries to rise while, at the same time, cooler water falls from the top. Under these competing flows the water is now far from equilibrium and it contains a mixture of flows, eddies, and whorls. . . . In fact, chaos has set in.

As the rate of heating continues to rise, however, a critical point is reached at which the whole system moves from disorder into order. This occurs when heat can no longer be dispersed fast enough through random movements alone and the tiny eddies suddenly become magnified into large-scale flows. Almost magically, movement in the liquid shifts from chance into a series of stable convection currents which have the effect of producing a regularly ordered lattice of hexagonal currents.

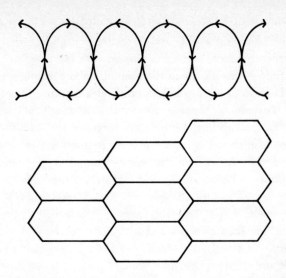

Large-scale convection currents in a heated pan of water result in the formation of hexagonal cells that can sometimes be seen on the surface of the water by viewing it from a glancing angle. Similar patterns form in desert sand as a result of night-time cooling of the air.

These Bernard cells can sometimes be seen on the top of a cooling cup of coffee when it is viewed at a glancing angle. Similar patterns can be seen if one flies over the desert in the evening. Large-scale convection currents, rising into the cold night air, lift tiny particles of sand and then deposit them into hexagonal mounds. For Prigogine the onset of global order is a "spectacular phenomenon," for millions upon millions of molecules suddenly move coherently rather than in a random way— an phenomenon that recalls the cooperative movement of cells in the slime mold or electrons in the plasma.

All such dissipative structures are maintained at the expense of a constant consumption of energy, or flow of matter and, therefore, release large amounts of entropy into the external environment. In this sense the second law is never violated, for all dynamical structures, from cells to cities, dump their high-entropy waste products into their surroundings. It is not difficult to discover a host of such examples from the living and the nonliving worlds and to realize that inanimate dynamical structures have much in common with life itself.

Termites running about the ground, each carrying a particle of dirt, seem to act at random until, at a certain critical point, their movements become cooperative and one of the piles grows in size while the others are forgotten—the first stage of nest building has begun. On a freeway in early afternoon each driver feels independent, free to accelerate, change lanes, and slow down as he or she wishes. But during the rush hour each car is part of a single flow—now the driver is driven by the traffic itself, and a stable, dynamic flow structure is present.

Prigogine has also pointed to a series of curious chemical reactions—termed autocatalytic—in which oscillating patterns are produced in space and time. These patterns can be remarkably stable, provided that a proper flow-through of fresh reactants is possible.

The living cell is the supreme example of a dissipative structure; by taking in building materials and chemicals rich in energy from its environment and expelling entropy-rich waste products, the cell is able to maintain its structure and growth through a constant process of renewal. In a similar fashion, cities are born out of the disordered arrangement of villages and settlements. Cities maintain themselves by gathering in raw materials from their environment (energy, people, food, and building materials) and expelling waste. The entropy production needed to maintain the city's dynamic structure is found in air and water pollution and the growth of city dumps and car wrecking sites.

From the perspective of the second law, the city and the cell are equally alive. The city lives only by virtue of a constant exchange with the environment; in a sense the environment flows through the city. Once this constant renewal ceases, the city begins to die, its center is deserted, services and facilities grind to a halt, and eventually the buildings themselves will fall apart. The "living universe" therefore appears in many different disguises and the emergence of meaningful patterns are ubiquitous in nature.

STRUCTURE AND SYNCHRONICITY

The structures of the "linear world" are built through the ordering and arrangement of elements. Bricks are arranged in rows and cemented together to form a wall; walls in turn are arranged to form a house. The parts of a child's construction set are locked and bolted together to build bridges and towers. In each case the final structure is built from simpler parts and its final form is not explicit in any one of these parts. Such structures could be termed *constructs*, for they are made according to an external design and with the aid of a builder. The house requires plans; the child's toy needs an act of human imagination. The meaning of these static structures is, therefore, found external to them and is imposed through the ordering of their parts.

By contrast, nonlinear systems can evolve forms that are maintained through a process of constant change. In a paradoxical sense, the fountain of water in the center of a city maintains its shape because it is never the same; it is constantly born through the flow of water. Each of these dynamic, nonlinear, dissipative systems is, therefore, an expression of the whole system and requires no external act of construction to give it life. It is, therefore, a self-sufficient form and could be said to *contain its own meaning*, or rather to be an explicit expression of *the meaning of the whole system*. No external plans or designs are required, and in a sense, the emergence of each novel form is, from the start, implicit or enfolded within the whole system as its potentiality.

It is now possible to make use of these ideas as a metaphor for synchronicity. Synchronicities take the form of patterns that emerge by chance out of a general background of chance and contingency and hold a deep meaning for the person who experiences them. Often these coincidences occur at critical points in a person's life and can be interpreted as containing the seeds of future growth. Synchronicities could, therefore, be said to involve the meaningful unfoldment of potential.

Meaning is also implicit in the forms and structures that have been explored in this chapter. They emerge collectively

out of apparently chaotic or individualistic behavior. Within each of them is enfolded some greater whole, and likewise, the form itself unfolds over this whole. Each structure emerges at a critical point, a juncture in which its potential is at first embryonic and then flowers into a living form. No external plans or builders are needed for these patterns, since they are expressions of their own meaning as they emerge out of the chaos that surrounds them.

The particular dynamic structures of this "living universe" all owe their existence to a wider whole, which may ultimately involve the entire universe itself. It is characteristic of such systems that they are born out of an underlying ground, persist for a time, and then die back into this ground. As a metaphor for mind this is suggestive of the feelings of vastness, wholeness, and the dissolution of the ego that accompanies certain transcendent states. For the mystic, the ego does not have a primary reality in itself but is simply a pattern that, for a time, appears within the unknowable.

The images of this chapter suggest that consciousness may involve a form of meaning that emerges out of a deeper ground and is sustained by it. Like dissipative and nonlinear structures, mind may contain, in some enfolded form, the whole nature of this ground. In this way the meaningful patterns of synchronicity, which manifest themselves in both matter and mind, represent the unfolding of a deeper order that lies beyond the distinction of either. Synchronicity is therefore the expression of the potential or meaning contained within a certain point of existence. It acts as an intimation of the meaning that lies hidden within a particular life, relationship, or historical moment. For Hellmut Wilhelm, a historical moment sounds as a single chime, the meaning of which is to be found in "immanent powers." Could these immanent powers be an expression of the entire universe, material and nonmaterial?

These metaphors for synchronicity are intended as signposts along the road that leads in the following chapters to notions of archetype, psychoid, implicate order, and unconditioned creativity. However, at this juncture, it is necessary to add a note of caution. In creating analogies between synchronicity and

dissipative, nonlinear, and cooperative structures, this should not be taken to imply a new form of reductionism, in which synchronicity and mind are to be explained in terms of, for example, the mathematics of nonlinear differential equations. There is a current trend of thought which suggests that the exotic and curious phenomena of modern physics can be used as a foundation or justification for mysticism, the paranormal, and the religions of the East. This implies a reductionism in which, for example, mind is explained by reference to faster-than-light particles or the collapse of the wave function. In place of the Newtonian billiard balls, therefore, a new worldview is to be based on quantum fluctuations.

But what is being suggested here, however, is rather that residue of the Newtonian heritage still tends to mesmerize thought and leads to a view of nature in terms of linear causality in which all phenomena are reduced to their simplest elements. In the face of such a worldview, it becomes extremely difficult to accommodate synchronicity. However, as science is explored in new ways, an approach is developed that is not entirely incompatible with, for example, synchronistic thinking. Therefore it is not so much that science is being used to *explain* synchronicity, but rather that a consistent attitude can be developed toward both fields. No longer is it necessary to wear one hat in the laboratory and another on Sundays. In this way the scientific accounts of nature, what the ecologist of mind Gregory Bateson calls "just so stories," can take their place beside the accounts of religion, art, and psychology, offering an illumination into the nature of synchronicity.

Conclusion

The illustrations of this chapter were taken from "the living universe" and include everything from the ecosystem of the slime mold and the human body to the individual cell and the evolving city. Significant parallels were discovered between these organic systems and the cooperative and emergent behavior of the electron gas, superfluid, nonlinear, and dissipative systems. In each case novel forms are found to emerge at

certain critical points and new forms of order are enfolded within chaos. Each of these systems displays a powerful relationship between the whole and its parts and, in the case of the soliton for example, the whole of a system could be considered to be enfolded within each element.

The image of novel patterns unfolding out of a general background of apparent chaos is a persuasive one when it comes to synchronicity, particularly when the form of these structures is a function of their meaning. In the chapters that follow, the inner nature of these various patterns and the laws associated with their unfolding will be explored.

NOTES

1. A. Koestler, personal communication with the author.
2. Hellmut Wilhelm, *Heaven, Earth and Man in the Book of Changes* (Seattle and London: University of Washington Press, 1977).
3. H. C. Yuan and B. M. Lake, "Nonlinear Deep Waves," in *The Significance of Nonlinearity in the Natural Sciences*, eds. B. Kursunoglu, A. Perlmutter, and L. F. Scott (New York: Plenum, 1977).
4. J. Scott Russell, *Report on Waves*, report of the British Association for the Advancement of Science, 1845.
5. For more information on solitons and other nonlinear phenomena, see F. David Peat and John Briggs, *Chaos and Order*, to be published by Harper & Row.

4 PATTERNS OF MIND AND MATTER

The special flavor of a synchronicity lies in its being, at one and the same time, a unique, individual event and the manifestation of universal order. Wrapped within the temporal moment, a synchronicity exhibits its transcendental nature. It is in this relationship between the transcendent and the coincidental arrangement of mental and physical happenings that the synchronicity acquires its numinous meaning.

In moving away from the mechanistic order of the second chapter, novel patterns and structures have been found to emerge in an organic fashion from the background of apparently chaotic movements. In this chapter the internal structure of these patterns will be explored in order to reveal the deeper order that is enfolded within a single moment of time and the causal conjunctions of a person's life.

DIGESTING THE WORLD

Each life experience begins with the unique flavor of the moment. The events of our life are like a sculptor's blocks of marble, for we are drawn into their individuality and learn their particular meanings through our senses. To the sculptor, each stone is different, and so the sculptor must learn its strengths and weaknesses, in what directions it can be pushed, and where it will lead.

The mind and body are almost prehensile in the way they envelope the world around them. Just as a baby learns by placing the objects it encounters into its mouth, so we too savor events for their individuality. We reach out with our senses to envelop the world and digest it in our thought. In this fashion, personal experiences are almost synchronistic in their nature for they are always concerned with *the way things happen together*.

An individual moment is bathed in sounds, sights, tastes, smells, and textures. A party from childhood is remembered by the taste of its candy, the feel of a party dress, the pattern of wrapping paper, the drowsy sensation of being driven home. Each element is part of that very unique moment and its conjugation cannot be dissected without, at the same time, destroying the very essence of the experience. In a similar way, synchronicities have their origin in combinations of mental and physical events that produce, for the experiencer, a strong sense of meaning. This meaning is found both in the very uniqueness of the conjunction and in the universal order that lies beyond it.

Experience begins with the immediacy of particular events. How is it possible to look beyond these events and perceive the deeper order that lies at their ground? For the sculptor, every block of marble is a living thing with its own unique story to tell. To the scientist, however, each block is a manifestation of the same general order. No matter how much the surface and shape of these stones may differ, the scientist is still aware of the same internal crystal lattice that gives rise to its form and, beneath this lattice, of the electronic structure of its constituent atoms. Within each accidental form of nature, the scientist touches something universal. Nothing could differ more from a block of marble than a ripe apple, a speeding tennis ball, or the drifting moon, yet each is governed by Newton's laws and each is subject to the same universal attraction of gravity. Newton's triumph lay in his insight and ability to move beyond the surface of phenomena and so uncover the universal order that is inherent in all matter.

Whether scientists are concerned with the trajectories of Newtonian particles, the interference patterns of Hamilton-Jacobi waves, or the nonlinearities of a quantum field is not at issue here. Rather it is a matter of the staggering power of scientific abstractions to move beyond the surface of nature— toward her interior relationships. These laws of nature manifest themselves in the orders, structures, arrangements, and transformations of matter and energy. However, the laws are themselves abstract things and must, therefore, be realized in the material world of space-time, matter, and energy. If such laws are immanent in the patterns and behavior of matter then could there not exist other, deeper laws that manifest themselves in both matter and mind? A synchronicity would, therefore, represent the fusion of inner and outer orders in the meeting of surface and spirit.

However, to treat physical laws as if they were somehow immanent in matter has all the appearance of a logical blunder. To argue, for example, that the second law of thermodynamics *causes* the running down of a clock or the rusting of an automobile seems to be as muddled as to suppose that a baseball commentary actually *determines* the state of the game. Science has always treated its laws as mathematical abstractions, descriptions after the fact, rather than laws in the judicial sense that determine and direct behavior. Therefore to speak of such laws as being *manifest* or *realized* in matter, so that they play a formative role, sounds absurd.

But suppose that this orthodox view of science is strictly limited; suppose that, at some level, a formative and ordering principle does indeed operate within the universe. Such a principle would act to generate the novel forms and structures of nature and would be the motivating force behind all patterns and conjunctions. Clearly a formative principle must be very different from what is normally meant by "a law of nature," which is the abstraction and generalization of scientific experience. But what could it be, this principle of animation and generation that differs in such a radical way from the conventional laws of physics?

Physicist John Wheeler put the dilemma in a particularly graphic way during a discussion with Paul Buckley and myself:

Imagine that we take the carpet up in this room, and lay down on the floor a big sheet of paper and rule it off in one-foot squares.

Then I get down and write in one square my best set of equations for the universe, and you get down and write yours, and we get the people we respect the most to write down their equations, till we have all the squares filled. We've worked our way to the door of the room. We wave our magic wand and give the command to those equations to put on wings and fly. Not one of them will fly. Yet there is some magic in this universe of ours, so that with the birds and the flowers and the trees and the sky it flies. What compelling feature about the equations that are behind the universe is there that makes them put on wings and fly?[1]

But the equations of physics will never take wings and fly for they are simply mathematical descriptions, abstractions in thought. Suppose, however, that these laws are themselves the mathematical manifestations of something which has hitherto only been dimly grasped. What if the laws of nature—the ones that really fly—are not simply abstractions of experience but are the realization, within the world of mind, of something that is creative, generative, and formative, of something that lies beyond mathematics, language, and thought?

This generative power cannot lie within the mental or material worlds alone but rather has its place in some, as yet unexplored, ground that lies beyond the distinctions of either. The nature and name of this generative power will be discussed later in this book. For the present, it will be referred to as an "objective intelligence" or "creative ordering" that manifests itself in both the mental and the physical realms. Normally this ordering is only dimly grasped but within the operations of a synchronicity it may be apprehended more directly for it produces a sense of the underlying unity and integration that is possible within nature and in an individual's life.

THE PATTERNS OF MATTER

To understand what could be involved in an "objective intelligence" which brings about a dynamic ordering of matter and mind, think first of more specific and concrete forms of order—the patterns and symmetries that are exhibited in the natural world. Take, for example, the fivefold symmetry of the star-fish; the sixfold symmetry of a snowflake; the lateral symmetry of a leaf, fish, or human body; the branching order of a seaweed; the curving growth of a ram's horn or a nautilus shell. Clearly each of these objects possesses a basic form of order which relates to the way they occupy and grow in space.

The lateral symmetry of a violin, triangle, maple leaf, human face, and butterfly is observed when the left-hand side of the object reflects into the right. It is a very basic form of symmetry which allows for the balancing of masses and forces and for the duplication of organs. On the other hand, the rose window of a cathedral along with the daisy, starfish, and snowflake possesses a rotational symmetry such that an imagined rotation of the object brings it into exact coincidence to itself.

The branching of tree roots, the delta of a river, the interior of a lung, and a piece of seaweed are all the results of finer and finer divisions during growth. This property of treelike growth is also shared with the exponential increase of binary decisions within a computer's search program. Ordering that arises through growth is also found in the pattern of seeds in a sunflower and the curving of shells and horns. While this order may seem more subtle than the rotational symmetry of a flower, it nonetheless follows inevitably from a simple law of growth. In this case, the numerical Fibonnaci series operates. Discovered during the Renaissance, it applies to the above forms of growth, as well as to the increase in the population of breeding rabbits, and how certain irregular tiles cover a floor.

Each of these symmetries arises out of the way matter occupies space, the way atoms and molecules pack together, the geometrical structures which minimize energies, and the balancing of forces. It is for this reason that the same spatial symmetry can underlie such a wide variety of different structures and that photographs of natural and man-made objects, taken on many different scales, bear such a striking resemblance one to another. While the material basis of each may be as different as a soap film and a steel rope, collagen and

concrete, bone and aluminum, in each case the different structures are united by the same underlying symmetry.

The symmetries of this section could all be termed *constitutive*
in their nature for they arise within the very constitution of the
objects themselves. The pattern within a beehive arises out of
the actual packing of hexagons together; the structure of a
diamond is determined by the way carbon atoms arrange themselves in space under the action of the atomic forces between
them. The bones of a bird's wing arise from the balance
between strength and lightness.

But these symmetries are also *descriptive* for they arise
within the mind. No symmetry of nature is totally ideal, since
structures are perturbed by their environment and growing
things are subject to accident and attack. Nevertheless, we
immediately respond to the symmetry that is implicit within a
particular form or perceive the more complex orders that are
present within a dance, poem, sculpture, or piece of music.

The mind is capable of generating extremely subtle degrees
of order and symmetry and of projecting these onto nature.
Thus the symmetries of this section are all double-edged, for
they are both *constitutive* and *descriptive*. They are descriptive
and subjective because their total order is immediately perceived within the mind of the observer, but they are objective
and constitutive for these symmetries are an integral part of the
constitution of material objects. This duality between the objective and subjective aspects of pattern and symmetry is also
a recurring motif in the discussion of synchronicity since it
demonstrates yet again how meaning is generated out of the
intersection of the inner and outer aspects—the mental and
physical sides—of events in nature.

BROKEN SYMMETRIES

The symmetries discussed above are relatively straightforward
and it is only in exploring the more abstract symmetries associated with elementary particles and consciousness that the domain of objective intelligence and creative order is approached.
One of the most powerful aspects of symmetry that has been

exploited in physics over the last few decades is that of broken symmetry, which provides an inroad into the archetypes and immanent orders that we will explore later in this chapter.

As a first step, suppose that the starfish of the previous section had been attacked in an undersea fight. A lone arm drifts in with the tide and is deposited on the beach. What can be inferred from it, of the original symmetry inherent in the whole animal? By itself this arm has lateral symmetry, for its left side is similar to its right. But the rotational symmetry that was essential to the constitution of the starfish is now lost; it was literally broken in the fight and the explicit form of the arm will never reveal what is missing.

One could imagine a host of similar examples of lost symmetry in which a structure is damaged, attacked, or modified in ways that destroy the spatial self-similarity of its original form. It is as if a jigsaw puzzle, exhibiting a given picture, was broken apart and constantly shuffled on a table. Each piece of the puzzle shows a small part of the total picture but it would be only by chance that all the pieces came, for an instant, in exactly the right configuration to display the full symmetry of the original picture.

Does this image of the jigsaw puzzle with a broken symmetry that is momentarily restored by the random configuration of its component parts stand as a metaphor for synchronicity? Clearly not, for such a pattern is destroyed as quickly as it is formed. It is purely descriptive in the way it arises out of its elements, unless, for example, each piece fits firmly into its neighbors. Synchronicity is more than a mere chance arrangement of disconnected parts into a pattern, for it involves a conjunction of the individual and the global, and arises out of the operation of some deeper principle that binds elements together into a fundamental pattern.

Some hint as to how such a principle could operate can be found from those symmetries that operate in a *dynamic* rather than a *static* way. In such cases, form and pattern emerge as the system grows and evolves and it is therefore possible for symmetries to be broken and then restored as a structure changes and its individual parts disperse and regroup. In other words, something like a symmetry can emerge out of an apparently chaotic ground, in response to some underlying symmetry principle.

In the example of the jigsaw, each element of the picture is explicitly present on a particular piece. When the puzzle is broken apart, therefore, the total picture is lost and only small, individual features remain. In such a case the *whole is no more than the sum of its parts*. Within the previous chapter, however, systems were discussed in which *the whole is enfolded within each element*, so that every aspect of the system is at one and the same time global and local. It is therefore possible for a symmetry to be broken, in an explicit way, yet still present in an implicit or enfolded sense. This hidden symmetry will therefore exert a formative influence on how each element behaves and unfolds. Symmetries, in this sense, could be said to have a *constitutive* potential in that they govern the motion and evolution of each of the system's parts. When an explicit symmetry emerges out of a system it is not by chance, as with the jigsaw puzzle, but out of the very essence and existence of the system. If such symmetries and patterns are enfolded in both matter and mind then a synchronicity could be thought of as the simultaneous unfolding of a broken symmetry.

Several examples of such dynamic, broken symmetries have already been given. Within each slime mold cell is enfolded the pattern of a moving slug. This slug represents a synchronicity, a collective form which evolves out of the enfolded patterns present in each individual cell. Likewise, physicists consider the plasma vibrations of a metal as arising out of a broken symmetry. The original full symmetry was present in the electromagnetic field of interaction that stretches out symmetrically in all directions in space from each electron. This symmetry is broken by the random motions and interactions of the electron gas. However, at a certain critical energy, the gas begins to vibrate as a whole and exhibits a new symmetry to its motion which partially restores the original broken symmetry of the electromagnetic interaction.

In a similar fashion the homogeneity of space is broken when an atomic lattice forms in a metal. While the lattice has its own particular symmetry, it does not possess the full rotational and translational symmetry of empty space because certain directions and positions are singled out by the particular arrangement of atoms. But the original, full symmetry is still present in an implicit way within the lattice. Although it would require some mathematical subtleties to show why, this enfolded symmetry has a formative action on the lattice and reveals itself through the cooperative vibration of the lattice atoms, what physicists call "phonons." An even more complex manifestation of hidden symmetry occurs when the electron gas and the lattice vibrations couple together to produce the large-scale behavior of the superconductor with its wave function of global proportions.

In the first chapter, Pauli's exclusion principle told of the subtle dance of electrons that is governed by an "acausal connective principle." Again, symmetry and pattern are not explicitly present in any one part of the system but are revealed through its overall behavior. The operation of broken symmetries therefore has a formative and constitutive nature; they represent a potential which brings objects together in particular patterns and movements. These dynamic, broken symmetries take us from the realm of static structures with explicit spatial symmetry to the world of unfolding patterns that display themselves as a dance in space and time. In later chapters these broken symmetries, which lie at the forefront of modern physics, will be used to create a powerful analogy to the "immanent powers" of the ancient Chinese that manifest themselves in the *I Ching* as meaningful clusterings.

ABSTRACT SYMMETRIES

In the first years of this century it was natural to speak of the elementary particles as being the "building blocks of matter." At that time, matter was believed to consist of atoms made up of a tiny nucleus surrounded by a cloud of electrons. The nucleus in turn was built of protons and neutrons so that the whole of nature could be broken down into three elementary units—the electron, the proton, and the neutron. Using the

laws of quantum theory it was possible to reconstruct molecules, gases, liquids, and solids through a combination of
these internal building blocks.

However, as the internal structure of the nucleus was probed,
a whole new generation of elementary particles was discovered.
Mesons were found to be responsible for the strong forces
between nuclear particles. The symmetry inherent in certain
nuclear disintegrations led Pauli to propose the massless and
chargeless neutrino. As experiments became more and more
refined and particle accelerations were pushed to higher and
higher energies, the number of elementary particles that were
discovered rose from five or ten to almost a hundred. This
proliferation of particles posed a considerable problem, for if
nature, at its most fundamental, is supposed to be simple, then
why had its "elementary building blocks" grown into a veritable
zoo of different particles? Surely something was profoundly
wrong with this "ultimate level of reality."

Shortly before his death, Werner Heisenberg, the creator of
quantum theory, argued that what was truly fundamental in
nature was not the particles themselves but the *symmetries* that
lay beyond them. These fundamental symmetries could be
thought of as the archetypes of all matter and the ground of
material existence. The elementary particles themselves would
be simply the *material realizations* of these underlying
symmetries.

Heisenberg argued that ultimate reality is to be found not in
electrons, mesons, and protons but in something that lies
beyond them, in abstract symmetries that manifest themselves
in the material world and could be taken as the scientific
descendents of Plato's ideal forms. While the notion of an
"ultimate reality" raises many questions, it is certainly possible to accept these abstract symmetries, or rather the principles that lie behind them. Hence, in addition to being *constitutive*
and *descriptive*, these symmetries have an immanent and *formative*
role that is responsible for the exterior forms of nature. Is it
possible that archetypal symmetries of this nature could also
manifest themselves in the internal structures of the mind?

The symmetries of the elementary particles are quite different from the static symmetries exhibited by the rose window, snowflake, and starfish, for they exist not in individual objects themselves but in the way the elementary particles can be grouped together and mathematically transformed one into another. In this way these symmetries are similar to the broken and collective symmetries of the previous section, for they are not so much explicit in an object as existing by virtue of family resemblances between them.

These new symmetries are, however, far more abstract than anything dealt with so far, for they cannot be referred in any direct way to the properties of space and time. Take for example a familiar-sounding property, the "spin" of the proton or electron, one of those quantum properties that gives rise to the symmetry patterns of the elementary particles. At first sight this evokes the picture of a tiny ball spinning in space. However, it is clear that such a simplistic interpretation—a spinning ball—cannot be applied to quantum particles. Indeed, it is not strictly possible to speak of the proton or electron as having any dimensions at all. Rather the mathematical transformations of the proton's wave function have all the appearance of something analogous to spin. The proton, therefore, does not spin—its mathematical wave function simply transforms in a way that is analogous to the mathematical description of a spinning ball.

But the abstract nature of elementary particle symmetries goes even further. Along with the spin of the proton, there is another quantum factor termed the *isospin*. Not only does the proton spin—in a mathematical sense—without having spatial dimensions, but in addition, it has a second type of spin that does not take place in space at all but in an abstract *isospace*. Therefore not only does the proton have spin without spinning but it has a second "Cheshire cat" spinning that takes place in a space that is not space at all!

Indeed, the symmetries of the elementary particles are all of this general abstract nature. They do not refer to the normal operations of reflection, rotation, and translation in our familiar space but to abstract operations that take place in various mathematically defined spaces. In addition, of course, the full symmetry is not explicit in any one particle but in the grouping of the particles as a whole. This does not mean to say that the particles actually congregate together in space to form a pattern. Rather, it is their individual dynamic activity that, taken together, forms a pattern of mathematical transformations.

In moving from starfish and snowflakes to elementary particles, from static structures with simple spatial symmetries to complex dynamic patterns in a multidimensional space, the following question suggests itself: Are the abstract symmetries of the elementary particles nothing more than descriptive devices, mathematical artifacts that have been projected onto quantum matter by human imagination? Or do these symmetries point to a constitutive and formative potential? Are they perhaps the ghosts of Heisenberg's fundamental symmetries that, he argued, underlie all of nature?

Earlier in this chapter, it was suggested that an objective intelligence or creative ordering lies within nature. It now appears that the elementary particle symmetries could give a clue to such a formative potential. That is, of something that does not exist primarily within the material world but nonetheless manifests itself through the phenomena of quantum matter. But this should not be taken to imply that the current supersymmetric and grand unified theories of elementary particles, with their attendant symmetries, are necessarily correct; rather that the evidence of a wide variety of such theories points in the same direction—toward an underlying unification in terms of symmetries. The elementary particles may therefore be closer to the gestures of a dance or the movements of a piece of music than to "elementary building blocks of matter."

In summary, nature contains certain archetypal patterns and symmetries that do not exist in any explicit material sense but are enfolded within the various dynamic movements of the material world. Matter, according to such a view, does not represent a "fundamental reality" but rather is the manifestation of something that lies beyond the material domain. Within the following sections a similar investigation will be applied to the world of mind to see the activities of the conscious and the unconscious mind as the result of orders and patterns at some archetypal level. In this way it will be shown that there is no ultimate distinction between the mental and material so that synchronicities represent the explicit unfolding of deeper orders.

THE UNCONSCIOUS

Since we live out our lives with all the appearance of freedom, it is difficult to consider the possibility of underlying patterns and structures to the human mind. We make decisions, change our opinions, will our actions, and create in the arts and sciences. Why then need there be an internal structure to consciousness?

However, no one would deny that the language we speak has an internal structure. It is governed by semantics and syntax, yet each of us is perfectly free, if we are able, to construct entirely original plays, novels, and poems. Likewise a piece of music is the free creation of the human mind. Nevertheless all music is governed by laws of structure, such as modulation, counterpoint, resolution, and tension, as well as by the physical properties of overtones, scales, and harmonic progressions. So it is not impossible for freedom and creativity to exist side by side with internal structuring. Likewise it is possible for the mind to have a hidden, archetypal structure while, at the same time, operating in a creative fashion. As to whether these internal structures could themselves be changed in creative ways is a deeper question.

All artists owe a debt to the inspiration and insight that lies in a region beyond their direct control. While relaxing after many months of compositional struggle, Wagner heard the ceaselessly repeating modulations of the River Rhine in his imagination and the opening bars of *Das Rheingold* were born. Similarly, "Here the Khan Kubla commanded a palace to be built," followed by some two or three hundred lines, occurred to Coleridge as he lay in a "profound sleep" induced by opium. The basic insights of quantum mechanics were perceived by Heisenberg after walking and swimming while on vacation from the intellectual controversies of the University of Gottingen. In each case, inspiration lies beyond the control of the ego, and creativity cannot be summoned up by conscious will.

For the Greeks, inspiration was given by Athena, the goddess born from the head of Zeus. To "primitive" tribes the trees, rocks, and animals have voices and speak words of wisdom during dreams. Indeed dreams were of paramount importance to many early peoples. Dreams appear as pure creative acts, autonomous in nature, that contain significant messages for the tribe. In some groups, for example, a special dreamer would act on behalf of his or her tribe and offer dreams for interpretation.

For the artist and shaman this powerful world of symbol and inspiration that lies beyond the conscious mind is a firm reality. In the West, generations of writers and painters have deepened our understanding of the unconscious domain. Shakespeare's *Macbeth* demonstrates the nagging power of denied guilt upon perceptions and actions. Dostoevsky's *Crime and Punishment* shows how repressed wishes can surface in dreams. However, it was with Sigmund Freud that the investigation of the unconscious mind reached its greatest refinement. Led by a desire to understand how abnormalities of behavior could be produced in the absence of lesions to the brain, Freud began to investigate the symptoms of hysteria, depression, compulsion, anxiety, and the other neuroses. He argued that exceptionally painful experiences in early formative years are not always recognized directly but may be forced, through repression, into the unconscious. A constellation of repressions could therefore persist, in its initial primitive state, well into adulthood, still charged with its original, violent energy. When some new, unpleasant experience acts as a trigger, it, in turn, becomes associated with the repressed material. In this way complexes are formed which produce bizarre and inappropriate behavior in their victims.

Through careful observation, Freud was able to piece together the various mechanisms which operate in the unconscious mind such as displacement, rejection, repression, substitution, transference, and association. Through the method of psychoanalysis, he argued, repressed material can be brought to the surface and confronted, whereupon its associated energies are dissipated. In this fashion Freud's first therapy sessions showed remarkable success in curing the various symptoms of hysteria.[2]

For Freud, the contents of the unconscious mind were predominantly personal for they consisted of repressed memories and desires from significant periods of each person's life. However, to the extent that every infant passes through similar stages of development, and within our Western society families and their relationships are broadly similar, there exist collective qualities to this unconscious mind. Many societies, for example, are focused around the close-knit family, and in such cases, Freud argued, each male passes through an Oedipal phase of desiring the mother and wishing death to the father who possesses this love object. It is not surprising, therefore, on Freudian grounds, the Oedipal myth should have such a universal significance and that the associated neuroses should be so widespread.

Nevertheless Freud placed most emphasis on the individual nature of repressions and it remained to his "spiritual son," Carl Jung, to discover what he called the collective unconscious. For Jung believed that it is only within the objective layers of the mind, deep below the levels of personal repressions, that the energies and patterns of synchronicity are to be found. Indeed the deeper we dig into the mind the more we discover that the distinction between mind and matter is dissolved and the operation of the objective intelligence begins to manifest its power.

The Collective Unconscious

The patterns and energies of the collective unconscious were to occupy Jung for much of his life. The origin of this important concept can be discovered in two incidents that took place early in his career—one, a dream, and the other, a patient's fantasy.

Around 1906 Jung noticed that one of his Zurich patients, a paranoid schizophrenic, was squinting at the sun while moving his head from side to side. The patient explained to Jung that the sun possesses a penis which is the origin of the wind and that by turning his head from side to side he could make this penis move. The fantasy sounded quite irrational; nevertheless Jung made a note of it, a fact that was to prove particularly significant several years later.

By 1909 Jung's star was ascending and he traveled on a lecture tour of the United States with Freud and another analyst, Sandor Ferenczi. During their trip the three men decided to pass the time by analyzing each other's dreams. Jung related a dream which began on the third floor of his home. The rooms, however, appeared to have been built and furnished in the eighteenth century. The dreamer explored

In Jung's dream, the human skulls were associated with the deepest levels of the collective unconscious. This Neolithic skull, decorated with mud and cowrie shells, is over eight thousand years old and was excavated from the city of Jericho. To look at this skull is to see back into the childhood of the human race. (Copyright British Museum.)

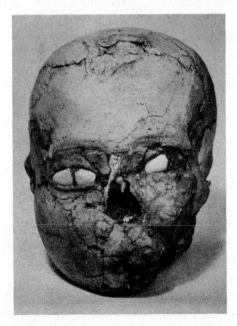

further and discovered that the ground floor was arranged in the manner of a sixteenth-century house and below was a cellar built of Roman brick. In the floor of the cellar Jung noticed a square stone with a ring attached and, lifting the stone, he looked down into a cave filled with prehistoric pottery and ancient human skulls.

Freud interpreted the dream in terms of personal repressions and suggested that Jung desired to destroy someone close to him but had buried the wish deep within his dream house. The Swiss analyst disagreed strongly with Freud's views but, for the time, kept his own counsel. Later, in writing about the dream, Jung argued that it represented the history of European consciousness from its neolithic origins, through the rise of Rome, the late Renaissance to the enlightenment of the eighteenth century. Just as the physical brain contains anatomical remnants of its evolutionary origins so, the dream indicated, the mind itself contains primitive, hidden memories of its remote past.

These speculations received a powerful confirmation when Jung came across a Greek account of an ancient Mithraic ritual which tells of a tube, let down from the face of the sun, which is the origin of the wind. Here was a striking correspondence between a two-thousand-year-old myth and the fantasy of a modern Swiss patient. How could a schizophrenic's mind have come up with an image that was identical to one once believed in by the followers of Mithras? Jung began to delve further into this mythology and discovered a number of other correspondences that had surfaced over the last two thousand years. Medieval paintings, for example, show divine rays emanating from the sun, and some legends claim that the Holy Ghost impregnated the Virgin in a similar fashion. In addition, the visitation of God is often experienced as a divine wind. It appeared, therefore, that a certain essence of this myth of the sun had been common to minds over the past two thousand years.

Over the decades that followed, Jung collected manuscripts from the Middle Ages, Gnostic texts, and classical works from China, India, and Tibet. He analyzed the many dreams and waking fantasies of his patients and traveled to Africa and India to hear dreams, myths, and legends at their source. Again and again he discovered that similar dreams, images, and myths were surfacing in remote parts of the world and in very different cultures and historical periods. The result was a little like studying the languages of Western Europe and discovering that, with minor exceptions such as Basque, they all have a common origin in Latin. Then, on widening the scope of the investigation discovering that Latin itself has its root in a proto-Indo-European tongue.

Just as the German and English languages have too many points of similarity to be ascribed to pure coincidence and, therefore, suggest a common origin, so Pauli's dream of the world clock and the vision that occurred to a medieval monk suggest that they originated in the same ground. Through his travels and researches Jung discovered that the images of the hero, the twin brothers, the sun, the eternal feminine, the underground journey, the serpent, the mandala of wholeness, and the dynamism of opposites occurred again and again, each time clothed in the particularities of a local culture yet exhibiting the same underlying form. Jung's conclusion was compelling, that the unconscious mind had a *collective* level that is common to all humankind. Jung's dream in 1909 had been a graphic illustration of the collective layers of the unconscious mind.

While Freud's unconscious contains personal experiences and desires which have been repressed out of awareness, Jung's collective unconscious consists of material that has *never before* attained consciousness in the mind of the individual. The deeper levels of mind are therefore *objective*, for they belong to the entire human race rather than being the personal and subjective property of a particular individual. They are unconscious, not by virtue of having been forgotten or repressed but because they exist in a hidden or enfolded form that is not normally accessible to active attention. The contents of the collective or objective unconscious are a little like a message that is sent by a spy to his intelligence agency. Since the message is in code, it cannot be directly apprehended but must first be passed through an electronic decoding device which converts it into normal English. In a similar way, the deepest levels of the unconscious could not, in Jung's opinion, be brought to the surface directly. It is only when certain aspects of the collective mind are projected into attention, clothed in the images and symbols of our particular culture, that we become aware of something universal that has come into the mind.

The discovery of the collective unconscious probably stands as Jung's most original contribution to psychology; indeed, he referred to it as his "personal myth." The physicist Pauli was particularly struck by the correspondence it created between physics and psychology. For centuries physics had been the objective study of nature, but with the advent of quantum theory, it now appeared that the observation of nature also contained a subjective element—the irreducible link between observer and observed. Likewise the personal nature of mind had now been shown to contain an objective, impersonal level. Pauli believed that this dualism between objective and subjective was particularly significant and indicated that a much deeper unification existed between matter and mind. As the structure of matter is probed in finer and finer detail, it dissolves into the indeterminacies of the quantum world. Below the everyday appearances of matter, in which the scientist acts as an impartial observer, are encountered quantum processes in which observer and observed are intimately linked. Below this level, Heisenberg and others have hinted, there may no longer exist a fundamental ground of matter but, rather, fundamental symmetries and ordering principles. In a complementary way, when the first layers of mind are probed, the subjective realm of personal repressions is reached, but at deeper levels lie the objective contents that can no longer be observed directly but are hidden in symbolic forms. Just as the electron cannot be directly apprehended but must be inferred from, for example, its tracks in a bubble chamber, so the contents of the collective unconscious cannot be brought directly to the surface of awareness but are deduced through their tracks or shadows that appear in awareness and the personal unconscious in the form of myths, dreams, fantasies, powerful images, and works of art.

At their deepest, the objective layers of mind and the subjective layers of matter are both hidden from direct apprehension, so that their existence can only be inferred from their impacts at higher levels. However, below the quantum phenomena there are hints at a new, nonmaterial level of symmetry or order. Could it also be true that below the level of the collective unconscious there does not exist simply "mind stuff" but something that is beyond mind, a fundamental dynamic ordering perhaps? At such a level the division between mind and matter would no longer apply and the domain of creative ordering and objective intelligence would have their ground.

But again it must be stressed that all of experience cannot be reduced to a single, fundamental level or the universe to a single level of description. Such simplistic reductionism can never work; rather, the arguments above should be taken in a pluralistic fashion in which no one of them is to be taken as an absolute ground. For what appears, at first sight, to be a fundamental ground may, on closer examination, prove to be conditioned and defined in terms of other levels. The quantum level of matter, for example, which appears to underlie all material phenomena is itself dependent upon the classical level for its definitions and for any measurements that are made. Hence, while it is always possible to analyze higher levels in terms of lower, it is also true that the higher levels may condition the lower and may contain unexpected and novel forms of behavior. The complexities of matter and mind are therefore like images reflected in parallel mirrors that can never be grasped in a unique way. Just as the deepest levels of matter are irreducibly connected to higher levels, so too may it be discovered that the deepest regions of the collective unconscious are in some degree dependent upon and conditioned by conscious awareness. In Chapter 6 this interconnection of levels will be explored in greater detail in the case of the explicate, implicate, and super-implicate orders.

MATTER, MIND, OR SPIRIT

The physics of the material universe can be understood in terms of the orders of its patterns, symmetries, and relationships. Indeed it has even been suggested that the notion of elementary particles as fundamental building blocks should be replaced by that of fundamental symmetries. Could it be that "objective intelligence" and "creative ordering" are the generative principles that give rise to this underlying order of matter? In a similar sense the origin of mind may be discovered in the dynamic orderings that lie at a level of objective intelligence that is neither matter nor mind, but the source of both.

It was Carl Jung who first suggested that below the familiar levels of awareness and of Freudian repression there lies an objective level of mind. Indeed, in certain of his writings he even suggested that this objective unconscious merges into the instinctual responses of the animal kingdom. In a sense therefore its order may encompass the whole of life and possibly beyond, into all matter itself. Just as the material structures of the previous chapter were sustained, not through the static locking and balancing of elements and forces but through a constant dynamic renewal, so too may the collective unconscious be found to maintain itself through the dynamics of fundamental principles of creative ordering which Jung called the archetypes. Just as a waterfall exists by virtue of its continuous change in which it is reborn, so too may the ground of mind lie in a continuous, creative rebirth at the archetypal level.

The dynamic structures of matter, it will be recalled, all contain and unfold out of their own meaning, as opposed to static structures that are created according to the design of some external agency. Likewise the essence of the collective unconscious lies in the meaning of its archetypes, those dynamic patterns and symmetries that maintain its internal structure. Meaning, therefore, is the kernel of both material structures and of the collective unconscious. This meaning is at the heart of the "objective intelligence," that formative, generative principle that is neither matter nor mind.

The archetypes, which provide the dynamic basis of the collective unconscious, cannot, of course, be directly apprehended in their naked forms for they are not of the same nature or essence as thought. An analogy may serve to illustrate this point. The brain possesses nerves which tell when the body moves; they indicate the disposition of the arms and legs, the process of digestion, and the sensation of the heart when it is stressed. However, the brain has no nerves to tell us how it is operating. I do not receive a sensation of fullness when I read Shakespeare or of pain when I reflect on my income tax. While the brain contains a display of the body's activity, it does not display its own internal operation. Similarly, the structure of the mind is the result of the dynamic play of the archetypes and these can never be displayed directly. Rather, the archetypes leave their footprints in the mind and project their shadows across thought. While it is not possible to observe the archetypes directly, their movements can be sensed through the numinous images, myths, and happenings that enter consciousness. Whenever something is experienced that exhibits a universal power, then it is a good indication that the dynamics of the collective unconscious are being stirred into new activity and that the archetypes are entering a new constellation. A dream whose profound effects remain for several hours after waking suggests that the archetypes are at work.

Popular accounts of these archetypes generally focus on their more static manifestations, such as various mandalas and paintings of wholeness. But the archetypes are essentially dynamic in nature and unfold their projections in time. The whole pattern of an individual's life, for example, may be the gesture of an archetype. The stormy seas of a marriage indicate the constellation of particular archetypes. Jung has even suggested that archetypes can unfold over hundreds or thousands of years and they manifest themselves in a series of historical events within a particular nation.

The quantum level of matter has been written about to such an extent that it will be relatively familiar to most readers. However, the idea of an objective level to mind has not been as extensively explored in popular books. Jung's dream of the house suggests that the human mind is like an onion that can be peeled to reveal many levels, down to a neolithic origin and possibly beyond. Likewise, the fantasy of one of his patients indicated that the essence of a particular ritual can resurface two thousand years later in the mind of a twentieth-century man. How can it be that images and memories are encoded and stored over tens of thousands of years of the mind's evolution? If the basis of mind lies in the dynamic ordering of the archetypes then what correspondence do they have to the physical organ of the brain and to its evolutionary history?

The brain itself is often pictured as containing a series of evolutionary levels beginning with its primitive reptilian brain stem and working upward to the higher primate functions of the cortex. In addition, there are probably a number of evolutionary remnants present in the chemical pathways of the various neurotransmitters, peptites, and other chemicals used by the brain. Since related structures and functions have been studied in animals, it is possible to identify regions of the human brain with particular outputs. This correspondence can be confirmed in cases of brain injury and selective anesthesia where the functioning of higher levels is suppressed or lost.

In this fashion, particular human reactions have been ascribed "to the results of our primitive ancestors." Some commentators have even suggested that we are like those sea creatures that first ventured onto land—the human race represents a major evolutionary leap forward, yet it still does not wholly belong to one environment or the other.[3] Humans, according to this argument, may create great works of art or make leaps in science and mathematics but they are still in the grip of more ancient areas of the brain. Put a sensitive poet in the midst of a chanting, flag-waving crowd and the "animal" areas of the brain override more civilized behavior.

Such arguments, which contain more speculation than fact, suggest that the unconscious mind arises out of a more primitive layer of the brain which is not yet capable of secreting "higher" conscious thought. The activities of these earlier evolutionary structures have a direct effect on the mind's activity through various physical changes within the chemistry of the body and brain. In addition, the output of these lower levels may have some direct influence on thought. Everyday consciousness, in this view, is constantly moved by forces that are not of its own making, so that it must try to interpret them as best it can in the form of dreams, fantasies, drives, and irrational emotions. Excessive patriotism, for example, would be the response of the lower brain to an emotionally charged symbol such as a waving flag. The overriding flood of activity in the lower brain then floods into the higher areas, where it becomes rationalized into loyalty, honor, truth, and national pride.

Such a view denies the ground of consciousness as being an infinitely subtle and creative thing but rather suggests that, just as the body's structures are inherited and encoded within its DNA, so too is the mind based on certain inherited brain structures. The archetypes and instincts would therefore have evolved through random mutations and natural selection into the collective unconscious of today.

While it is possible that certain instincts and fixed structures within the brain and mind are the evolutionary remnants of an earlier mind, it represents a considerable leap of faith to suggest that similar changes took place between Roman Europe, the Middle Ages, and the Age of Enlightenment. For Jung suggests that each age contributes its levels and structures to the collective unconscious. Jung has even argued that a North American has a special layer of the collective unconscious that differs from his or her European counterpart through the addition of images from the original native population. But how could such recent additions be explained on a mechanistic basis, in terms of mutations of the central nervous system that are passed on through the DNA? It is possible, however, to approach the problem from another direction and consider how mind, brain, and the collective unconscious could be related.

The connection between thought and the physical brain is infinitely more subtle than a simple correspondence between behavior and gross physical structure. One of the leading researchers on neural networks, Eric Kandel, has written:

. . . even during simple social experiences as when two people
speak to each other, the action of the neuronal machinery in
one person's brain is capable of having a direct and long-
lasting effect on the modifiable synaptic connections in the
brain of the other.[4]

The brain is not something static and fixed that determines
our behavior. Rather, the brain is fluid, a constantly changing
instrument of extreme subtlety. Each experience, action, or
thought feeds itself back into the brain to modify synaptic
connections and produce changes in neural networks. During a
conversation, Kandel suggests, two highly complex and adapt-
able neural networks are interacting and changing each other.
Just as no one can step into the same river twice so too can no one
think the same thought twice. For the act of thinking changes
the thinker. Indeed, just as there is an irreducible link between observer and observed in the quantum theory, so, within
consciousness is there an irreducible link between the thinker
and the thought. Indeed the thinker *is* the thought; the thought
gives birth to the thinker who, in turn, creates the thought
anew. Therefore, rather than the brain creating thought, it is
thought which generates the brain. Or rather, that the brain
and its activities are inseparable and through their constant
activity both brain and mind are created and maintained.

Kandel's example of the conversation provides an image of
two neural networks engaged in the dance which modifies and
maintains them both. Minds are the unfolding of thought.
Meaning is once again discovered to be crucial in determining
the world. It is the unfolding of this meaning in time which
produces the whole gesture of the mind's dance. Within this
gesture, brain and consciousness are sustained just as the
fountain lives by virtue of the water that flows through it.

It is now possible to offer complementary accounts of the
collective unconscious. At one level its origin lies in the
metabolic pathways and architecture of the networks of the
brain which are inherited genetically from generation to
generation. In this sense the archetypes are fixed and reach
down to our animal origins. They can be modified, according

to conventional biological theories, only through random mutations.

But since the activities of the brain itself can feed back and modify its own structure, it is also possible that certain aspects of the collective unconscious are created by the society we live in. Ritual, symbol, and image make their impact upon the brain not only on awareness but at the more primitive levels where meaning is transacted and transformed. In this way the collective unconscious can be modified by society and, in turn, acts back on that society to determine its internal, social structure. According to this second view, society and the collective mind are inseparable.

Finally, it has been suggested that the structure of the material universe is the manifestation of something deeper— the objective intelligence. It is now possible to speculate that the origin of mind lies in a similar ordering that is neither matter nor mind but obeys laws that were hinted at in earlier chapters of this book. At this deepest level, the collective unconscious is maintained by a constant dynamic activity and by the unfolding and unfolding of meaning and pattern. While such a level is inseparable from society and from our evolutionary past, it is nonetheless capable of changing in novel and creative ways.

The collective mind contains levels that stretch back into the remote past of the human race, but at the same time, it is constantly being restructured by dynamic forces that lie below the level of mind. In this way the door is opened for the collective unconscious to change its contents and structures creatively. No single level in mind or matter can be taken as absolutely fundamental since it is always being conditioned by the levels above and below it. In a similar way, therefore, it becomes possible for the conscious mind, through its perceptions, insights, and reflections, to act back on the collective unconscious and change it. Inspiration wells up into the mind of an artist from its collective depths. In the light of consciousness this material is molded and worked on. Transformed into marble, paint, language, or dance, it becomes an act in the external world. But this creative action, produced in full consciousness, can also act back on the hidden, collective uncon-scious and modify or add to it. So consciousness and the collective, light and dark, are in a constant interaction, each transforming the other.

Such changes need not take place at the level of mind alone but may also affect the structure of matter. Since the brain itself is responsive to changes in meaning, it is possible for its internal structure to be changed in creative ways by means of the dynamic interplay of the collective and unconscious minds. It is even possible to go further and suggest interactions at the generative level of the objective intelligence itself so that conscious actions may ultimately have an effect upon the evolutionary structure of the brain itself. At this level the personal consciousness begins to touch something that is liter-ally collective and universal. To plunge into the symbols and images of the collective unconscious is to enter a realm that lies beyond space, time, and matter. It is like descending a dark passageway through a rockface and emerging into an underground ocean in which all minds have their origin. Within this hidden realm can be found the rhythms of the whole universe and the generative power of all that is matter and mind—the wellspring of synchronicity is uncovered.

CONCLUSIONS

Synchronicities are characterized by a unity of the universal with the particular that lies within a coincidence of events. This essence of the universal is also discovered in science, where patterns, symmetries, and mathematical laws are found to interconnect a multiplicity of individual events. While sci-ence has conventionally accepted that its laws are purely descriptive in nature, it is possible that behind the phenomena of the material world lies a generative and formative order called the objective intelligence.

Below the layers of consciousness and Freud's personal unconscious lies a collective and universal level of mind. Just as the elementary particles are maintained by a dance that transcends the world of matter, so, too, is mind sustained by dynamics that lie beyond both mind and matter. Beyond mind and matter there are therefore patterns and symmetries which have a generative and animating effect. During a synchronicity it becomes possible, for an instant, to touch these regions so that within the conjunction of coincidences is enfolded something truly universal that lies at the heart of all creation and touches the most basic rhythms of existence.

In the following chapters, the dynamics of this hidden region will be explored, along with theories that have been proposed by Rupert Sheldrake and David Bohm. In addition alternative visions of nature, in which rhythm and synchronicity have a primary place, will be explored through the dreams and oracles of the Naskapi Indians of Labrador and the Shang of ancient China.

NOTES

1. Paul Buckley and F. David Peat, *A Question of Physics* (London: Routledge & Kegan Paul, 1979).
2. In recent years Freud's theories and the effectiveness of his methods have come under increasing scrutiny. A. Grunbaüm in *The Foundations of Psychoanalysis* (Los Angeles: University of California Press, 1984) provides a careful analysis of the issues.
3. See, for example, Paul D. Maclean, "The Paranoid Streak in Man," in *Beyond Reductionism*, eds. A. Koestler and J. R. Smythies (London: Hutchinson, 1969).
4. Eric R. Kandel, "Small Systems of Neurons," *Scientific American* 241 (September 1979): 66–76.

5 PATTERNS IN THE BONE

In the previous chapters, the meaning of synchronicity was gradually unfolded to reveal a vision of the universe that is very different from the scientific worldview that has flourished over the last five hundred years. Synchronicity is, however, a little like a candle flame when compared to the light of the sun, for the scientific view of nature has by now permeated every aspect of life in the West. Strongly based on earlier notions of determinism, causality, and the linear unfolding of time, it leads to the belief that all difficulties can be resolved through a process of analysis which leads to control or reorganization. Nature and society, it is believed, can both be understood by reducing complex problems to more simple elements.

The result has been a science which has made considerable strides in explaining, predicting, and controlling the natural world. On the other hand, these scientific explanations sometimes fail to capture the essence of actual experience, for they are unable to address our subjective reactions to nature. Therefore, despite its power to shape the modern world, science has little to say about the way in which people live their daily lives; enter into relationships; experience love, birth, and death; give value to the world; and respond to new situations in creative ways.

Alongside the triumphs of science has developed an ever increasing tendency to fragment knowledge and experience into various areas of specialization. In this way knowledge in a particular field becomes rigid and has restricted relevance to the concepts and questions of other fields. By limiting the context of a particular branch of knowledge, the solutions to the world's problems often generate unforeseen complications that end up being worse than the original situation. For example, advances in agriculture, nuclear energy, the control of social behavior, new forms of health care, and mass communications have all produced crises of far-reaching consequences. Faced with these new difficulties, science tends to react, yet again, from its fragmented categories of knowledge and attempts new forms of control. In this way an endless spiral of crises and solutions is generated.

The problem of the fragmentation of knowledge and understanding extends far beyond science into fields such as economics, sociology, psychology, practical government, human relationships, indeed to the very fabric of society. It is almost as if the twentieth century had lost its ability to perceive the larger patterns of nature and the broad contexts in which events happen. A particularly significant area of concern is that of the meaning of life and of personal values, subjects that science finds particularly difficult to measure, analyze, and quantify.

Synchronicity, by contrast, begins with the very fact of meaning in life and in nature. Its strength lies in its power to address the subjective side of experience and its value therefore involves the possibility of combining the subjective *meaning* of phenomena with *objective* explanations. By combining the objective and subjective elements together, synchronicity has something to say to both the artist and the scientist.

In addition, synchronicity is concerned with pattern, with correlations between dissimilar forms and structures, and with connections made between physical processes and mental states. Synchronicity could therefore be thought of as a counterbalance to fragmentation, for it always deals in the widest context and seeks its patterns across boundaries and categories. Clearly if the scientific and analytic approach to nature could be integrated with the more holistic, pattern-seeking, and meaning-valued aspects of synchronicity, then a creative surge of considerable energy would be possible.

FLATLAND SYNCHRONICITIES

But what could be the objective side to an "acausal correlation"? In the previous chapter, it was suggested that a pattern of internal and external experiences may arise out of an order that is common to both. Synchronicities therefore have their origin in a ground that lies beyond the particular categories of knowledge and defies all attempts to place boundaries or erect mental divisions between particular areas of experience.

In other words, synchronicities are manifestations, in mind and matter, of the unknown ground that underlies them both. In this way similar orders are found in both consciousness and in the structuring of matter. The parallelism between the objective and the subjective aspects of the universe do not so much arise through causal connections, or linear patterns in time, but out of underlying dynamics that are common to both. Synchronicities therefore introduce meaning and value, in an essential way, into nature. The meaningful patterns of the world, which transcend all our attempts to limit and encompass them, arise not so much through the mechanisms of external orders but through the unfolding of their own internal significance.

A simple illustration may help to indicate one aspect of this notion of synchronicity. It should not, however, be taken as a picture of the way things are but, rather, as an allegory that is being used to point our perceptions in a new direction.

Suppose there exists, unsuspected by us, a race of two-dimensional beings who live out their lives on a flat, two-dimensional plane. These Flatlanders go about their business, preach their philosophies, and have even developed a physics to account for the various phenomena observed in their two-dimensional universe. Suppose, however, that events from our own three-dimensional world now begin to intrude on their flat universe.

One day a baseball falls through their world. The instant the ball intersects their two-dimensional universe, a single point of contact is made. The point grows, as the ball moves, into an expanding circle, until it reaches its maximum size, where-

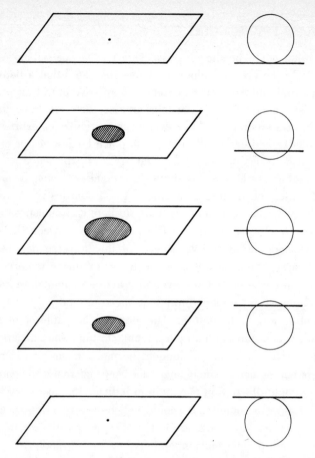

A ball falling through Flatland produces a circle that widens, contracts, and then vanishes.

upon it contracts to a point and vanishes again. The ball has left their universe.

Flatland scientists busy themselves in attempting to account for this curious phenomenon when, on the following day, a pipe slowly enters their world. At first they believe that this is a repetition of the phenomena of the previous day, for a point of contact is made which begins to expand into a circle—the bottom of the bowl of the pipe has just met their universe.

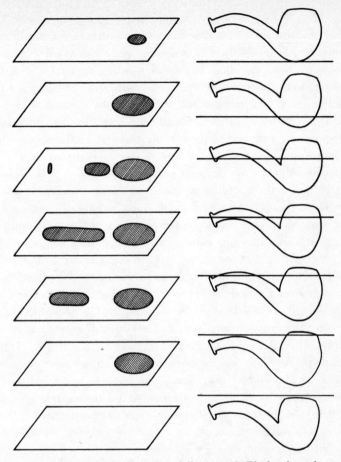

*A pipe or other complex object that falls through Flatland results
in a correlated series of events that are separated in space. Events
that appear normal in our three-dimensional world may look like
synchronicities in the flat world of two dimensions.*

But next the tip of the stem enters. A line of contact is
discovered some distance from the expanding circle. This
widens into an ellipse, which deforms until it meets the expanding circle. Finally this distorted shape vanishes, leaving
only a circle which remains of constant size until it suddenly
vanishes.

On the following days even more bizarre events are observed

by Flatland scientists. A coffee pot, a trumpet, a vase of flowers, and even a waving hand make journeys through their universe. What do the Flatland scientists make of all this? As soon as the pipe had begun to manifest itself, scientists rushed to the spot and, with their measuring apparatus, tried to determine what force was acting between the expanding circle and the deformed ellipse. Clearly these two events, although distinct and separate in the two-dimensional Flatland, were in some way correlated. In the weeks that followed, some scientists postulated a new force of nature, as yet undetected, which gives rise to the coordinated motion of distant events. For they believed that all correlated events must be causally connected in some way. Others speculated that Flatland synchronicities were at work, involving correlations and coordinations in which no causal connections can be involved. The circle and the ellipse, for example, were taken to be true acausal connections.

A few scientists, however, speculated that their universe did not contain the whole of reality but was, in fact, embedded in a greater three-dimensional world. The acausal correlations that were being observed, between, for example, a series of oscillating circles were nothing more than the Flatland manifestation of a single underlying event—the movement of a three-dimensional hand. What appeared to be the correlations of different events were simply the movements of structures within a higher-dimensional world, in which their own was embedded.

One of the more daring theoretical physicists even went so far as to propose that this hypothetical three-dimensional world was itself only a part of further dimensions of an unimagined complexity. In this way, ever more phenomena of the flat world could be expected to arise from the order of this higher-dimensional reality. What had appeared, at first sight, to be almost magical in nature was now turning out to be the projection of a higher-dimensional order, into a world of two dimensions.

Here the allegory ends. It would be tempting but, at this stage, foolish to suggest that we too are part of some "higher-dimensional reality" and that the order of this reality manifests itself in what we take to be synchronicities or the patterns of growth, harmony, and form within our universe. This could be expanded to suggest that "mind" arises out of some of these dimensions. Or that the underlying reality out of which mind and matter emerge is a multidimensional ground with its own particular and highly subtle orders. The "meaning" of a synchronicity and the pattern of its internal and external events would therefore be a manifestation of this underlying order. But the Flatland illustration simply cannot be pushed that far. The whole notion of spatial dimensions, for example, would lose all its significance long before this ground was approached. In addition mind cannot simply be tagged onto matter as a "further dimension," for the relationship and meaning of mind and matter is far more subtle. Finally the whole allegory is based far too strongly within our conventional worldview of nature to be taken any further. At best it makes a point, and directs our perceptions along a particular path, and nothing more.

WORLDVIEW AND PARADIGMS

Why then introduce the Flatland allegory in the first place? The reason is that, without such graphic, if simplistic, illustrations it is very difficult to accommodate the notion of synchronicity in any successful way. Over the past five hundred years the West has been committed to a scientific worldview that has been variously described as mechanistic, reductionist, and analytic. Beginning with Galileo, modern science made striking advances in its abilities to probe the secrets of nature as well as in prediction and control. The worldview that gave rise to all this is not, however, simply confined to physics and chemistry but has had profound influences (and indeed gave rise to these very subjects and their subdivisions) on psychology, biology, economics, and sociology. Even the study of such "humanistic" topics as history and literature, for example, the ways in which people watch a film or read a book, are deeply affected by the overall worldview that first arose in science. In other words the worldview that predominates in the West now pervades all aspects of life and profoundly influences not only the way the world is seen but the perceptions people have of themselves and the values they give to society.

The historian of science Thomas Kuhn made use of the word "paradigm" to describe such a state of affairs within science itself. A paradigm is not simply a given branch of knowledge that is explicitly learned. But rather it includes the whole set of skills, attitudes, and approaches that are absorbed during each scientist's training and apprenticeship. This paradigm therefore has a deep influence on the way each scientist approaches and thinks of nature and communicates his results and attitudes to others.

The particular scientific paradigm that came into existence during the Renaissance, and has flourished ever since, is now so all pervasive that its influence has extended beyond the purely scientific domain into all aspects of life. This attitude to nature, and to ourselves, is far more than a highly organized branch of nature for it is a communal attitude of mind, a way of perceiving the world, of being disposed to act and to communicate that, by now, appears wholly natural. Indeed it is no longer possible to see this worldview or paradigm but rather everyone perceives *through it*.

The inhabitants of the Emerald City, in Frank L. Baum's *The Wizard of Oz*, saw that everything about them was green, the houses, clothing, and even other people. The reason for this uniformity of color arose not in the reality of the city itself, but because each citizen wore green-tinted spectacles. Since everyone saw the city through the same-colored glass they held a common worldview on the colors of things. Green spectacles were the paradigm through which the citizens of the Emerald City perceived their universe. Science is the paradigm through which we perceive ours.

Since this view of nature, dominated by causality, analysis and reduction, linear time, and explanations in terms of elements, is so pervasive, it is particularly difficult to come to terms with the full force of synchronicity, a phenomenon which demands a very different worldview. Indeed synchronicities themselves often appear to disturb the foundations of this ordered, scientific world and leave us disoriented and shaken.

Synchronicities, in such cases, can appear magic and irrational, as the jokers in nature's pack of cards.

Within the first four chapters of this book, an account was given of how synchronicities may be accommodated without entirely abandoning the current, scientific framework of thought. But in order to go further, it is necessary, at least provisionally, to drop this traditional worldview and explore alternatives. In the chapters that follow, some approaches to mind and matter that break, to a greater or lesser extent, the conventions of our contemporary worldview will be examined. These include Sheldrake's morphic fields, Bohm's implicate orders, and Jung's notion of the pleroma and psychoid. While each is still grounded within a scientific perspective, they may go some way toward illuminating what W. Pauli may have meant when he told his assistant, H. B. G. Casimer:

> There must come something else. I think I know what is coming. I know it exactly. But I don't tell it to others. They may think that I am mad. So I am rather doing five dimensional theory of relativity although I don't really believe in it. But I know what is coming. Perhaps I will tell you some other time.[1]

Nevertheless it still requires a considerable creative step to produce a unified vision of the world which accommodates causality and acausality side by side, or as the dualities suggested by Jung and Pauli's diagram in Chapter 1. It demands an approach that gives equal weight to the subjective aspects of experience as well as to their objective analysis, and allows meaning to assume a significant role in science. It is the very seductive power of our present worldview that hampers us from taking a leap into the unknown.

For this reason there follows an exploration of worldviews that are totally alien to us and in which synchronicity plays a central role. But this should not suggest that the ways of understanding nature, described below, are somehow preferable or more accurate than our own. Rather they may help the reader to gain some insight into a "consensus reality" that was very different from that of the West yet was sufficiently consistent and coherent to support a whole culture and bind it together. By considering the worldviews of the Naskapi, the Shang, and that implied within the *I Ching*, it becomes possible to speculate how much our own world, and our understanding of ourselves and our society, must change in order to accommodate causality and synchronicity side by side.

NASKAPI: DREAMERS OF LABRADOR

The vast tract of land between Hudson's Bay and the Labrador sea in northeastern Canada is so barren and inhospitable that it supports only a few thousand Montagnais and some three hundred Naskapi Indians. Before the coming of the white man, native peoples in other regions of North America had developed full social structures involving governments, systems of communication, elaborate rituals, and works of art. The Naskapi, however, were forced by their environment to concentrate on their inner, spiritual environment. This small group of hunters has no true government, social institutions, or organized religion and few formal ceremonies. They hunt alone or in small family groups, and although the modern Naskapi today make use of rifles and snowmobiles, one anthropologist has described them as having reached only the "snowshoe" stage of civilization.

In place of material wealth and a desire to dominate nature, the Naskapi face a wilderness that must feed and support them. Their survival is therefore based on a cosmology that stresses the individual's harmony within a living world of nature. Central to this worldview is Manitu, which inhabits all things and brings individual hunters, men and women, closer to the rhythms that surround them. It is difficult to determine if the Naskapi ever developed the notion of "High God" or Supreme Being, as other North American native people have done. It is possible that such a concept was imported into the region by earlier missionaries. (In addition, such a concept can sometimes be projected upon a culture by a visiting anthropologist, an example of the seductive power of a worldview that appears so natural that it must be universal.) At all events, the idea of a High God appears to have little significance to the Naskapi. Rather it is Manitu which assumes importance. Manitu is the essence of all things and resides in them. Each species of animal has its own Manitu, which gives meaning and power. Manitu is also immanent in invention and procreation, and was even ascribed to the first steam engines seen by the hunters.

Each Naskapi possesses Manitu. He or she is not a creature apart, a Western-style Lord of Creation, who stands outside nature to observe and manipulate, but is simply one element in the overall pattern of nature, who must respond appropriately and respect all life and growth. Within the hunter is a center, or focus, that has been variously called the Great Man, Shadow, Soul, Footprint, or My Friend. "My Friend" is born with the hunter, lives in his or her heart, and at death, goes to play among the stars and the northern lights. "My Friend" will help in hunting; it is made happy by drumming, smoking tobacco, and singing; it speaks to the hunter in dreams.[2]

The Naskapi owe their existence to the caribou and the bear. Human and animals are linked together in such a way that the hunter and the hunted each fulfill the other's destiny. The Naskapi believe, for example, that caribou will not be killed unless the spirit that controls the herd agrees to the hunt. Likewise, the bear in his cave must be addressed in a respectful and oblique fashion. Following the kill, he is treated with great respect and feasting.

Central to the life of the Naskapi is the big Dream, in which the hunter goes on the trail, meets friends, and locates herds of caribou. It is not unusual, after experiencing such a dream, for the hunter to wake and immediately begin drumming and chanting in order to amplify the dream and tell it to those around him. In this way the dream is believed to be broadcast to the spirits of the animals in the bush. A friend, Dr. Alan Ford, who has lived and hunted with the Naskapi told me of the amused puzzlement of a group of hunters when he told them that he never had any big dreams on waking.

If a hunter behaves well and respects the animals and his fellows, then his dreams will improve and he will become a great man. But if he violates these codes, then dreams may desert him. Today, as civilization encroaches on the lives of the Naskapi, the big dreams may not be as frequent as they were when the first anthropologists visited the Naskapi. However, certain of the older and more experienced hunters are recognized as great dreamers who must be consulted before any expedition is made. In this world of dreams the Naskapi encounter old friends, recognize various points on the trail, and learn of the movements of game.

Frank Speck has also written of the bear hunt, in which a Naskapi enters a sweat lodge containing hot stones. Inducing a fever, the hunter spends several nights in the lodge dreaming of the bear and the hunt. After meeting the bear in his dreams in this way, the actual hunt is itself almost a formality.

In addition to their dreams the Naskapi also engage in a number of divinations, the most important of which involves consulting the bone oracle. Animals are sacred; they consume the herbs of nature, and indeed to eat bear and caribou is to take medicine. (A medical officer of health for the Labrador region told me of a general deterioration in health that followed the importation of meat and other foods into the region. Arctic game is particularly low in saturated fats, and despite an almost exclusive meat diet, the Indian and Inuit do not suffer from a high incidence of heart disease.) This power or Manitu is also present in the bones of animals and can therefore be used to reveal the location of game. A hunter will throw a bone into the fire and then study the patterns of cracks and dark spots, which are interpreted as trails, lakes, herds, hunters, and strangers. The Naskapi believe that the spirit of the fire also enters into the bone, and if the diviner has great power and is in harmony with the spirits of the animals, then the outcome of the divination will be successful. Some hunters will use only the bones of small animals, for they believe that the powerful moose and caribou bones can be used only by those with great Manitu.

The survival of the Naskapi people depends on each hunter's being able to recognize the patterns and flux of nature and to live in harmony with them. It is through the bone oracle and dreams that the hunter is able to maintain contact with the Manitu within and, in this fashion, respond to patterns that are manifest in the external world such as weather, migrations of game, habits of the bear, and the travels of other hunters.

The Naskapi live in a world of meaningful pattern in which no distinction exists between what we have come to call mind and matter. For Manitu operates in all things and causes the movements and currents of the natural world which appear in dreams. These patterns are also displayed in the art of bone divination, which occurs when the Manitu of the diviner comes into conjunction with the Manitu of bone and of fire. To ask if the oracle actually *predicts* the future or if nights spent in the sweat lodge actually *cause* the success of a bear hunt would be an absurd question for these people. When all that happens is part of the one universal pattern and Manitu can be found without and within, then the way of knowledge that is based on causality and analysis must appear irrelevant.

What is perhaps most striking about the Naskapi's bone oracle is that today, on the other side of the world, in remote mountains of China, a similar ritual is practiced. Taking a sheep or goat bone, the Chinese shaman will burn or strike it and then interpret the pattern of cracks. The ritual begins by addressing the bone and charging it to answer a specific question. The diviner speaks to the bone and argues that, since the sheep or goat lives only on clean grass and drinks pure water, the "universal" will be strong within the bone so that it can see and hear. The shaman may then offer the bone a little rice and, after charging it not to lie, writes his question on the bone and causes the cracks to be made.

"Will this couple have sons and grandsons?" "Will their marriage be good, bad, or not so bad?" A young couple wait for the bone's verdict on their future as the shaman studies the patterns of cracks on the bone. If the crack extends to one side, the prognosis is good, but if it moves in the other direction, things may be bad. Whatever the outcome, the shaman is confident that the "universal," an echo perhaps of Manitu, which is in all nature and has been absorbed by eating and drinking into the sheep, will give power to the oracle bones.

But divination with oracle bones is not confined to the Naskapi of Labrador or to the mountain people of modern China it has been found in many subarctic regions and is used by the Dog-Rib Indians of northern Canada and the Chuckchi of Siberia to tell of the approach of weather, the onset of disease, attacks by wolves, movements of the camp, and successes of the hunt.

THE SHANG OF THE YELLOW RIVER

The twentieth-century Chinese shaman who ponders over the cracks in a sheep bone is in fact the heir to a legacy that stretches back over five thousand years, to the dawn of Chinese civilization, a period in which early hunter-gatherers discovered the rudiments of farming and began to settle in small villages. The bone oracle was particularly significant to the Longshang, a neolithic people who gave the greatest importance to religion and ritual in their lives. The Longshang were already more advanced than their hunter-gatherer ancestors for they buried their dead with special care and developed a sophisticated art in the form of pottery and polished jade objects, such as the mysterious Zong.

A major advance in the civilizations of China, and the full flowering of the bone oracle, began with the emergence of the Shang peoples from the Yellow River area, around 1700 B.C.[3] As we shall see, the government and religion of the Shang centered around bone divination, which makes them, unequivocally, a civilization built on synchronicity. Under the Shang, cities grew, farming improved, and a system of grain storage was introduced. A special class of craftsmen was maintained to produce pottery, jades, and bronzes of exceptional beauty.[4] Their government and bureaucracy were sophisticated enough to undertake great building projects, such as the wall at Jinhuan, which, it is estimated, took 12½ years and 10,000 laborers to build.

For these Bronze Age people there was no sharp distinction

The complex design on this ritual vessel of the Shang Dynasty is based on that of a face. The casting of these bronze vessels demands a consummate skill. (Copyright Royal Ontario Museum.)

between mind and matter, heaven and earth, the living and the dead. The cosmos was a harmony, the universe was cyclical, and the role of humankind was to maintain this balance through right conduct, ritual, hunting, and planting crops. While the ultimate cause of the universe was impossible to conceive, there did exist a High God, Di, together with lesser gods, important ancestors, and even beings whose special concern was for a particular village or home. Religion for the Shang was not a formal matter, residing in the hands of a priest class but was part of daily life, in which small sacrifices could be made and rituals observed by everyone.

However, it was not given to the ordinary people to intercede with the greatest ancestors or gods and so the Emperor evolved to become the intermediary between the highest heaven and his people. It was the Emperor who made major decisions, gave orders, declared war, began work on new buildings, and concerned himself with the bounty of the earth and its crops. Yet none of these things happened through his efforts alone for he was a vehicle for the harmonies of the universe.

This oracle bone, used by the Shang, clearly demonstrates the type of cracks used in divination. The inscriptions are in an archaic form of Chinese characters. (Copyright Royal Ontario Museum.)

Along with the change in society and religion that gave central place to the Emperor came the development of the bone oracle, from the Longshang's use of shoulder bones, in which cracks were produced by hot brands, to the great rituals of divination by tortoise shells used in the Late Shang, also called the an-Yang, Yin or Historical Period.

At the height of the Shang, the Emperor consulted the tortoise oracle on everything from military campaigns, weather, hunting, building, and administrative orders, to toothaches, dreams, children born to concubines, requests to an ancestor, as well as prognostications for the week, day, and night. Each day for up to several hours, the Emperor of the Shang took part in the rituals of divination. Indeed it has been calculated that some three million man-hours were spent working with the tortoise oracle during the Late Shang period.

Divination began with the preparation of the tortoise shell itself.[5] So many of these animals were required for the royal divination that they had to be imported from several other areas of China. A hundred thousand inscribed and polished shells have been discovered in one pit alone. First, the shell itself was cleaned, cut, and carefully polished until it shone like jade. Next it was inscribed with a catalogue number, its origin, and the method of preparation, and finally a series of indentations were drilled into the shell to form a pattern which followed the symmetry of the shell itself. This whole process would have taken some ninety hours.

With the shell prepared, the daily divination could then take place. The Emperor stood before an altar of earth on which rested a number of the shining, polished shells. He first made a "charge" to the shell. For example, "There will be good hunting tomorrow." Then a hot brand or poker was applied to one of the indentations until a sharp crack was heard and a crack appeared on the other side of the shell. This process was repeated until a pattern of cracks was made, each radiating from one of the burned hollows.

In many cases the name of an important ancestor would be involved to assist with the charge and divination. If the first reading was clear, then an animal would be sacrificed and

The tortoise shell oracle used by a Shang Emperor. On the reverse side, a pattern of carefully drilled indentations can be seen along with the scorch marks produced by hot brands. The front exhibits symmetrical, wavy lines, which are the natural joins of the animal's shell. In addition, crack lines produced by heating can also be seen. The reading corresponding to this pattern of cracks is also inscribed in the shell. (Copyright Royal Ontario Museum.)

disemboweled and the divination repeated to confirm that the ritual was acceptable to that particular ancestor. If, however, the reading proved to be unclear, then the whole process would have to be repeated. In some cases a series of divinations was required, each one establishing an answer to a yes/no question, in order to establish the best decision for some important action. It may have been necessary, for example, for the Emperor to consult a series of shells in order to determine, through binary questioning, which god or ancestor should be appeased.

Finally, several hours later, the divination was complete and the shells were given to scribes, who engraved the reading onto the shell and, later, added the outcome or verification. After this, the shells were stored in a vast, Bronze Age filing system and left for archeologists to discover three and a half thousand years later.

It is clear from the extent and importance given to the tortoise oracle that divination had become the focus for the life of the Shang.[6] As we have seen, in the transformation from the Longshang to the Later Shang, the process of divination had reached a high art. No longer was it sufficient to throw a buffalo's shoulder blade into the fire, or burn it with a hot brand. For now the vehicle of divination had to be prepared with great craftsmanship and the readings themselves were accompanied by an important ritual.

The synchronicity represented in the bone oracle had evolved, in the Shang period, to have such significance that it no longer applied simply to the meaning and experience of a single individual but to a whole civilization. The conjunction of the Emperor with the tortoise shell was a central, meaningful event for the whole Shang people. The act of divination therefore involved the inner questions of the Shang, as expressed through their highest representative, with external manifestations of the shell, and through this unity with all the harmonies of heaven. The pattern of cracks, together with their interpretation, formed an "acausal parallelism" with events in nature and society, so that the microcosm of the act of divination formed a mirror in which were reflected the patterns of the macrocosm, from the movements of game and the ripening of crops, to the building of palaces and the death of Emperors. Within the bone oracle, heaven and earth, microcosm and macrocosm, coexisted and intersected so that the inner and outer worlds were able to contain and reflect each other.

It would never occur to the Shang, for example, that the Emperor somehow "caused" an event to happen, through the act of divination, or that a link of causes could be discovered between a pattern of cracks in the tortoise shell and, say, the birth of a son. The oracle was an expression of the harmonies of heaven and earth so that its acausal parallelisms, for the Shang, were a manifestation of the underlying movements of the universe. It is appropriate to recall here the story of the Chinese rainmaker (Chapter 1), who did not so much "cause" rain to fall as to place himself, and the village, in harmony with the natural processes of the world, including rain itself.

The Shang civilization was therefore based on a worldview of global harmony in which it was considered perfectly natural for "unrelated" events to happen together and thereby form patterns. Central to such a perception was that what appear, to us, to be unrelated, such as mind and matter, heaven and earth, god and humankind, internal and external, were, for the Shang, taken as being without division or distinction. How curious would have appeared our scientific obsession with analysis, our search for causal chains, our attempts to unravel the patterns of nature into linear time scales, and our belief that understanding comes from an exploration of the elementary units of any system.

Through the ritual of reading cracks on the shell of a tortoise, the Shang were able to organize and maintain their complex culture. By no means can their worldview be dismissed as simply the aberration of a backward and obscure people, for the Shang are considered as one of the world's major early civilizations. Their culture survived for a longer period than that of the British Empire. Indeed their synchronistic worldview lasted longer than post-Renaissance science has existed!

Today the tortoise oracle has become the rich history book of the Shang. For every detail of their daily life is recorded on these shells—the weather, seasons, political decisions, births, marriages, deaths, the planning of campaigns, and negotiations with outlying tribes. One inscription even gives details of the appearance of a nova in the sky. The actual form of the inscriptions themselves proved a scholar's gold mine, for the three thousand characters that appear on the shells form the nucleus from which Chinese writing evolved.

At sometime around 1030 B.C. (some scholars have put the

date between 1122 and 1018 B.C.), the Shang were conquered by the Western Chou, and like all victors, the Chou rewrote history. The bone and tortoise oracle persisted sporadically right down to our own century, but never again was it to achieve the central position in a major civilization. It has been replaced by an equally ancient but more flexible method of divination known as the *I Ching*.

THE BOOK OF CHANGES

It is with the *I Ching* that the Chinese view of synchronicity reached its most advanced philosophical form.[7] The considerable collections of writings that surround the *Book of Changes* contain a theory of synchronicity and of the order of harmonies that is in remarkable accord with the arguments of this book. In addition, the *I Ching* was of fundamental influence on the thinking of Carl Jung.

It is easy to forget that the *Book of Changes* contains a cosmology, philosophy, and theology as well as providing significant insights into farming, psychology, and good government. For in the sixties, the *I Ching*, along with miniskirts, flower power, LSD, macrobiotic foods, and the Beatles had become just another part of Western culture. The *I Ching* was, to the sixties, what seances, Ouija boards, tea leaves, and palm readings were to the superstitious Victorians. But it must not be forgotten that for several thousand years the Chinese believed the *I Ching* to contain the patterns and dynamics of the universe, and to stand as a mediator between heaven and earth.

To consult the *Book of Changes*, the questioner, having a clear and tranquil mind, first manipulates the stalks of the sacred milfoil (or in later versions, tosses three coins). The oldest existent text, the *Zhouyi*, describes this process of randomly dividing and setting aside the stalks and counting the numbers in each pile until a series of numbers are arrived at, which represent broken and unbroken lines:

The number of the total is fifty. Of these, forty-nine are used. They are divided into two portions, to represent the two primal forces. Hereupon one is set apart, to represent the three powers. They are counted through by fours, to represent the four seasons. The remainder is put aside, to represent the intercalary month. There are two intercalary months in five years, therefore the putting aside is repeated, and this gives us the whole. . . . Therefore four operations are required to produce a change; eighteen mutations yield a hexagram.

The random division of stalks is therefore used to generate a number which is, in turn, represented by a single broken or unbroken line. The whole manipulation is repeated and a second broken or unbroken line is set down above the first and the process continued until a hexagram of lines is produced. Finally the *Book* itself is consulted, and corresponding to that particular hexagram, a decision, an image, and a commentary are studied, along with the particular interpretations for the overall hexagram and each of its lines.

Mythology tells us that the *I Ching* had its origins in the trigrams (trios of broken and unbroken lines) that were created by the legendary Fu Hsi, inventor of cooking and farming. Another myth tells of a tortoise which emerged from the Yellow River carrying hexagrams on its back, a story that suggests an obvious connection between the *I Ching* and the tortoise oracle of the Shang. The *I Ching* itself records that the hexagrams were created by King Wen, destroyer of the Shang, and that the commentaries were written by his successor, the Duke of Chou. Other legends claim that Confucius himself added to the *Book of Changes*.

It is clear that some form of divination by means of vegetation stalks had been practiced from the earliest times by the Chinese people. As far back as 3000 B.C., symbols and trigrams corresponding to those used to denote the hexagrams were inscribed on bronze vessels. One inscription reads:

It wax the eighth month, after the dying moon, *wu-yin;* the king was at the Si pavilion in Pangjin and personally ordered Scribe Yu to perform a milfoil divination. The king called out to Yibo to award Yu cowries. Yu bowed and touched his head to the floor, and to respond to the king's munificence herewith makes [this] Father Ding treasured urn.[8]

Some archeologists in China believe that the *I Ching* may have developed from the bone oracle, while others hold that it is a more ancient or a parallel system of divination.

The written interpretations of the *I Ching* were, by tradition, first composed between three and four thousand years ago, with later additions being made in the Ch'in and Han dynasties. The book that is on sale in bookstores today is therefore the translation of a complex text containing many layers, each written and rewritten at different historical periods, and interleaved together for each hexagram. At various periods the *Book of Changes* was interpreted as a treatise on magic, a handbook of statecraft, a philosophy, a system of divination, and a theory of the universe. Recently, a version of the *I Ching*, written on silk, was found in a tomb of the Han dynasty, dating from 180–170 B.C., which has different arrangements of the hexagrams and simpler interpretations. Possibly it was intended for use by ordinary people, as opposed to priests and those trained in divination.

The most striking aspect of the *I Ching*, for the modern mind, is that it appears to be based on a binary code. The hexagrams are constructed out of broken and unbroken lines; in other words, they are built on binary numbers that correspond to yes/no, Yin/Yang, or the 0,1 of a modern computer. In 1779 the philosopher and mathematician Leibnitz published his *De Progressions Dyadica*, which described the binary number system. Some twenty years later, during his correspondence with a Jesuit missionary in China, he was struck to learn of the *I Ching* and realized that its hexagrams could be interpreted as a binary representation of the numbers 0 through 63.

On closer examination, however, it turns out that the numerology of the *I Ching* is more subtle than is implied in a simple binary code. Each line is, for example, given a number—6, 7, 8, or 9—which has particular mystical and cosmological importance. (The numbers 1, 2, 3, 4 were used during the Tang dynasty.) These indicate if the line is broken or unbroken, moving or stationary. Where a "moving" line occurs, it is able to change its value, from broken to unbroken

Ch'ien   Kun   Ken   Sun

Tui   Ken

                                       Ch'ien

                Ta Kuo   Kuai

or vice versa, and hence produce a transformation from one hexagram to another.

The lines themselves are first grouped into trigrams. Since each line has two possible modes, broken and unbroken, there are a total of eight (2 × 3) trigrams which display all possible threefold interactions of yin and yang. For example, three yang lines are called *Ch'ien:* the Father, Heaven. Three yin lines are called *Kun:* the Earth, Mother. If *Kun* is modified by replacing a "masculine" yang line in the "third place," numbering from the bottom, then Ken: Water, the Eldest Son, is produced. Modifying *Ch'ien* with the feminine principle yields *Tui:* Lake, the Youngest Daughter.

Reading the trigrams proceeds, as with the tortoise oracle, from bottom to top, in the opposite direction to normal Chinese writing and reveals the movements and oppositions between the forces of yin and yang that are displayed in nature, the state, and the family. Yin and yang proceed from the Tao; they are the forces or principles of nature that balance and move against one another. Displayed in the ancient trigrams of the *I Ching*, they give an image of eight basic situations.

The next stage in the evolution of the *I Ching* was to combine all eight pairs of trigrams to produce sixty-four (8 × 8 = 64) hexagrams. By placing one trigram, or situation of nature, above the other, sixty-four different states are produced. For example, to place *Ken*, the Mountain, against itself produces the hexagram *Ken*, Stillness. But place *Sun*, the Wind, over *Ken* and the result is *Ch'ien*, Gradual Advance. Corresponding to each hexagram is a particular image of nature which comes about through the opposition or balance of the forces in the trigrams. Hence within the hexagrams can be read the overall tension and harmony of its various lines.

Ken
Mountain

+

Ken
Mountain

=

Ken
Stillness

Sun
Wind

+

Ken
Mountain

=

Ch'ien
Gradual Advance

In the opinion of Dr. J. Hsü of the Royal Ontario Museum in Toronto (which houses one of the world's major collections of oracle and tortoise bones), as the Chinese society became more complex, the interpretations of the *I Ching* had to become increasingly more subtle to allow for less clear-cut situations. In this fashion the "moving" or transforming line was introduced. Depending on the number produced by the division of milfoil stalks, a yin or yang line may find itself in a moment of transition as it moves to its opposite polarity, the broken becoming unbroken and vice versa. A moving yin line in the first position will therefore take *Ta Kuo*, Excess, into *Kuai*, Renewed Advance. When this occurs, the hexagrams are read in succession and the questioner realizes that a particular situation is in a period of transition. In this sense the *I Ching* may reveal the inner dynamics of a process of society or of nature.

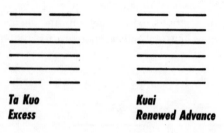

Ta Kuo
Excess

Kuai
Renewed Advance

Compressed within the hexagram and its arrangement of yang and yin lines is a whole cosmology, a sociology, a psychology, and an image of how the archetypes of nature can move into balance, oppose each other, precipitate change, or produce temporary stability. Through contemplation of society and nature and by study of the hexagrams, generation upon generation of Chinese thinkers have been able to add their comments to the *Book of Changes*. Even Confucius is reputed to have said, "If years were added to my life, I would devote fifty of them to the study of the oracle, then might I avoid committing great errors."

Early this century, Richard Wilhelm was introduced to the *I Ching* by the master Lao Nai-hsuan. Interrupted only by World War I, he made a translation into German of what he believed to be one of the most important books in the world's literature. For Wilhelm, the *I Ching* contained the origins of Taoism and Confucianism as well as the seeds of Chinese natural science. Through him, the full meaning of the *Book of Changes* came to the attention of Carl Jung, who saw in it a confirmation of his own theories and connections to the gnostic traditions of Europe and the philosophies of India. He referred to it as an "Archimedean point" from which the Western attitude of mind could be shaken to its foundations. "Like a part of nature, it waits until it is discovered." At critical times in his own life Jung consulted the *Book of Changes* and encouraged certain of his patients to work with it as well. Yet as to its ultimate meaning, he cautioned:

> The less one thinks about the theory of the *I Ching*, the more soundly one sleeps.[9]

The "theory of the *I Ching*," as embedded in the book itself, comes strikingly close to the ideas of synchronicity that are explored in this book. To appreciate its full significance, it is important to remember that the Chinese do not structure their world, as does the West, into causal terms but through clusterings, coincidences, and correspondences. For example, as Jung's colleague von Franz points out, a Chinese history book does not try to trace causal connections between events but rather it records the clusterings and happenings that took place during a particular reign:

> . . . the question is not how has this come about, or what factor caused this effect, but what likes to happen together in a meaningful way at the same moment. The Chinese always ask: What tends to happen together in time?[10]

In the cosmology of the *I Ching*, humankind is seen as the mediator between heaven and earth. Human beings have their existence in both spheres, and by means of the *I Ching*, a traffic between these two worlds can be established. Everything that takes place within the earthly universe is an unfolding of patterns that exist in the higher world which is inaccessible to the normal senses. All these patterns and changes coexist timelessly so that the processes of nature and society are temporal images of the eternal. The sages of old had intuitions of this higher world and set down their insights in the *Book of*

Changes. These patterns of symmetries have their ground in a timeless state which then manifest themselves as an unfolding, in time, within the reality of our perceptions.

When the *I Ching* is cast, an image is created or unfolded of the particular moment in time which includes the questioner, the question, and all that surrounds him or her. Just as in quantum physics the observer, or questioner, is included within the general description of reality, so is the questioner irreducibly linked to the divination. The microcosm of this meaningful instant is represented by a particular hexagram, within which are contained the balance and opposition of the various forces of nature, the yin and the yang. In a sense, therefore, the moment of divination and the hexagram that is obtained are an image of the seed out of which the future is born. Although the *I Ching* brings the questioner into contact with the world of eternity, Hellmut Wilhelm, son of the translator of the book, believes that no special training or wisdom is required to understand it, only the highest integrity "to see things as they are."

By reading and interpreting the *Book of Changes*, the questioner therefore comes to know the significance of a particular moment in time, the seed from which future events will flow. By taking right action in the light of the divination, he or she will assist in the harmonious movements of nature. The *I Ching* therefore deals in pure synchronicity since its hexagrams, produced by chance, are meaningful images of the universe and act as signposts to its direction of unfolding.

Divination through the *I Ching* does not, of course, imply a deterministic universe whose future can be "predicted" through the random movement of a handful of plant stalks. Rather, the *Book of Changes* seeks to expose the essence and the implications of a given moment and guides the questioner in taking responsibility for actions and decisions. It perhaps conjures up the image of one of those bifurcation points, regions of extreme instability, out of which Prigogine's dissipative structures are born. These are the nucleii in space and time which contain the implications of future structures. At such a point of chance and change, a system may move in one of several possible directions, each of which will unfold to give a new structure. The questioner stands at such a point in time and, through the act of divination, exposes the various forces and patterns that are at work.

DIVINATION, WORLDVIEWS, AND LANGUAGE

What significance does the tortoise shell oracle of the Shang or the milfoil divination of the *I Ching* have for us in the West today? Clearly the *Book of Changes* had deep meaning for its translator, Richard Wilhelm, and appeared to speak directly to Carl Jung. It is equally true that many people in North America and Europe, who may be largely ignorant of Chinese philosophy and customs, nevertheless use the *I Ching* as a method of divination and a guide in their daily lives. The question essentially is, to what extent can the Chinese methods of divination address the worldview that prevails in our modern world?

To understand this question, it is necessary to recognize that the *I Ching*, the oracles of the Shang, and the bone divination of the Naskapi are all associated with particular, strongly held worldviews. Such a worldview goes far deeper than just a particular branch of knowledge or a paradigm of science, for it pervades the whole of life and disposes each individual to deal with the world in a particular way. It determines how society is organized and the particular image each individual has of her- or himself. But all of this is largely tacit and unconscious so that it enters even into the way that people perceive the world (both in their mind's eye and through the senses) and communicate with each other. Even the spoken language, therefore, reflects an overall worldview.

One can recall here the famous example of the large number of different names used by the Inuit to describe snow. Snow is of enormous importance in the lives of the inhabitants of the North American Arctic and Greenland, who must be able to distinguish particularly subtle differences in their environment. Differences which, to us, would probably seem unimportant. This niceness of distinction is therefore reflected in the number of different names that are used to describe the various forms of snow. But this relationship between perceptual differentiation and language works in both directions, for the very richness of the names in turn disposes an individual to look for and make fine distinctions. In a similar way our single word "snow" has the effect of lumping together all our different perceptions of the winter into one category and thereby obscuring them. Of course a painter may learn to distinguish many different forms of snow and explore their appearances and effects on canvas. Yet he or she would probably find it difficult to verbalize exact feelings about these perceptions and would have to call on a variety of analogies and metaphors to convey the impression in words.

The linguist Benjamin Lee Whorf argued, in the first half of this century, that language is strongly related to cognition and that enfolded within each language are ideas about nature and society. Whorf's notion, that the structure of the language predisposes its speaker to think and act in a certain way, created a considerable controversy amongst linguists. However, in *Science, Order and Creativity*, David Bohm and I argue that the whole area of perception and communication must be considered as an indivisible whole.[11] Language, the whole activity of communication, and perception through the senses and the mind all act on each other in particularly subtle ways. In this way a worldview and language are able to reinforce each other so that everyone who speaks that language is unconsciously disposed to see the world in a particular light.

Such a dynamic combination therefore goes beyond a mere theory, or area of knowledge, and spreads out into the whole culture, pervading every aspect of life, including the social structure along with its customs, beliefs, activities, and the very relationships between individuals. This is, of course, why it is so difficult for the West to accommodate the Eastern view of the universe and its preoccupation with synchronicity. Even before the time of the Shang, an overall vision of the wholeness of things, with an emphasis on conjunction and harmonies, must have developed in China which permeated social institutions, language, and all aspects of daily life. It would therefore be as difficult for the ancient Chinese to call into question the notion of synchronicity as for the average Westerner to question the notion of linear time and the historical succession of events.

It is true, of course, that during the present century China has undergone economic and cultural revolutions and, today, is accommodating more and more Western ideas. But only time will tell, in the decades to come, how profound this change has been and whether a more ancient worldview, which must still be enfolded deep within the language and customs of these people, will have an influence on the future.

At all events the more subtle elements of the Chinese, and for that matter, the Naskapi view of nature, are hidden from us in the West. Only those who have taken the trouble to study the customs, philosophies, and languages of these people may hope to obtain a direct experience of the deeper levels of their worldview. Nevertheless some claim, through their intuition perhaps, to have direct knowledge of the *I Ching*. Possibly Jung, for example, was able to achieve an insight into what the Chinese sages had discovered and set down in their book. For in bypassing the surface layers of Eastern and Western culture and addressing the archetypes directly, which Jung believed have a universal component common to all humanity, he may well have arrived at a deeper truth.

How do people today approach the *I Ching*, or the bone oracle, and in this way come to terms with a whole society based on synchronicity? Within the Western worldview several questions immediately suggest themselves: Does the *I Ching* really work? Does it predict the future correctly? How can the manipulation of milfoil stalks be related to the complex events in society or within an individual's life?

A conventional answer to these questions is to suggest that the readings, which correspond to each hexagram, form a screen onto which the questioner projects various concerns, beliefs, and questions. Just as the complex refractions and reflections of the crystal ball, or the random pattern of tea leaves in a cup, were used by Victorians as the complex patterned background into which their imaginations, instincts, and intuitions could read, so does the subtle language of the *I Ching*, like the pattern of cracks on a bone, provide a canvas on which the questioner's concerns can be painted. It is certainly true that the highly symbolic language of the *I Ching* and the rich system of images it draws upon are open to many interpretations and therefore lend themselves particularly well to such "reading in" by the imagination. In addition, the situations described in the *I Ching* are generally archetypal in nature, so that it is quite probable that the questioner will discover a powerful resonance between her or his current state of affairs and the situation and advice given by the hexagram.

Another "Western" approach would be to suggest that, subliminally, the actual casting of the hexagram, or the cracking of a bone, is influenced by what the questioner desires to learn. Through unconscious manipulations of the milfoil stalks, or the oracle bone, the background of chance events is therefore directed toward a particular goal. In this way the act of casting, and the subsequent reading are open to the subtle promptings that are undetected by the conscious mind. By influencing the reading, the *I Ching* therefore acts as a vehicle through which the unconscious mind can be made manifest.

Other explanations for the working of Chinese divination could involve such notions as precognition and the possibility that the future can in fact be predicted, or that the forces and wishes of the unconscious could have some actual effect on external events.

It should also be pointed out that the *I Ching* contains the distillation of thousands of years of wise advice pertaining to the outcome of many archetypal situations and can therefore be used as an experienced guide to life. Finally it must not be forgotten that many people seek a meaning in their lives and may be attracted to a religion, an individual, or a book which claims to provide an answer. From being initially drawn to the *I Ching* by curiosity, some may eventually come to rely heavily upon it and structure their lives accordingly. The belief of such individuals that the *I Ching* is working for them would therefore become an almost self-fulfilling situation.

The significant point about these various explanations is

that while they may be satisfying to us, they would not appear to be particularly profound or even relevant to the Chinese sages of old. No doubt they would point out that our attempts to pin down the heart of the *I Ching* misses the whole essence of the book. Their benign indifference to our efforts would cause us to realize, yet again, the considerable gulf that separates one worldview from another. The *I Ching* is a universe unto itself and cannot easily be encompassed within the Western approach.

The Chinese and the Naskapi demand no explanation, for the operation of synchronicity and for the patterns and harmonies they see around them. If pressed, their reaction may be similar to ours when asked why time flows from the present into the future: "But that is simply the way the world works." Indeed our worldview, of the past five hundred years, is so powerful that, like sunlight that renders the stars invisible by day, it tends to obscure the subtle patterns and meanings that may be revealed within nature, society, and the life of the individual. For hundreds of years the Shang civilization was guided by the divinations of the bone and tortoise oracles. After this, the *I Ching* offered its own wisdom. Worldview, civilization, and synchronistic divination were irreducibly linked together in ways that may seem alien to our own "causal" and "temporal" approaches. It may well be that for us, in the late twentieth century, to accommodate the ideas of synchronicity in any fundamental way will require a profound transformation of the way in which we view ourselves, nature, and society.

CONCLUSIONS

What meaning can synchronicity and the divinations of the Naskapi, the Shang, and the classical Chinese have for the West? Clearly there would be no point in exchanging computers and radiotelescopes for tortoise shells and milfoil stalks. Indeed it is not even possible to make a conscious decision to change a worldview, for this is tacitly and largely unconsciously enfolded within the whole society. However, we can at least entertain the possibility that different worldviews may in fact work for other societies. Indeed, by attempting to hold together a number of such different approaches in the mind, it may be conceivable that creative new insights will be born.

While science has an awesome power to predict and control, it is also clear that its essential fragmentation of nature is no longer able to address all the major problems that face the world today. Synchronicity, however, with its sensitivity to harmony and the indivisibility of consciousness, humanity, and nature at least opens up the possibility of a new approach. But again this does not mean making a choice to "adopt" synchronicity or to "replace" some of the approaches of science with those of synchronicity. Rather, by being perceptive to these issues it may be possible to move, in a creative way, in an entirely new direction.

One step toward becoming more sensitive to the duality between these different worldviews is to begin to question the whole current order of science and to develop new ideas and theories that have a more holistic approach. In the next chapter, some of these new notions will be discussed and an attempt will be made to give an account of the *I Ching* which fits more satisfactorily into a new scientific account of the universe.

NOTES

1. H. B. G. Casimir, *Haphazard Reality* (New York: Harper & Row, 1983).
2. Frank G. Speck, *Naskapi: The Savage Hunters of the Labrador Peninsula. The Civilization of the American Indian*, vol. 10 (Norman: University of Oklahoma Press, 1977). I have also learned of the Naskapi from my good friend, Dr. A. J. Ford of the University of Montreal, who has lived and hunted with these people.
3. Te-k'un Cheng, *Archeology in China*, vol. 2 (Cambridge University Press, 1963).
4. J. Rawson, *Ancient China: Art and Archeology* (London: British Museum Publications, 1980).
5. D. N. Keightley, *Sources of Shang History, The Oracle-Bone Inscription of Bronze Age China* (Berkeley: University of California Press, 1979).
6. There have been suggestions made by some scholars in the West that divination was used to give the appearance of divine approval to a particular system of political control. Indeed, during one period the

method of preparation of the shells may have enabled the diviner to predict the directions of the cracks. This method, however, soon changed, and in the opinion of most authorities, the Shang employed the oracle with great reverence (discussion with Dr. J. Hsü, Far Eastern Department, Royal Ontario Museum, Toronto).

7. R. Wilhelm, *The I Ching or Book of Changes*, trans. C. F. Baynes (Princeton University Press, 1950); A. Douglas, *The Oracle of Change* (Harmondsworth, Eng.: Penguin, 1971); G. Whincup, *Rediscovering the I Ching* (Garden City, N.Y.: Doubleday, 1986); H. Wilhelm, *Heaven, Earth and Man in the Book of Changes* (Seattle and London: University of Washington Press, 1977); and Ching Chem Shiu-Chin, "How to Form a Hexagram and Consult the I Ching," *Journal of the American Oriental Society 92:2* (1972): 237.

8. Chang Cheng-Lang, "An Interpretation of the Divinatory Inscriptions on Early Chou Bronzes," *Kaogu Xuebau* 4 (1980): 403–415.

9. From C. G. Jung's foreword to R. Wilhelm, *The I Ching or Book of Changes*, Eng. trans. C. F. Baynes (London: Routledge & Kegan Paul, 1951).

10. M-L von Franz, *On Divination and Synchronicity* (Toronto: Inner City Books, 1980).

11. David Bohm and F. David Peat, *Science, Order and Creativity* (New York: Bantam Books, 1987).

6 MIND, MATTER, AND INFORMATION

A synchronicity is an origin, the creative moment from which the whole pattern of order in a person's life can be perceived as it spreads out into the future. But synchronicities can also act as the jokers in nature's pack of cards, for their unexpected conjunction of events can disrupt a person's confidence in a rational, ordered picture of the world. They are as much concerned with meanings, values, and inner experiences as they are with external events. Indeed Wolfgang Pauli was struck by this duality between the objective and the subjective in nature, and he pointed out that just as quantum physics has introduced the subjective observer into its description of reality, so has Jung's collective unconscious revealed an objective layer to mind.

Unless mind and matter are to be treated as two aspects of a single whole it will be difficult to make further progress in understanding the nature of synchronicity. The challenge, presented in the first chapter of this book, of understanding how matter and mind could emerge out of a single organic unity, remains to be answered. For the Shang and the Naskapi, however, the whole universe was ripe with meaning so that no discontinuity was perceived between mind and matter, human beings and nature. In this way all events were believed to flow, and unfold out of a timeless pattern of synchronicities rather than through a sequence of causal connections in a linear time.

In earlier chapters a series of examples showed how the familiar notions of causality could be modified in order to view nature in a more organic fashion. But it still remains to demonstrate, in a convincing way, how this new worldview could encompass consciousness. It is the purpose of the present chapter to develop new notions of order that can embrace the phenomena of both mind and matter.

UNITY OR DUALITY

In the seventeenth century, when the more subtle properties of matter were unknown, it was natural to contrast the evident "grossness" of the material world with the more mercurial aspects of mind. Even the most ingenious of machines could be seen to operate using a system of cogs, levers, springs, governers, and counterweights, all of which moved in a mechanical and repetitive fashion. While a Swiss clock or a mechanical robot may have represented the highest state of engineering, nevertheless its deterministic principles were obvious and explicable in terms of a few simple laws and principles. By contrast, the mind moved with extreme subtlety and speed so that its operation was evidently of an entirely different order than that of matter.

For the philosopher Descartes, mind and matter had such different behaviors and demanded such irreconcilably opposed descriptions that he concluded that they were quite different substances. This difference was emphasized when it was later discovered that all matter can be described through Newton's laws, which are deterministic in nature. In particular when the movement of an arm, for example, changes its quality (momentum), this is only possible through the application of a physical force (for example, the energy of the muscles or some external pull on the hand). But since all movements of the body are the result of physical forces, which obey Newton's laws, how is it possible for the mind to influence the body in any way at all? For if the mind can exert a material force, then it too must be governed by Newton's deterministic laws and therefore no freedom of will, or subtlety of application, is possible.

The best that the Cartesians could do was to suggest that mind and body are like two clocks in perfect synchronization.

While no causal interaction passes between the clocks, nevertheless when the hands of one point to the hour, the other chimes. By a curious irony, Cartesian dualism had been forced to invent a form of synchronicity. In order to preserve the duality of mind and matter, the Cartesians insisted that inner experience is the result of acausal coincidence with external, material events.

While it has been hotly debated by many generations of philosophers, the Cartesian split still comes down to us, in one form or another, today. Even though our understanding of mind has become more acute, and our knowledge of matter more refined, nevertheless these two are, in one way or another, taken to be difficult and irreconcilable substances with an obscure form of interaction between each other. Or, alternatively, it is claimed that mind does not in fact exist, only complex neurochemical processes that direct behavior.

This Cartesian split is, however, in total contradiction to immediate experience. A person feels thirst and reaches for a glass of water. An arm is burnt and pain is experienced. These are rather obvious and simple examples, but even more impressive are the uncountable number of ways in which each person experiences mind and body as an undivided whole. There is no need to propose, in everyday life, the existence of different substances in order to understand human activity. While rocks and stones appear very different from minds, nevertheless the human body is composed of matter too, and few readers would admit to feeling a definite Cartesian split in their experience.

But to go beyond this fact of immediate sensation and experience, and to develop it into a rational, scientific account of the unity of mind and body, is particularly difficult. Philosophy is often blocked at this very point in making any creative progress forward. Possibly it is the hidden power of many centuries of a particular worldview which prevents new insights. But unless this particular problem is resolved, there seems to be little possibility of encompassing synchronicity within a rational view of the world.

Several thinkers have sought ways out of this dilemma by

insisting on a real connection between matter and mind. But it is difficult to do this in any truly successful way if it implies a link between something that is free and creative and that which is assumed to be mechanistic and determined.

One solution is to consider the mind as analogous to the driver of an automobile, who operates outside the mechanisms of the engine and simply directs its output. In this way mind is assumed to be a superior force that can in some way intervene or overrule the mechanisms of the body. Sir John Eccles, the Nobel Prize–winning neuroscientist, has postulated an actual region of the brain where this interaction is supposed to take place. The liaison area of the brain, according to Eccles, acts as an interface between the twin substances of material brain and disembodied mind. In this way the mind is able to direct and oversee the operations of the body.

Some thinkers have suggested that quantum mechanics could provide the loophole through which mind acts on the material universe. As long as every aspect of matter, including the body and its nervous system, is governed by causal, deterministic laws, then it is very difficult to see how the mind has freedom to operate. But the indeterministic, chance processes of quantum matter suggest a possible area where mind could act. If quantum processes are so finely tuned that their outcome is a matter of pure chance, then could mind "bias the odds" as it were and, in subtle ways, influence the microscopic processes of the brain and nervous system? Because the brain is of such complexity, an amplification of very small effects may occur and in this way mind's activities may manifest themselves on a global scale. Indeed it should be emphasized that the nervous system does, in a sense, have a quantum nature, for the eye is able to respond to individual photons of light and the nose can detect the presence of individual molecules.

The physicist Eugene Wigner has used a version of this argument to help him resolve the measurement problem, one of the major areas of controversy in the quantum theory. The details of this problem lie outside the scope of this book, but in essence, the problem is the search for an explanation of why, in an indeterministic and probabilistic theory, there are definite outcomes to experimental measurements. Wigner has suggested that these definite outcomes are produced by the consciousness of the human observer acting on the quantum system. In fact, mind is supposed to act at the quantum level to "collapse the wave function" of the system into a well-defined state. In such an explanation, mind continues to stand outside the material world as the superior substance that directs and influences certain material processes.

An alternative approach is to suggest that the realm of mind is an unnecessary concept, for science is able to account for human behavior on the basis of the electrochemical reactions of the brain itself. Scientists point out that the sea slug, a simple animal with an elementary nervous system, nonetheless exhibits several different forms of behavior. The sea slug has a form of memory, it recognizes simple patterns of stimuli, and it can be sensitized and habituated so that it is able to learn and become conditioned.

Scientists such as Eric Kandel at Columbia University have studied the individual nerve pathways and synaptic connections in the sea slug and have been able to explain various forms of behavior in terms of electrochemical reactions in the network of nerves. In this way, it is claimed, the simplest elements of behavior can be explained in terms of material processes. While it takes a considerable leap of extrapolation to go from the sea slug to the human being, many neuroscientists argue that it is simply a matter of the degree of complexity of the nervous system. In other words, human behavior can be broken down into a complex sequence of simple elements, each of which can, in principle, be associated with an electrochemical process in the brain. There is no need to involve the "deus ex machina" of mind to explain human behavior.

But what of the experience of consciousness itself? Resisting any appeal to the disembodied mind, some scientists speak of consciousness as being an epiphenomenon of the brain. A simple analogy will illustrate what they mean. Early computers had several rows of flashing lights which went off and on when a particular region of the machine was processing data. Thus while the computer was working out a problem, a complicated dance of lights would appear on the console. People joked that this was the computer "thinking," almost as if the dancing patterns of lights were the computer's mind and that they directed the actual processes occurring inside. However, it was clear that these lights were totally inessential to the proper operation of the machine; they were nothing more than a convenient display, an epiphenomenon of the computer's internal electronic processes.

Just as the pancreas secretes a fluid to aid in the digestion of food, so does the physical nervous system secrete consciousness to provide a display of the brain's operation. This display has obvious evolutionary advantages, for it presents the current state of the brain's various activities and strategies and assists in their modification. But, the argument goes, it no more directs the physical brain than the lights on a computer direct its internal working. Additional evidence for such an approach is given by the next (fifth-generation) stage of computer design, in which some essential display of goals and strategies will be built into the machines to assist them in modifying their own problem-solving abilities.

These various attempts to come to terms with the complexity of consciousness and human behavior, in one form or another, all preserve features of Cartesian duality, for mind and matter are taken to be different orders. This duality seems to result from treating mind and matter as *substances* so that matter becomes the substance that can be held in the hand and mind becomes the invisible, intangible substance. But, of course, the whole notion of matter has changed radically since the time of Descartes, for in addition to stones and cannonballs, the world has been found to contain invisible fields of energy and elementary particles that cannot be said to have paths or even properties that can be unambiguously specified in the absence of the observer. Indeed it may no longer be possible to divide the modern world into such simplistic categories. Rather, it may be more appropriate to inquire into the whole *order of matter* and the *order of mind* and in this way determine if these two orders are in fact irreconcilable and therefore dualistic, or if they lie within a common spectrum of orders.

If mind and matter can be understood as emerging out of a common order, then it will no longer be helpful to think of them both as distinct substances but rather as inseparable manifestations of the one undivided whole.

THE SUBTLE ORDERS OF MATTER

The history of science can be thought of as the discovery of progressively more subtle levels within nature. In other words, the scientific understanding of the stuff of nature has constantly been extended to include new and ever more complex forms. While it is often claimed that science reduces all experience to a materialistic explanation, it is really more appropriate to say that science has been forced to extend its horizons as to what matter could be. In the present century the ultimate level of nature appears to be that of space-time and the infinite energy of the quantum field. But there is no reason to suppose that the ground of reality lies there and that there may not be an uncountable number of yet more subtle levels to be discovered. Indeed it is possible that the level of mind and matter emerge out of a common ground, for the history of science is one of reconciling apparently incommensurable aspects of experience.

In the Middle Ages the heavens were considered to be of an entirely different order from that of the earth. It was evident that the heavens behaved in a radically different way, for while stones and apples fell to the ground, with the minor exception of shooting stars, the heavens had never been known to fall. Moreover Aristotle had taught that bodies move only under the influence of a force, and when that force is absent, the body will come to rest. But the sun, moon, and planets visibly continue in their eternal movements with no apparent effort. Since the orders of heaven and of earth were so different, it seemed reasonable to conclude that they were composed of entirely separate substances.

It remained to Newton, and his laws of motion and principle of universal gravitation, to show that there was nothing special about the order of the heavens and, in particular, the motion of moon and planets. For the moon does indeed fall, just like an apple. However, its inertial tendency to move in a straight line creates a centrifugal force that generates an outward falling which exactly balances the inward falling under gravity. In this way the moon is maintained in an eternal elliptical orbit. In addition, scientists had discovered that Aristotle's theory of motion was incorrect, for all bodies move in a straight line (or stay at rest) in the absence of a force. Even matter on earth would move unceasingly if it were not for the opposing forces of air resistance and friction. So by introducing new ideas such as gravity and inertia, it was possible to extend the concept of matter to include the heavens as well as the earth.

In the eighteenth and nineteenth centuries, advances were made in understanding the nature of energy and it was discovered that heat, electricity, chemical activity, and even the dissipation of work in a machine were all related by one substance—*energy*. In this way many different forms of behavior in nature could all be encompassed within the one order of energy. But clearly this order was very different from that of matter, for energy was an intangible thing. But during the nineteenth century even that distinction became blurred. The Hamilton-Jacobi theory of motion, for example, pictured material bodies and their paths as being less substantial and involving complex forms of wave motion. In addition, fields of energy were introduced by J. C. Maxwell which united the phenomena of light, magnetism, and electricity in one electromagnetic field. Finally in the first years of the twentieth century, Einstein showed that matter and energy are entirely equivalent, and the quantum theory demonstrated that both matter and energy share in a dual particle/wave nature.

The order of the world had thus changed to become more like a spectrum with mechanical motion of solid bodies at one end and continuous fields and wave/particle dualities at the other. A similar enrichment in understanding the orders of nature took place as a result of the rise of organic chemistry. It was once believed that since life behaves in a very different way from inanimate matter, there must be some essential difference in their orders. Life, for example, is characterized by movement and growth and its organization is considerably more complex and delicate than the most ingenious machine. On the other hand, matter was believed to be essentially deterministic and mechanical. However, it was also true that when a living thing died it could be reduced to simple, inanimate components. It therefore appeared that the phenomenon of life involved a special "life force" which entered into matter, causing it to congregate into complex, animated forms. In this way nature was considered to contain both the order of inanimate matter and the invisible order of the life force.

However, as the unique potential for bonding of the carbon atom began to be understood, scientists realized that this atom could enter into a multitude of complex and subtle reactions with oxygen and hydrogen, and to a lesser extent with nitrogen, chlorine, sulphur, and a handful of other elements. In this way collections of rings, long chains, and other complex shapes could be formed. In addition, these complex molecules readily entered into extremely subtle reactions with each other, which involved the exchange of very small amounts of energy. Thus, with an organic system, a very large number of chemical reactions could be linked together in such a way as to give rise to a vast network of feedback loops and structure-building and energy-carrying processes.

In this fashion the complex chemistry of carbon-based reactions, when combined with the insights of biology, were able to explain many of the rich processes of life. Again, by increasing the notion of the order of matter, it was possible to include a whole new range of phenomena that had hitherto been considered irreconcilable. Rather than life's requiring a new "life force" in order to explain its order, it turned out that the whole phenomenon could be understood by assuming that matter contains a new range of complex and subtle orders.

In other words, it is now possible to see the evolution of science in a totally new light. Rather than nature and the heavens being *reduced* to "mere matter," the reverse has in fact taken place. The whole notion of the material world has been constantly extended into regions of greater and greater complexity and subtlety until, today, it is possible to speculate that this subtle order can be extended into deeper and deeper regions without limit. The order of matter has therefore become far removed from that of the billiard balls and falling apples of the Newtonian world. Rather than nature being *reduced* to the material, the whole notion of the material has been extended into regions of indefinite intangibility.

THE MECHANICAL ORDER OF MIND

Just as matter has been discovered to have increasingly subtle levels of behavior, so does mind appear to have associated with it mechanical orders of operation. For example, at one time it was assumed that solving problems, doing mathematics, and playing chess were among the most advanced things that the human mind was capable of doing. But today these activities can be carried out, to a passable level, by electronic computers. Does this mean, as some people think, that computers are actually becoming intelligent and "mindlike" or does it suggest that certain of the mind's functions can be broken down into sequences of essentially mechanical steps?

By building in the ability to recognize certain patterns of data, compute various permutations of a particular situation, search a solution space, and operate simple strategies, it is possible for a computer to solve apparently difficult problems. In addition, the combination of large numbers of rules and facts into a vast network of "knowledge" enables a computer to operate as an "expert system" which can outperform human experts in particular fields of medicine, computer design, electronics, prospecting, and mathematics. In turn, cognitive psychologists have discovered that certain aspects of human performance can indeed be broken down into sequences of rather mechanical steps that are carried out rapidly and largely unconsciously. In this way it appears that certain activities of the mind have a largely mechanical order.

But there is no need to turn to computer analogies to see this. You have simply to be aware of your own behavior and internal thought processes. While thought can range far and free, engage in particularly subtle meditations, and break into fresh areas by an intuitive or creative leap, it is also true that some thought is highly repetitive and mechanical. If you examine your past life, or that of your friends, it becomes apparent that certain aspects have a rather repetitive, mechanical behavior associated with them. A man may become engaged in a long series of broken relationships with essentially the same type of woman, a woman may come in constant conflict with a figure of authority. Similarly there may be neurotic areas in a person's life that are concerned with sex, travel, food, work, or, for example, the need to avoid cracks in the sidewalk and to make elaborate preparations before taking a journey. Often this repetitive, mechanical behavior is triggered by the same stimulus each time. During these neurotic attacks it is possible to observe thought going round and round inside the mind, like a clockwork toy. Sometimes even a word will act as a trigger to a host of strong feelings and produce an obsessional stream of thought, or speech, in response.

Not only the repetitive use of language and thought but also emotion can be involved in a mechanical order, for strong feelings and reactions can be turned on by a simple symbol. Show patriots a flag and they will cheer or fight for it. Show a bigot a member of an abused race and immediately strong feelings of fear and anger will surface.

A little reflection on the part of the reader will show that in many ways the mind is not free and creative but obeys, in certain of its operations, a mechanical order that is not too different from that of a computer or a sophisticated machine. However, it must be emphasized that this mechanical order is only one aspect of the total behavior and even neurotic behavior cannot be fully explained by an appeal to even the most sophisticated computer. For the repetitive response to a stimulus and the different ways in which behavior can become conditioned or triggered all depend on perceiving a context. But contexts themselves are very subtle things that depend on nuances of observation and the ability to integrate together a multitude of features from the environment. As an example, for a particular word or gesture to become an insult, it must be perceived in the right context. In a theatre, between children or lovers, or when relating an anecdote, this word will not be taken as an insult, but when delivered with clenched fists or a sneering face, it may trigger off a sequence of hostile actions. So the context is as important as the gesture, for it is not so much the formula of words or the contortion of the face that conveys a message as the whole context in which it is placed. A context establishes a meaning, no matter if it is a president's speech or the ringing of a bell in Pavlov's laboratory, and these contexts require intelligence of a nonmechanical order to be appreciated.

It should therefore be clear that while mind does in fact contain certain mechanical orders of operation, these all emerge out of a much deeper nonmechanical ground. The order of mind is therefore particularly subtle and can never be reduced to that of a machine. However, it is also true that the order of nature also extends far beyond the mechanical orders of Newtonian matter and embraces fields of energy and the whole order of quantum theory. The question may therefore be raised: Does matter have an unlimited range of orders which merge into those of mind?

MORPHIC FIELDS

In Chapter 3 a series of cooperative structures were described whose order is very different from that of a machine. Clearly, powerful principles of organization are at work when the individual cells of a slime mold colony suddenly congregate together to form a single, unitary slug. Likewise when electrons in a metal begin their collective dance to form a plasma, or move with the integrated flow of a superconductor, something more than the mere statistical averaging of a large number of mechanistic individuals is at work.

In the case of the development of a human embryo, something even more subtle takes place, for the exact coordination of all the processes involved is of almost unimaginable complexity. Cells migrate, divide, die, or differentiate at exactly the right moment; organs coordinate their growth and secretions; various syntheses and metabolic processes switch off and on in harmony with other events taking place in remote areas of the organism. The optic nerve, for example, must develop within the embryo in such a way that the two ends of this complex bundle of nerves make exact connections between the 100 million receptors in the eye and the various areas of the visual cortex.

As S. J. Snyder of Johns Hopkins University put it in an editorial in the magazine *Science:*

> One of the major questions in all biology is just how discrete portions of the body come to be where they are and adopt their characteristic appearance and function. . . . What tells a group of cells in an embryo to sprout an arm? Why do some cell groups develop into the liver, others into the adrenal glands and yet others into the gonads? The brain is a single organ which, in many ways, displays a greater complexity than the entire rest of the body. In embryonic life thousands of discrete neuronal pathways must meander through often convoluted itineraries before reaching their adult locations.[1]

Clearly the development of the embryo represents a staggering challenge to biologists, who must explain exactly how the fetus is able to develop in exactly the right sequence to form a unique human being. The conventional account is that the genetic blueprints of life are contained within the DNA of each cell. Through various chemical triggers, the synthesis of proteins which act as enzyme catalysts or building materials is switched off and on at precise moments. In this way the metabolism and growth of the cell are controlled. In turn, cell secretions and other chemical messengers maintain a traffic of information across the embryo to ensure perfect coordination of its growth.

Individual sequences of the genetic code have indeed been translated and synthesized in the laboratory. In this way, small strands of code have been introduced into yeasts or bacteria, and the production of proteins has been demonstrated. In addition various molecular "switches" have been discovered which turn cell processes off and on. Many chemical messengers are known to carry information between cells and to coordinate the function of different organs. But in spite of all these advances, there is a considerable distance to be traversed in both theory and experiment before the whole theory of cell function, let alone the development of the embryo, is established. In short, it is still only a hypothesis and *not* an established theory that the functioning of any living being can be completely explained in terms of DNA and cell metabolism. Certainly this hypothesis is well accepted by the biology community and it is believed that, as more and more research accumulates, the various gaps in theory will be filled in. Eventually, it is assumed, the whole phenomenon of growth will be explained in terms of these mechanisms.

Not everyone, however, is convinced by this hypothesis, and from time to time a few maverick biologists have argued that the genetic picture, while containing essential aspects, is too simple to provide an exhaustive explanation for life. In addition to the problem of development, biologists have also pointed to the problem of evolution. While the conventional argument, that new varieties are produced by changes in genetic material, must certainly be part of the truth, it does not always seem to give a satisfactory account. How, for example, does a totally new species evolve? How do complex organs such as the eye develop? Can random mutations explain the jump from reptile to bird? The evolution of flight, for example, required the coordinated development of a large number of factors, any one of which, taken on its own, would not have appeared particularly favorable.

Could a theory based upon the chance mutations of DNA explain the rich variety of form in nature, and the speed with which new species have appeared? Without sacrificing Darwin and the theory of natural selection, would it be possible for information from the environment to have an active role in shaping the mutation of forms?

The eminent biologist C. H. Waddington was never entirely satisfied with the conventional explanations of genetics and used the image of the developing organism as moving through an "epigenetic landscape." Just as a traveler descends from the hills to a fishing village by skirting hillocks, rocks, and sudden drops, so does the organism develop in time by selecting the most effective path in a landscape that has been laid down through its evolutionary history. Waddington was not, however, too specific about the nature of the processes involved beyond stressing that growth involves an element of wholeness that represents the expression of the global, epigenetic landscape and is not, therefore, totally determined by DNA in an hierarchical fashion. It appears that Waddington was moving toward a notion of development in which living matter in some way responds to a field of information which exerts a formative power over the processes of the cell.

More recently these ideas have been taken much further by the biologist Rupert Sheldrake, whose theory of morphic fields has aroused considerable controversy.[2] Sheldrake has proposed that such fields of information do exist and influence the structures not only of living organisms but of inanimate matter as well. According to Sheldrake, all matter has an associated field of memory which plays an active role in guiding the formation of structures and various processes. Clearly if Sheldrake's idea is taken seriously, then it would extend the nature of matter by introducing a new level, that of active information.

What is most striking about the proposal is that these morphic fields, as they are called, act not only on developing embryos and other biological systems but on all matter. The theory has therefore been applied to the crystallization of new synthetic substances and to the formation of molecules out of constituent atoms. In the conventional explanation, molecules form when atoms approach each other in space. A variety of quantum mechanical forces are exerted on these atoms, whose strength and direction depend upon the various orientations and patterns that are being formed. In the case of a rather simple molecule, such as O_2, the form of oxygen we breathe which is formed out of two oxygen atoms; the situation is often pictured in terms of a car on a roller coaster. The hills and valleys of the coaster represent the forces or energies of the various atomic configurations and the car represents the actual state of the system at any particular point in time. Clearly the most stable form is that with the lowest energy, represented by the car coming to rest at the bottom of the lowest valley. For example, as two oxygen atoms move together, the car is pictured as rolling downhill to its final, equilibrium position.

With more complex molecules there may be a whole series of valleys and hills; indeed the situation will be more like that of a landscape, in many dimensions, consisting of hills, valleys, rocks and flat planes. The path taken by the roller coaster will now be very complicated indeed. In some instances it may get trapped in a narrow valley that lies over the hill from a much deeper one, which represents a more stable end point. But according to quantum theory, given sufficient time and nudges of energy from the environment, the roller coaster will eventually find its way to the lowest valley.

Sheldrake has argued, however, that this piecewise, random search for the most stable molecular structure is inefficient, unpredictable, and time-consuming. By contrast, the processes of nature often tend to be smooth, and fairly reproducible. He concludes therefore that the roller car is actually directed, or *informed* about the whole landscape, during its path downhill. Under the action of a morphic field, the incoming atoms are steered in the right directions so that molecules are formed in an efficient manner. While the actual driving force is still the quantum mechanical desire to minimize energy by moving to the lowest valley, the actual process is given form by information in the fields themselves.

In this fashion molecules, crystals, plants, and animals all develop according to their proper form. In the absence of these fields there would simply be too many alternatives and contingencies for nature to exhibit the sort of unity in diversity that is seen in the structures of matter and living things.

The first time a new molecule is created, or a crystal grows, it must follow a piecewise, blind path down the valleys and hollows of its energy landscape, determined by the various local forces that operate on it. But this process also gives rise to a morphic field, which is a kind of memory of the material processes involved. The next time this process takes place, it has the advantage, Sheldrake says, of being guided by information from the morphic field. With more and more repetitions of the process, the field builds in strength and is more active in its controlling the direction of the process. The whole effect is a little like skiers going downhill. The first skier must find a path between trees and hillocks but the ones who come after are guided by the tracks and able to move a little faster and avoid false trails. In each case it is the downhill pull of gravity that actually provides the energy for the skiing to take place, while it is the information in the track marks that enable each skier to choose the best way down the hill. In a similar fashion, quantum mechanical forces determine the overall process of molecular formation, while the information in the morphic field steers the process in the most effective direction.

When it comes to more complex processes, such as the growth of a cell or the development of an embryo, Sheldrake hypothesizes a whole hierarchy of morphic fields to guide all the processes involved. Morphic fields direct not only the formation of structures but their actual behavior, for the reflexes and patterned responses of animals are also supposed to be directed by such fields.

The hypothesis is certainly a bold one, but what evidence is there for these hypothetical fields of memory? It turns out that most arguments are anecdotal, or depend upon the reinterpretation of earlier experiments. Little in the way of original research has been done, so that the overall weight of evidence is not particularly compelling. One example is the formation of new crystals. According to Sheldrake's theory, the first time a novel substance is synthesized it should be very difficult to crystallize, until morphic fields have built up to assist in the arrangements of atoms in a lattice. Indeed this has been found to be true, and the second and subsequent processes of crystallization are always found to be easier than the first. What explanation does conventional science have for this effect? It is generally argued that tiny microcrystals, floating around in the laboratory and left over from the first experiment, will contaminate the solution and act as nuclei around which the second set of crystals can form. In this way, as accidental contamination builds up, each act of crystallization becomes a little easier.

But what if the first experiment is done in Oxford and the second in Chicago? Here the explanation becomes rather bizarre, for scientists have suggested that microcrystals are carried around in the beards and clothing of visiting scientists from Oxford who in this way introduce the nuclei for future crystallization into other laboratories.

A further anecdotal piece of evidence comes from the behavior of sheep. In many districts of Britain, a grid of metal rollers is placed at the entrance of a field to allow farm traffic to pass but to prevent sheep leaving—the animals do not like to step on these rollers. Recently, however, some sheep were observed to escape from a field by lying down and rolling across the grid. Shortly after, similar sightings were made in other parts of the country. Had a new morphic field for sheep behavior been created? Or had this bizarre form of rolling been always present but simply not recorded before? Or had maverick sheep escaped to inform their enslaved colleagues across the country?

The problem with these sorts of examples is that they are difficult to present in any acceptable scientific form. Indeed the scientific community has not been particularly attracted to Sheldrake's ideas and has treated them with everything from indifference to outright hostility. There has simply not been enough serious interest to subject Sheldrake's hypothesis to a rigorous theoretical and experimental examination. Indeed I confess that I do not find the evidence for Sheldrake's hypothesis to be particularly convincing; in addition, I have difficulties in accepting several aspects of his theory as it is presently stated. However, new ideas are like delicate plants; they deserve to be nurtured for a time and allowed to unfold their full potential, rather than being uprooted and dismissed out of hand. It is certainly true that Sheldrake is pointing to something that is very important. The processes of nature, he suggests, are far more subtle than is presently supposed and, in fact, contain an aspect that is very close to what we would normally call mind. Matter and mind, it would appear, are no longer distinct and different substances but may be a part of a much larger spectrum. Even if the overall details of Sheldrake's morphic field hypothesis are rejected by the reader, then at least this notion of a new and subtle, mindlike, level to the unfolding processes of nature should be given serious consideration.

These morphic fields are a type of memory that acts like a formative pattern with regard to material structures and patterns of behavior. In this sense they are related to Jung's archetypes, which could be thought of as formative fields of the collective unconscious. Just as the whole evolutionary and developmental history of an organism is supposed to be enfolded within its hierarchy of morphic fields, so is the history of a people, and indeed of the whole human race, supposed to be enfolded within the archetypes. Is it possible therefore that the archetypes and the morphic fields have a universal aspect, being formative fields of information that have an active role within the processes of matter, thought, and behavior?

The notion of a field of information that can have an active role upon material processes could be compared with the formation of a picture on a television screen. The incoming signal contains a large amount of information but its energy is negligible compared to that which powers the TV set itself. However, because of the internal complexity of the set, this negligible energy of information is able to shape the electronic processes within the circuits and form a series of images on the screen. Formative information may work within matter in a similar way, provided that the internal structure of matter is of sufficient complexity.

Sheldrake's idea could be developed by suggesting that even elementary matter has an internal structure of great complexity and, associated with it, a field or more subtle level which contains information about the entire environment. While atoms and molecules move under the normal quantum mechanical forces they are also able to respond to the information actively present in these fields. So that enfolded within any region of space or particle of matter would be information that potentially applies to the whole universe.

Evolution would therefore be driven both by internal molecular processes, produced by random mutations of DNA, and also by the active information of the whole environment. In this way the developing organism can have an effect on its environment and, in turn, the environment can act back on the developing species to help it follow more appropriate pathways of growth.

Such a hypothesis would, however, require the internal structure of matter to become increasingly subtle and complex as more and more microscopic levels are revealed so that ultimately the complexity of the universe is enfolded in the most elementary level of matter. In this fashion, process and change need not take place in a blind or piecewise manner but would be determined by the global nature of the whole. This picture is not dissimilar to that of the Hamilton-Jacobi theory, in which all matter is considered to be built out of a complex intersection of wave motions, and the path of an individual particle is the result of the wave processes of the whole.

The idea of an active field of information that unfolds in the various structures and processes of nature, and of matter that has endless levels of subtlety suggests that the whole order of nature may be more complex than was ever supposed. It is also possible that, as suggested by Jung's archetypes, these fields of active information may act in both consciousness and matter so that the deeper the mind is explored, the more complex is its structure. Indeed both consciousness and matter may be discovered to evolve out of a common order where the processes of matter and the activity of information are two sides of the one reality. These fields of active, formative information are more general, therefore, than those of Sheldrake. They are not simply fields of habitual response but are closer to some form of intelligence that wells up from an underlying creative source. While certain aspects of nature are dominated by the relatively habitual, repetitive, mechanical nature of these formative fields, other aspects may be more dynamic, able to respond in new and creative ways.

These ideas are, of course, highly speculative and can be developed in a number of different ways. In a sense they provide another image, or metaphor, of how mind and matter interpenetrate each other at all levels of nature. They suggest that it may well be possible to imagine a universe in which the physical and the psychological are no longer separated by a great barrier and in which synchronicity plays a complementary role to causality.

ACTIVE INFORMATION AND THE IMPLICATE ORDER

The idea that information can have an active or formative effect on matter has been investigated by David Bohm. His causal interpretation of the quantum theory presents a detailed description of what may actually take place during quantum processes, such as the disintegration of a radioactive nucleus, while avoiding the traditional problems of interpretation. The theory involves new assumptions about the nature of matter, and while it yields numerical results that are identical to conventional quantum mechanics, it has not yet been examined in a serious way by the physics community.

The theory assumes as its starting point that elementary particles do not actually have a wave/particle nature but instead are particles with considerable internal complexity. In the more advanced version of the theory this particle is, in turn, represented by fluctuations within a quantum field. In addition to the normal electromagnetic force that acts on the elementary particle as a result of its electrical charge (and the weak and strong nuclear forces) Bohm's theory postulates a new *quantum potential*. The quantum potential is of a particularly novel nature, for unlike the other forces of nature, it is subtle in its form and does not fall off with distance. Because of this, even objects which are at remote distances from the quantum particle can still have a profound effect upon it. In addition, the quantum potential's action does not take the form of a mechanical push or pull, like an ordinary force, but acts more like a guide wave. In this sense the quantum potential has something in common with the way a morphic field acts on a developing organism. Or to make use of an analogy, it acts like a radar signal received by a ship at sea. The energy in this signal is negligible compared with the energy that powers the ship yet the *information* in the signal, about harbors, fog, icebergs, and other shipping, has a formative effect upon the course of the ship. In an automatic system, for example, this radar signal may be processed by a computer and in this way play an active role in steering the ship.

In a similar sense the quantum potential carries information about the environment of the quantum particle and thus *informs* and effects its motion. Since the information in the potential is very detailed, the resulting trajectory is so extremely complex that it appears chaotic or indeterministic. In this way the indeterminism of quantum events is accounted for by the complex nature of the quantum potential. In addition, since this quantum potential does not fall off with distance, it is in general not possible to analyze a quantum system and its environment into separate parts; rather the system must be treated as a whole which is guided and formed by active information in the quantum potential.

Bohm's causal interpretation suggests that matter has orders that are closer to those of mind than to a simple mechanical order. Information is given an active, formative role so that an individual elementary particle is linked through the quantum potential to the entire universe. Moreover this suggests that the elementary particle must have a complex internal structure in order to be able to respond to information within the quantum potential.[3]

These novel features can be seen even more clearly in the more advanced, quantum field version of the theory. Here the elementary particles become a manifestation of a quantum field. This recalls the Hamilton-Jacobi theory, in which matter and all its movements were produced by an underlying wave motion. In the Hamilton-Jacobi theory, a collection of wavelets in a small region of space has the appearance of a material particle. This group of wavelets constantly folds in and out of the general wave motion of the background much like a large wave of water is produced by the overall motion of the ocean. In this way a constant process of enfolding and unfolding gives rise to an object that has all the properties of a mechanical particle moving on a deterministic trajectory through space.

In a somewhat analogous sense, the elementary particles arise out of a global quantum field. However, in the causal interpretation the folding and unfolding of this field is guided or *informed* by a super-quantum potential. In this way information again plays an active role in giving rise not only to quantum processes but also to the elementary particles themselves. Active information is responsible for the way in which quantum processes unfold out of the quantum field of the universe. For this reason it is clear that the inner structure of the elementary particles may be of unlimited complexity, for they are in essence an expression of the entire universe.

There is no reason to suppose that these structures end at the level of the super-quantum potential and do not extend to further levels of subtlety. If this is so, then a level that in one context would be taken as a form of material process would be found, in a wider context, to be a level of active information. In turn, this level of information would gain its formative activity from adjacent levels of subtle material process. In this way a hierarchy of interleaving levels, and even cycles of feedback, may extend indefinitely. This speculation suggests that current quantum processes may not be the ultimate levels of matter and that future experiments may reveal even more subtle forms of behavior within nature.

These ideas can be explored in a more general way by referring to Bohm's concept of the *implicate* or enfolded order. In the quantum field version of the causal interpretation, an elementary particle is taken to be the manifestation of an underlying quantum field. This particle therefore represents the folding of a field into a localized region; likewise the annihilation of the particle is the unfolding back into the field. In this way the complex reactions of elementary particles can be thought of as enfoldings and unfoldings within a dynamic background.

Bohm has suggested that this implicate order, with its notions of enfolding and unfolding, is characteristic of all reality. Indeed the implicate order goes beyond the particular assumptions and details of the causal interpretation to describe not only the inner structure of matter but that of mind and society.

Even if we choose to reject Bohm's causal interpretation out of hand, the notion of an enfolded or implicate order should be given serious consideration.

The everyday world, of solid bodies that are unambiguously located in space and of sequences in a linear time, corresponds to what could be called the *explicate* or unfolded order. But this explicate order can now be seen as a manifestation of an unfolding from the deeper implicate order. An analogy may serve to illustrate this point. The fountain in an Italian square maintains its shape by virtue of the wave that flows through it. In this way its explicate shape is an expression of the constant flux of folding and unfolding. In a similar way the vortex in a river is an expression of the total flow of all the water, and its structure is constantly supported by the dynamics of the river as a whole. In a deeper sense the orders of matter, space, and time are all explicate manifestations of the underlying implicate order.

The explicate order corresponds to the Newtonian vision of nature, in which the paths of bodies are determined by local interactions and most boundaries are fairly distinct. Indeed the explicate order could be thought of as an extension of the order of Cartesian coordinates introduced in the first half of the seventeenth century. In the explicate order, bodies are exterior to each other and interact through local forces. By contrast, in the implicate order, structures enfold each other so that one structure can be simultaneously internal and external to the other. Since all forms unfold out of the same ground, there is no need to postulate the existence of forces between them for their whole dynamics is a function of the implicate order of the unfolding of explicate forms.

In Newtonian physics, the path of a falling apple or speeding ball is built out of a continuous succession of steps; it is a Cartesian order based on local forces and the Cartesian notions of time and space. In the implicate order, however, the particle itself arises as an explicate form which unfolds out of a deeper implicate order, persists, and folds back into the implicate order again. Successive unfoldments and enfoldments combine to give the impression of an explicate particle moving through space. In a similar fashion the collision and intersection of particles arises out of the implicate order. Clearly this whole mode of description is far more appropriate to the quantum world than is the Cartesian order of rigid forms. This picture of a particle as the explicate expression of an underlying ground recalls the solitons of Chapter 3. Those well-defined forms collide and interact with each other as independent bodies in interaction, yet at a deeper level they are simply the expressions of an underlying nonlinear field.

An analogy of this unfolding of explicate forms, from a more complex underlying ground, can be given by reference to human vision. It is well known that the illusion of continuous movement is produced in a movie by the rapid succession of still images. Even more striking is the fact that all human vision is built out of information gathered in the very short pauses between the rapid ballistic movements of the human eye as it scans an object. What is seen as a solid, explicate form is in fact built out of an extremely rapid succession of "snapshots," taken by the eye, of various parts of an object. As this jumble of discrete images enters the nervous system, it is unfolded across the various regions of the visual cortex and folded back again. The static painting that is seen on the wall of an art gallery is in fact the explicate manifestation of a complex implicate order within the mind, and is produced in the mind as a multiplicity of images enfold each other and then unfold into conscious awareness. Hence not only are the explicate parts of the world the result of an unfolding from a deeper implicate order, but the very sense impressions that we have of these objects unfold according to the same order.

David Bohm has also made use of the idea of a holograph to illustrate the concept of enfoldment of an implicate order. In normal photography, light from each part of the object is focused upon a corresponding region of the photographic plate. In this way the form of the image has an explicit correspondence to the form of the object so that each small segment of the photograph contains information about only a small segment of the object. In holography, however, light from each part of the object is folded over the whole of the photographic plate. In this way, every small region of the photograph contains information about the whole of the object. In the holograph, therefore, the relationship between object and plate is that of the explicate to the implicate and the image is reconstructed by unfolding this implicate order information.

The implicate order is also appropriate for the description of society. For example, a crowd of people consists of individuals, each of which has his or her own motivations and beliefs. Nevertheless in certain situations, a football game, a state funeral, a demonstration, a parade, the crowd also has a collective behavior, just as do the electrons in a plasma or the cells in a slime mold slug. In such a case the behavior of the crowd is enfolded in each individual and in turn each individual is unfolded within the whole crowd. In a more subtle way a society and its members are related through an implicate order of folding and unfolding.

The example of vision indicated that the implicate order may be the natural order of the mind. Indeed, influenced by Bohm's ideas, the neuroscientist Karl Pribram has proposed an implicate order model for memory. Just as information in the holograph is both enfolded into each small region of the plate and distributed across the whole, so, too, are memories not specifically located in particular cells or regions of the brain but have a distributed quality. Pribram suggests that incoming sensations fold themselves over large regions and, when recalled, unfold into specific memories.

Consciousness in general is much closer to the implicate order than it is to a mechanical order of succession. The "stream of consciousness" described by William James is not experienced as a causal succession of ideas, one following another like the railcars described in Chapter 2. Rather, thoughts seem to flow out of each other. A thought forms in awareness and may be enriched by many different associations and feelings. It may then dissolve into another related thought, or the mind may suddenly dart to something which is at first sight unrelated but on closer examination has a subtle connection to the earlier thought. The order of movement of thought is therefore much closer to that of the implicate/explicate enfoldments than to any mechanical analogy. This can be most clearly seen in dreams, where the control of "logic" or "reason" is not so apparent. In dreams, an image can unfold and sweep across the dream to reveal a host of other images enfolded within it. Just as the processes of the implicate order imply a notion of space in which objects can be simultaneously interior and exterior to each other, so are the images of a dream all contained within each other and are in a continuous process of transformation and unfolding.

In this sense, therefore, our thoughts are the explicate forms thrown up by the underlying movements of the implicate orders of mind. Like the vortex of a river, or the soliton of a nonlinear field, thoughts have no absolute, independent existence of their own but are constantly being supported by the underlying processes of their ground. Ultimately this movement of mind merges into that of matter so that the two should not be considered as dual aspects of nature but as arising out of the same underlying ground. In a similar sense, individual minds could be said to arise out of the one ground. They represent relatively stable forms, identities, as it were, within the underlying background. In this way it appears that individual minds have a common or collective origin that has something in common with that of matter. In a sense, therefore, mind is able to act upon mind, and mind and matter exert an influence one on the other. But this should be thought of not as some form of causal *interaction* since individual minds, and mind and matter, are not fundamentally separate but are simply the explicate forms that emerge out of a common, generative order.

Indeed the notion of time can similarly be developed in this way, for the implicate order is capable of evolving and maintaining certain different explicate forms. Within the order of the mind it may therefore be possible to sustain relatively mechanical orders of repetition. For example, while memory appears to be stored within the brain in some kind of distributed or implicate form, it also acts as a source of explicate forms. Thoughts which operate from a fixed memory will tend to be more mechanical in nature, being set off by relatively fixed, explicate forms of memory. In this fashion, relatively stable, explicate forms, which are identified with the self and all its memories, may be maintained in consciousness.

But mechanical processes are, of their nature, cyclic and repetitious, as opposed to the almost indefinite subtlety that is contained within the implicate order. Hence the relatively mechanical order that is contained within the mind is one of repetition and constant return, based within a broader stream of continual flow. But the combination of cycle with flow is exactly what is meant by time. Time is the "eternally recurrent" that is set against eternal change; time is the waxing and waning of the moon, the interchange of day for night, the cyclic swing of a pendulum, the oscillations of a quartz crystal in a clock. Science measures the passage of time by counting the cycles of repetition that are generated by natural processes in a background of continuous change. In the same way, time is actually created in consciousness by the appearance of relatively fixed mechanical responses in the background of constant flow. Time is therefore a creation of the mind that can be projected onto the processes of nature. Its origin lies in the explicate forms thrown up by the implicate orders of thought.

But, on reflection, it becomes apparent that the whole movement of mind must be far more complex and subtle than our present analysis suggests. While the image of thought as emerging out of an implicate order and of time as being created out of relatively stable explicate forms within this flow is a significant insight, there are other aspects of mind to consider. Perception, intuition, and creativity clearly go beyond this initial discussion and require more than the distinction between implicate and explicate.

The notion of an enfolded order takes us only so far. Clearly the whole nature of consciousness and mind must contain deeper levels that stretch down to a source of unconditioned creativity. Some speculations as to the nature of these additional levels are given in the last two chapters, but for the present, it is clear that certain aspects of the mind and consciousness do seem to be appropriate to a description in terms of implicate orders and fields of active information. Indeed the discussions of this chapter suggest that mind and matter may not be so far apart as is generally supposed since notions of formative and enfolded activity appear to apply to both and open avenues of speculation which may be profitably explored. Moreover it indicates that the orders of matter and of mind are not incommensurable but, in fact, lie on a whole spectrum of orders that range from the mechanical through the implicate order and possibly on to other orders of even greater subtlety. Since mind and matter arise out of a common spectrum of order, it is clear that their supposed duality was in fact a matter of illusion generated by concentrating only on the mechanical aspects of matter and the intangible quality of mind.

It is possible to extend this notion of an implicate order still further to include a second implicate order and, indeed, to suggest that the overall movement contains yet deeper enfolded levels and even more subtle levels of organization. The explicate forms of nature have been shown to unfold out of the implicate order, but this opens the possibility that the dynamics and structuring of the implicate order itself emerge out of a deeper second implicate order. In turn, the structures and relationships of the explicate order may provide information to this second implicate order so that a feedback loop or cyclic relationship is established. In this way the explicate forms of nature are sustained by the continuous movement of the implicate order. But these explicate forms supply information to the second implicate order, which gives form to the first implicate order. In other words, although thought and the explicate material forms of the world all owe their existence to a hidden, enfolded order, nevertheless they are capable of feeding back to the underlying movement and giving new form to it. This suggests that reality is reached through a dual movement. In a sense the whole of the universe is enfolded within each individual and within each region of space. The nature of this reality can therefore be touched both by reaching outward into the explicate forms (which feed back to the second implicate order) or inward to the implicate order itself.

An analogy of this cyclic movement of the implicate order can be obtained by referring back to Bohm's causal interpretation. There the elementary particles are formed, as explicate orders, out of an underlying quantum field. But this quantum field is, in turn, structured by the super-quantum potential which acts as a field of active information. This information includes details of the whole explicate order of nature, including a quantum system and its environment. In this way the explicate universe acts as part of the content of the active information within the second implicate order, and has a formative effect upon the quantum field of the universe, which is the source of all the explicate forms in nature. But this movement of implicate and explicate orders need not end at the level of the second implicate order but may extend indefinitely to deeper and yet more subtle orders.

This image, of the material world unfolding out of underlying implicate levels, may also apply in the case of the brain. The explicate levels could be thought of in terms of specific electrochemical processes that take place within the brain's structure. But these processes, in turn, carry information and have a particular meaning. In this sense they may also play the part of active information for other neural processes. In turn deeper, second-implicate and beyond, levels will give rise to the unfolding of active information within the neural processes and may, in turn, be conditioned or informed by it. In this way a series of interlocking levels of meaning, information, and electrochemical processes result. What appears, within one context, as a material process, albeit of considerable subtlety, will, from another context, appear as a form of active information. Likewise the formative, mental process, from another perspective, will manifest itself as some electrochemical, or more subtle, process of the brain.

In this fashion, mind and brain have the structure of a multiplicity or interleaving of processes, each with a dual aspect, that extends from the relatively mechanical to the extremely subtle. Material and mental, soma and psyche, are no longer different orders of experience but become the two sides of a single coin. In their ground they merge within a series of interlocking levels, and in their unfolding they appear, at their most divergent, as gross matter and subtle mind.

Within the nervous system, therefore, each process will

represent both an aspect of a material transformation, or un-folding, and a form of information which conditions other levels. Eric Kandel, for example, has noted that in the sea slug the overall meaning of a certain signal or situation will have the effect of modifying synaptic connections within the various feedback circuits of the slug's nervous system. Hence information about the environment has an active effect upon the material processes of the animal's nervous system and in a sense creates its "brain" afresh. In turn this new "brain" will gather fresh information about its environment and build a revised image of its environment.

Kandel is willing to extrapolate his results further and suggest that meaning has a constant, active effect on the human brain. Each time two people engage in conversation, a constant flow of active meaning is present. This meaning has the effect of making very subtle transformations within the brain which will, in turn, have their effect upon thought and action. Therefore, during each moment of the day the brain is structurally unfolding from a background of active information which is present both in its own structure and in the external environment. In turn the eternally fresh brain acts back upon the environment to change it and to create a new "reality." This reality will, of course, act back upon the brain through a constant process of formation and information.

The brain's structuring of reality does not simply include the direction of such physical actions as building cities, develop-ing new means of agriculture, or advancing knowledge of the inner structure of matter. It also includes human relationships, the nature of society, and the image each person has of him- or herself. The discussion above suggests that this is in a constant process of change. However, in most cases relatively mechani-cal forms of operation within the mind have an active role in "fixing reality" and leaving its structure relatively rigid and unresponsive. Clearly, however, a mind that remains flexible and sensitive will be in a constant process of creative change and will respond to the overall patterns of nature so that the individual can enter into these patterns in new ways. Synchro-nicity will appear very naturally to a mind that is constantly sensitive to change, for it reveals the overall patterns of nature and mind and provides a context in which events have their meaning.

When the mind, and its worldview, become fixated upon the explicate forms and relationships in space and time, the over-all meaning of synchronicity tends to be lost. In this way, knowledge becomes fragmented and the ability to see deeply into the structure of things is impaired by the failure to perceive wider patterns and contexts. Likewise a mind that is obsessed with synchronicity, as was the case with the Shang, will concentrate upon global patterns and meanings at the expense of analysis and concentration on the meanings of details of space and time and material structures. In this fashion, an exclusive adherence to either the way of causality and analysis or the way of synchronicity results in rigid, fixed structures of the mind and in civilizations whose creativity is ultimately blocked. The real message of synchronicity, for the Western, scientific view-point, is not to throw away all that is of value within the last five hundred years, but to be sensitive to new perspectives and to allow the mind its full creative potential.

REALITY AND REDUCTIONISM

The speculation that mind and matter arise out of a common range of orders that extends from the mechanical to the indefinitely subtle suggests that scientific analysis of matter may well be a quest that can go on forever. It implies that the current, quantum mechanical theory of matter is essentially limited and that it is possible to uncover a further series of properties and ranges of behavior.

What impact should all this have on the current paradigms of science? To begin with, it is certainly of a very different order from suggesting some new theory of the elementary particles or variant of the quantum theory. It is not at all clear as to how such proposals could be tested experimentally, in the immediate future at least. Karl Popper, the philosopher of science, has argued that the true criterion of a scientific theory is that it should be capable of being put to a crucial test. If the predictions of the theory are in agreement with the findings of this test, then the theory survives, at least provisionally; but if they do not agree, then the theory must be rejected. However, most experiments that are designed to probe the inner structures of matter are based upon the assumption of elementary particles and fields. Here something very different is being proposed and it seems unlikely that it could be explored experimentally within the next few decades.

But if the suggestion, that matter and consciousness are different aspects of the one underlying order of nature, cannot be put to immediate scientific test, then does it have any scientific significance at all? Does the content of this book amount to nothing more than loose metaphysics having no real practical significance? Some, no doubt, would argue that this is the case. However, there are strong reasons for thinking that these ideas, which after all are being proposed, in different forms, by many other thinkers, may have a particularly deep influence on the future of science. For, after all, is science concerned solely with predictions and experimental verification and with the accumulation of new knowledge? Science, I would suggest, is really about understanding, about understanding ourselves, the universe, and our position in it. Science, according to such a view, is not fixed but fluid, and its methods, approaches, and techniques must be always ready to change and to respond in creative ways to new demands and new situations.

The arguments of this chapter suggest that science may, in the end, have to look in new directions if its understanding of nature is to continue. Already many scientists are dissatisfied by the "reductionistic" nature of some branches of science and with the claim that an ultimate level of reality is shortly to be reached as a result of research on the elementary particles. Possibly science may have to follow new clues and ask new questions in the future.

Indeed the arguments of this book suggest that science requires a whole new disposition toward nature. From this will follow new orders of questions about the nature of life and evolution, the internal structure of matter, the subtle interrelationships that are found between various processes, the coincidence of similar forms at different scales, the nature of consciousness and its relationship to the body, and the overall structure of the universe. The idea that reality may unfold into a complex, and potentially endless, series of levels changes the whole meaning of reductionism, for example. Already Prigogine's objections to reductionism have been described. They are based on the observation that any level of scientific explanation depends on, and is conditioned by, concepts and meanings that arise in other levels. It is therefore logically impossible to construct a single, basic level of explanation upon which the whole of scientific knowledge is to be built. Such a level will be found, ultimately, to depend upon other levels and cannot, therefore, stand alone.

But now we see that as the microscopic levels of reality are probed, they must eventually open the door onto an entirely new domain consisting of endless levels of increasing subtlety. These levels may, of course, be probed by thought and experiment, yet in each case, an attempt to reach the "most fundamental level" will eventually lead to the uncovering of yet deeper, unexplained processes. Even more significantly, it will turn out that these deeper levels are themselves linked in delicate and subtle ways to higher, more explicate levels. For example, as attempts are made to explore the more microscopic levels of matter, the whole field may suddenly open out into the regions such as the entire structure of the universe and consciousness. Similarly the psychological exploration of deeper and deeper levels of the collective unconscious, as Pauli speculated, may suggest yet deeper connections to matter. In the end, the investigations of nature must unfold into a potentially infinite and creative universe whose particular manifestations are matter, life, consciousness, and society.

SYNCHRONICITY AND THE *I CHING*

In the light of this chapter it is possible to return to a discussion of the nature of synchronicity as expressed through the operation of the *I Ching*. According to the Chinese sages, the act of divination enfolds a moment that contains the essence of the present and the seeds of the future. Divination is therefore the microcosm that reflects the whole of nature and society and includes, within it, the observer.

The contemporary version of this ancient explanation is that within each process of nature is enfolded the whole. In this way the whole universe may be enfolded within a moment of time and within the act of divination. Within the *I Ching*, mind and matter are no longer perceived as a duality but in their essential unity, and the potential of the moment is explicitly unfolded within the pattern of the hexagram. In a sense therefore the *I Ching*, through the act of divination and interpretation, gives some insight into the nature of the information that acts upon mind and matter to give it form. The divination is therefore also a reflection of the eternal or timeless order in which all potentialities abide.

Within the activity of divination it is possible for creativity to operate. For the *I Ching* exposes the information that acts to structure a situation which is about to unfold in time. The act of perception that is involved on the part of the observer may cause the release of a creative energy that restructures this information and so breaks free of the bonds of time. In this way it is possible to reach down, through the patterns and levels shown within the *I Ching*, and to come into contact with the power of their source. Within this creative moment, observer and observed, explicate and implicate, information and structure, mind and matter, are indissolubly linked.

The creative energy that is let loose at this moment could be compared to that released in a nuclear reaction, when the internal structure of the nucleus is rearranged. Its power is sufficient to transform the whole meaning of the present and all the patterns it contains. In this way, energy dies to the mechanical order of repetition and its persisting state of confusion and is directed into new possibilities. The future and its endless possibilities becomes open again to creative change.

However, if the human subject does not possess that honesty of mind and purpose to see things as they really are, no matter what consequences will follow, then creativity is blocked and the patterns of the present will continue to unfold into the future. The *I Ching* not only offers an understanding of the nature of the present and the potentiality of the future, but also opens the possibility of effecting a total transformation in nature, society, and the individual. The creative nature of humanity and the great energy that is present within the unknown ground will be examined in greater depth in the next chapter, along with the nature of time and the possibility of the active transformation of the individual.

SUMMARY

Nature has been shown to reveal an order of unfolding and enfolding that is common to both mind and matter. In exploring the dissipative structures of Prigogine, the collective nature of the slime mold, and the electron gas, new principles of structuring have been discovered. These are very different from the mechanical orders of succession and of explicate objects with distinct locations in space and time and suggest that a whole new world of nonmechanical orders may be revealed. Through the theories of Rupert Sheldrake and David Bohm, it was discovered that these new orders involve the operation of active levels of information and of enfoldment.

The implicate order was discussed and shown to apply equally to matter and to consciousness. In turn, this enfolded order was found to be structured by an even deeper second implicate order. Indeed the possibility was explored that an endless series of such levels may operate in nature so that both mind and matter emerge out of a common order.

Within the implicate order it can be shown that all of nature is contained within a single element of space and time so that the formative principles of nature can be exhibited in microcosm. Within a synchronicity the meaning and potentialities of nature, mind, and society can be displayed. Moreover the perception of this moment by the individual may give rise to the release of formative energy that can be used to creatively change the future and even transform consciousness.

NOTES

1. 225 (1984): 1255.
2. R. Sheldrake, *A New Science of Life* (Los Angeles: J. P. Tarcher, 1982). See also John P. Briggs and F. David Peat, *Looking Glass Universe* (New York: Simon and Schuster, 1984).
3. See D. Bohm and B. Hiley, *The Causal Interpretation of Quantum Theory*, forthcoming. D. Bohm and F. David Peat, *Science, Order and Creativity* (New York: Bantam Books, 1987).

7 THE CREATIVE SOURCE

Synchronicity has gradually been enfolded into an entirely new dimension; in place of a causal deterministic world, in which mind and matter are two separate substances, appears a universe of infinite subtlety that is much closer to a creative, living organism than to a machine. From deep within this order there unfold harmonies that spread out across the mental and material realms in the form of meaningful patterns and conjunctions that act as intimations of the essential unity of all nature.

The world of explicate structures and sequential processes in time, which has been studied by science over the last centuries, now turns out to be the manifestation of a deeper, enfolded order that constantly sustains them. Causality, determinism, and reductionism, where they apply, now seem to be more appropriate to the relatively stable aspects of this explicate world, in which objects are distinct and separate in space and processes can be analyzed in terms of successions of events in time which take place under the influence of interactions in space.

But as the implicate world is investigated, it is discovered to be more appropriate to certain of the insights of quantum theory, such as Bohr's emphasis upon wholeness and to the nonlocal nature of space-time. Moreover, this deeper order has been found to be essential to the whole nature of thought. In this way, mind and matter appear to have something in common within their orders of activity. Indeed this leads to the general proposal that mind and matter are not separate and distinct substances but that like light and radio waves they are orders that lie within a common spectrum. A spectrum, moreover, which may include additional new orders that have mental and material components of varying degrees of subtlety, and possibly quite novel orders which go far beyond these realms. Such orders may have been hidden from the investigations that have hitherto been carried out in science and may be found to have relevance, for example, in living systems during periods of evolutionary change and within the operation of the immune and nervous systems. In addition, new orders may be found to apply to the operation of society as a whole, within unexplored regions of subatomic matter, and may even relate to the large-scale structure of the universe.

David Bohm, for example, has proposed an alternative interpretation of the quantum theory which, while it produces numerical results in exact agreement with the conventional approach, does contain a number of the above novel features. Quantum processes, in Bohm's approach, are interpreted as having what could almost be called a "mental" side, in that "active information" acts upon what is now found to be the extremely complex internal structure of the elementary particles. This active information then has a directing effect upon the various quantum processes that occur, and even plays a formative role in unfolding the elementary particles out of the quantum field which is their ground.

It is also possible to see that this movement, from the mental to the material aspects of nature, must go in both directions. For in one sense, information is impressed upon the material processes so that they are structured or *informed* by it. But in another direction, the explicate structures that result are themselves the information content of the deeper order. In a sense, therefore, this superimplicate order is able to "perceive" the explicate orders of the world and then use this information in an active way. The material level is thus perceived by the mental level, which then acts back on the unfolding of the material side. In this way, active information from within the deeper level is constantly changing in order to reflect the dynamics of relationships within the explicate universe. A two-way flow is therefore established between the mental and material orders of nature, which are, in a deeper sense, essentially indivisible.

Reality, in this way, is pictured as a limitless series of levels which extend to deeper and deeper subtleties and out of which the particular, explicate order of nature and the order of consciousness and life emerge. Synchronicities can therefore be thought of as an expression of this underlying movement, for they unfold as patterns of thoughts and arrangements of material processes which have a meaningful conjunction when taken together. But in fact, it is the essence of this whole vision of the universe that synchronicities, in themselves, are no longer unique, for a similar complexity is enfolded within each element of matter, each region of space-time and within the consciousness of each individual. A synchronicity can therefore be looked on as a microcosm which reflects the dynamics of the macrocosm as it unfolds simultaneously into the mental and material aspects of a person's life.

THE UNNAMED ORIGIN

In rejecting the dualism of mind and matter, which had its clearest statement with Descartes, the previous chapter presented an image of two orders or parts of a single spectrum which emerge out of a common source which is itself neither matter nor mind. Jung himself appears to have been exploring a similar idea when he introduced the notion of the *psychoid*, which, he said, contains both matter and mind and yet goes beyond them. Indeed Jung specifically made use of the image of a spectrum, in this case of vibrations, that possesses a threshold for human perception at both ends. In this case, vibrations enter human awareness at the low end of this spectrum as sound waves and at the upper end in the case of light. But of course, there is an enormous range of undetected vibrations in between. Moreover, Jung could have added, the vibrations of light extend far beyond this threshold into ever higher frequencies. While Jung's particular image is scientifically confusing and unclear (vibrations of light and of sound cannot really be compared on the same spectrum), it does suggest an analogy with the psychoid as a spectrum which contains mind and matter at its ends, as human thresholds, but with a whole range of hidden possibilities in between and even beyond. Synchronicity, for Jung, therefore had its origin in a "movement" of this spectrum which then manifests itself in its two extremes, as the simultaneous manifestation of a pattern in the material and mental realms.

This image of a spectrum of vibrations is replaced, in this book, by the idea of an order of orders, which are capable of extension to mind and beyond into indefinitely subtle levels at one end, and into the explicate orders of matter at the other. This order of levels of order itself springs out of a creative source. Clearly such a source must lie far beyond the orders of thought and matter; indeed it must be totally creative and absolutely unconditioned, beyond orders of extreme speed and subtlety.

But what then is the nature of this source? To attempt to capture its essence in thought or language would clearly be to limit it. Indeed Lao-tzu in the fourth century B.C. wrote of this source:

> The Tao which can be expressed in words is not the unchangeable Tao:
> For if a name be named it is not the unchangeable name.
> Without a name it is the beginning of Heaven and Earth.[1]

And, some six hundred years later, the Roman philosopher Plotinus wrote:

> What is This which does not exist? We must go away silent, involved in our thought in utter perplexity, and seek no further; for what could anyone look for when there is nothing to which he can still go on? Every search moves to the first principle and stops when it has reached it.[2]

If this source is truly the creative origin of all reality, then how is it possible to speak of it, or for that matter, to think of it?

For the absolutely unconditioned and eternally creative would appear to lie totally outside the experience of each one of us. However the ancients said that "man is the measure of all things." In the mystical traditions this was interpreted as meaning that "man" is the microcosm in which the whole universe is reflected. Similarly, the idea of an enfolded implicate order implies that the whole of reality is enfolded within each individual. In this way, the microcosm can stand as an endless series of analogies to the entire universe, which includes and yet goes beyond consciousness and matter. Enfolded within each one of us is the implicit ground which is sustained by the eternal spring which bubbles up from the unnamed source of creativity.

It is clear, therefore, that this creative source is present in each of us and its manifestation unfolds not only into consciousness and the physical body but into the whole culture, civilization, and the entire universe. Creativity is the very essence of each aspect of reality. But it is a creativity that is in no way contained or conditioned; it is not limited by anything that is external to itself. Like the pure spring that bubbles out of the rock unbidden, this creativity has no necessity and no end, and pervades all of existence.

Indeed within each moment of a person's life, or a speck of dust on the ground, is enfolded the whole universe, which is, itself, the manifestation of an unimaginable and unnameable creativity. While this creativity can never be captured in thought, nevertheless it may be possible to taste something of its flavor. By looking outward, into nature, with the artist, poet, and scientist, it may be possible to penetrate deeper and deeper into the nature of things and to peel away the layers of their complexity. Similarly, by looking inward with the mystic and exploring the hidden regions of the mind, it may be possible to see eternity enfolded within a second or reflected in a grain of sand.

At various times in human history, scientists, mystics, poets, and artists have attempted to capture something of the flavor of the creative source and to express it in the insight of a scientific theory, a new poetic metaphor, the movement of form and color, even the total abstraction of music. Another approach is to explore the various myths of origin that have been created by the human race, for it is possible that these may retain the shadow of a shared vision, which expresses the essential relationship between microcosm and macrocosm to the ground which sustains them.

The question of the origin of life, the universe, and indeed of all reality has preoccupied thinkers down through the ages. Indeed among the very earliest of surviving human artifacts are to be found the "earth goddesses," or primitive carvings and clay models of pregnant women, which suggests that the mystery of birth and fertility is magically tied to the whole essence of reality.

Many of the earliest creation myths involve a primordial state, or ground, out of which all nature emerges. With the ancient Egyptians, Atum-re raises himself out of the primeval ocean and brings the gods into being. According to one version of this myth, the universe is generated out of the power of duality. Atum-re fertilizes himself and gives rise to the gods of earth and sky, Geb and Nut, who then engage in intercourse and so create the universe. The act of separation of sky from earth is therefore equated with the birth of the material world.

In Babylon, this duality involved two oceans, one of salt water and the other of fresh, out of which the gods were brought forth. In turn, these gods gave birth to Marduk, who ordered the chaos around him. In Sumeria the primordial ocean, or mountain, separates the earth goddess Ki from the heaven god An. Out of their congress is born Enlil, the air god who separates heaven from earth and so brings the universe into being.

In these various creation myths from the Middle East, the origin of the world lies in the manifestation of order within a formless ground of absolute chaos. Once order has been established out of chaos then the various structures and appearances of the world can begin to emerge. The actual generative power that lies behind the various manifestations of the world, according to some myths, is to be found in the eternal movements of duality. This duality is created in the primal ordering. It is an act of pure distinction without reference to anything that has happened before, out of which emerge the twin principles of male and female, heaven and earth, night and day. In turn, these dualities enter into a congress where their distinctions are lost as they dissolve back into the formless ground.

The Egyptians pictured this generative movement as the intercourse of the gods Geb and Nut, an act which implies a constant separation and merging. The dualities manifest themselves, out of their ground, into separate polarities which dissolve back into the ground and then emerge again, bathed in the infinite energies of the source. While they are united in congress, the dualities become one with the infinite, unformed energy. But separated as pure polarities, this energy is transformed into an active potential that is capable of inducing transformation and change. So the cosmogony of the ancient Egyptians pictured creation as a constant movement, flowing from the first distinction, and an eternal movement of the potential out of the formless, of activity emerging out of an infinite sea of energy, that is brought into existence through the constant formation and dissolution of dualities in their act of congress. In a sense, a similar image was to surface several millennia later in the Jungian notion of the pleroma, as well as in certain insights related to the quantum theory.

THE VACUUM STATE

As civilizations waxed and waned, myth gave way to natural philosophy and more rationally satisfying accounts of the origin and nature of the universe were required. Democritus and Leucippus, for example, taught that the world is composed out of indivisible elements called atoms. Heraclitus, in contrast, considered nature to arise in a primordial fire or flux, in which there is a constant movement between unity and diversity. "What is drawn together and what is drawn asunder, the harmonious and the discordant," he wrote. "The one is made up of all things and all things issue from the one."

After the time of the Greeks, there were, of course, many other theories about the nature of reality, but each one of them, in one way or another, reflected the essential aspect of either the atomic theory or Heraclitus's theory of flux. Indeed it is only within this century that these two approaches have, to some extent, been resolved. At first sight the modern quantum theory, in which atoms and molecules are composed out of elementary particles, appears to confirm the intuition of Democritus and Leucippus, for the elementary particle is indeed the most fundamental unit of the material world. Yet within the quantum field version of this theory, elementary processes all take place within a background that seems closer to that of an eternal flux.

According to this latter theory, the elementary particles are in a constant state of formation and dissolution within what is called the ground state or vacuum state. In a certain sense, the elementary particle, like the vortex in a river, exists by virtue of its being constantly sustained through the activity of its background. The electron is continually being formed and sustained, while at the same time, it is dissolving into its background, where it transforms itself into other elementary particles, only to emerge back into itself again. To borrow from David Bohm, the explicate order of the electron arises as it unfolds and enfolds within the implicate order of the whole.

Paradoxically, the nothingness of the ground state, out of which the universe is sustained, is both a vacuum and a plenum. It is a vacuum because, as in the everyday idea of empty space, matter is able to move through it without interruption. But it is also a plenum because it is infinitely full of energy. Indeed, the observable material universe is nothing more than the minor fluctuations upon this vast sea of energy. And, it should not be forgotten, just as this infinite energy is used in the generation of matter, so is it also available to mind, through the deeper ground of its source.

As Atum-re brought the Egyptian gods into being out of the primordial ocean, so do the elementary particles, and the universe itself, arise out of a boiling "sea of energy," which has the appearance of nothingness. Moreover, in the scientific account of creation, this act of sustaining the whole of reality does not simply occur at a single moment of time, the "big bang" origin of the universe, but is a continuous process in which matter constantly renews itself out of its ground. But in a deeper sense, unconditioned creation also lies at the heart of this scientific account of the universe. For, in some way, it is at the heart of unknown, subtle levels which underpin the ground state of boundless energy itself and arise out of the creative source. Creativity is the secret force of animation that leads to the orders of matter and mind.

But what then is the nature of this vacuum state of the quantum field? Left to themselves, and in isolation from the rest of the universe, mechanical systems all tend to run down to their lowest energy levels, or ground states. A clock unwinds, water flows downhill, coffee cools, wood burns to ashes, iron rusts, a car battery goes flat, and, ultimately, the stars die. When a system has, in this way, dissipated all its available energy, its internal transformations and activities must then come to an end and the system is effectively dead. This, however, does not apply in the quantum world. For, by contrast, the vacuum state has infinite potential, and its boundless energy gives rise not only to the elementary particles and all the transformations of matter, but even to space-time itself.

John Wheeler, the theoretical physicist met earlier in this book, has graphically described the case of a space-time whose origin lies in the infinite sea of energy, known as the vacuum state:

> This quantum principle says that geometry, far from being smooth at very small distances, is instead like the surface of an ocean, which may look smooth to an aviator miles above it, but is seen to be covered with waves as he comes down to a few hundred feet above the surface. Then if he is precipitated into a lifeboat floating on the surface, he sees even those waves breaking into foam, in the same way that at small distances, by the quantum theory, space is predicted to have irregularities in its structure, so that if one gets down to sufficiently small distances the irregularities become so gigantic that it's like the foam on the surface of the ocean from the waves breaking. Space is built of a kind of foam-like structure.[3]

Space-time and matter not only originate in this primordial ground of infinite energy and quantum flux but are constantly sustained by it. But where did the ground itself come from? What is the nature of this ultimate origin of the universe in time? Most modern theories involve some version of a "big bang" creation at a definite moment in time. According to this approach, the laws of physics can be extrapolated back in time for 10 or 20 billion years until they meet a definite origin. At this initial $t = 0$, all equations and laws break down and infinities result; in mathematical terms, a *singularity* is encountered. As A. D. Linde of the P. N. Lebedev Physical Institute in Moscow, one of the creators of the current inflationary universe theory, writes:

> One may wonder, therefore, what was *before* the singularity? If our universe existed at $t = 0$ then how could it originate from nothing? The singularity problem is certainly one of the most puzzling problems of contemporary science.[4]

A solution to Linde's problem is offered by Stephen Hawking, who suggests that the universe in fact arose as a quantum fluctuation in a primordial wave function. Alan Guth, another of the creators of the inflationary universe theory, writing in the May 1984 issue of *Scientific American* with P. J. Steinhart, says:

> The inflationary model of the universe provides a possible mechanism by which the observed universe could have evolved from an infinitesimal region. It is then tempting to go one step further and speculate that the entire universe evolved from literally nothing.[5]

According to modern physics, therefore, all reality emerges out of a flux of energy that is in itself created by pure chance out of "literally nothing." David Bohm, however, is willing to peel away even deeper levels of explanation and suggest that below the quantum field there lie even more subtle levels of process that are involved in loops of active information. This whole hierarchy extends to increasingly more subtle levels in which both matter and consciousness are contained. In a sense therefore the universe may have emerged in a "big bang" out of a limitless energy. But looked at in another light, even this is only a small "ripple" within the immense activity of the ground, which in its turn arises out of an eternally creative source that lies beyond the orders of time.

But what of the scientific account for the emergence of material structures from the big bang? Within the first 10^{-43} of a second of creation (one-ten-million-trillion-trillion-trillionth of a second), space and time are still engaged in gigantic quantum fluctuations which take place on the scale of the universe itself. Over the next ten-thousandth of a second, space settles down and the elementary particles are produced. As the universe expands and begins to cool, at around 200 seconds, these particles are able to come together to form the isotopes of hydrogen and the helium nucleus. As minutes give way to millions of years, the whole universe is bathed in radiation and a swirling plasma gas of shockwaves. At around 100 million years the first stars begin to form out of this swirling dust, and within their hearts, hydrogen and helium fuse together to form the heavier elements, which, billions of years later, will find their way into our earth, and even into life itself.

The current grand unified theory of elementary particles lays great emphasis upon the role of abstract symmetries within the first fractions of a second of the big bang. Indeed, shortly before his death, Heisenberg argued that the deepest levels of reality do not involve *particles* but *symmetries*. So the electron, proton, neutron, neutrino, mesons, and the rest, are not in themselves fundamental but, rather, they are the realizations of underlying, abstract symmetries.

These symmetries are called abstract because they are very different from the usual symmetries, for example, found in snowflakes, flowers, and starfish, in which individual parts repeat themselves in three-dimensional space. Rather, they are the symmetries of quantum fields, which are defined on abstract mathematical spaces. According to these theories, the ground state of the vacuum has a very high degree of symmetry that is progressively "broken" by the appearance of the various elementary particles.

In a sense this symmetry breaking could be thought of as introducing distinctions or new information into the initially formless state of the universe. The breaking of a symmetry is therefore equivalent to the production of higher and higher degrees of order out of an initial ground that is empty of all distinctions.

In this fashion the various forces and particles of quantum matter are the manifestations of broken symmetries, and therefore, at a deeper level the matter of the universe begins in an act of ordering, in terms of abstract symmetries that evolve out of a symmetric ground state. Matter, in this sense, would be a reflection or the representation of these fundamental patterns; or rather, symmetry and material structure form two sides of a deeper order.

Indeed in the last chapter it was suggested that all these processes are themselves based on even deeper orders whose origin is a particularly subtle movement that is neither matter nor mind. The fundamental symmetries and their structures have their origin in something that is close to a pure intelligence which springs from an unknown creative source. The ground out of which matter emerges is also the source for consciousness, and indeed, since these two orders are essentially indivisible, it may be expected that "fundamental symmetries" play a role in the structure of consciousness as well. This is not to say that the particular symmetry groups of the elementary particles have any direct relationship to the structure of the mind. But rather, that both may arise out of a similar growth of distinction and active information that has its birth in a formless, symmetric ground that, in turn, is fed by the eternally *creative* spring.

THE PLEROMA

The key to Jung's cosmogony was the pleroma, an ancient term that has its origin in Gnostic creation myths and signifies a ground or "godhead" out of which all reality is born:

Hearken: I begin with nothingness. Nothingness is the same as fullness. In infinity full is no better than empty. Nothingness is both empty and full. . . . A thing that is infinite and eternal hath no qualities, since it hath all qualities.

The nothingness of fullness we name the PLEROMA. Therein both thinking and being cease.[6]

Like the vacuum state of physics, the pleroma is at once both empty and perfectly full, and as in Bohm's implicate order, a universe is enfolded within each of its points, for "Even in the smallest point is the PLEROMA endless."

Out of this formless, infinite ground emerges the creatura, a world of order and distinctions. Creatura is the world of created things for:

What is changeable, however, is CREATURA. Distinctiveness is CREATURA. It is distinct. Distinctiveness is its essence, and therefore it distinguisheth.[7]

Hence, in Jung's theory of the universe of mind and matter, all reality lies in the creatura, which has its ground in the fullness of the pleroma. Similarly, in the ancient myths of the Middle East, the animating power of the world arises within the movement of dualities. In the world of the pleroma, which is both empty and full, there are no distinctions. Rather, distinctions, or dualities of light and dark, empty and full, good and evil, the one and the many, appear in the creatura, where they arise out of what could be called an unconditioned act of perception. But the creatura, however, is not the eternal world, but a world of constant change. Likewise the dualities cannot be constant but, like polarities, must come together in a magical marriage in which all distinctions are resolved. "The pairs of opposites are qualities in the PLEROMA which are not, because each balanceth each." So, in unity, the dualities fall back into the nothingness and dissolution of the pleroma. Then in a creative act of distinction they are born into the creatura again. In a similar fashion, the vision of ancient Egypt has all creation arising out of the constant congress of dualities which move apart into pure potential and come together into formless energy and stillness.

It is within this basic movement that the archetypes must arise. Their ultimate domain, in this case, has been called by Jung the psychoid, which is both matter and mind and yet neither. To complete such an analogy, the archetypes, which are the formative elements out of which the mind's structure is formed, can in some sense be compared with the fundamental symmetries of physics and, finally, with the movement of the dualities in the creatura. The analogy between archetype and fundamental symmetry is, of course, a loose one and must not be taken too far, but it does suggest that the origin of structures and patterns does not lie in mind or matter as such, but arises in some more subtle level. Synchronicities, which have been called the activation of the archetypes, therefore no longer imply just an occasional form of coincidence but the essential meaningful relationship between the mental and material aspects of the universe.

Additional insights into these movements of distinction and duality, which give rise to the particular structures of reality, can be found in the work of the logician and mathematician, G. Spenser-Brown. Spenser-Brown is a rather enigmatic figure who first came to the attention of the aged Bertrand Russell in 1965:

> . . . a young mathematician, G. Spenser-Brown, pressed me to go over his work since, he said, he could find no one else who he thought could understand it.[8]

Russell was in some trepidation at reentering the field of mathematical logic after such a long absence.

> But when he came and I heard his explanations, I found that I could get into step again and follow his work. I greatly enjoyed those few days, especially as his work was both original and, it seemed to me, excellent.[9]

In addition to developing his new system of logic, Spenser-Brown had earlier made a critique of the way in which probability theory was being used to analyze the results of ESP experiments, a piece of research which aroused the interest of Jung. He also interacted with the psychiatrist R. D. Laing and with Gregory Bateson, whose interests extended from anthropology to information theory and the "ecology of the mind." Both Bateson and Laing were responsible for developing the "double bind" theory of schizophrenia, so it is clear that Spenser-Brown's approach to symbolic logic grew not only out of his expertise in logic but also from an interest in theories of consciousness.

The system which Spenser-Brown developed in his *Laws of Form*[10] is perfectly abstract, so it can be applied not only to the symbolic structuring of the universe, but also to the creation of forms and orders of thought out of some undifferentiated background. Just as the mythic and scientific accounts of creation begin with differentiation in an empty ground, so does *Laws of Form* take as its origin a basic act of distinction. This suggests that the creative source must, itself, act as a kind of immediate and unconditioned perception. This speculation will be unfolded in a little more detail in the paragraphs that follow.

The generation of form begins with nothing—a blank page in a logician's notebook, an empty void, a pleroma. Within this void is placed a single mark, a line on an otherwise blank sheet. This is the first distinction. It can be thought of as the initial act of creation, the drawing of a distinction within the void, and out of it will emerge a world of dualities and opposites, that lead on to the generation of form and of time.

Within empty space there can be no distinction, no up or down, no in or out, no above or below, no near or far. For empty space is totally symmetric, void of all information, so that, without an observer to draw distinctions and determine directions, every point is the same as every other. But once an active observer, or a creative act of perception, is admitted into this void, then it becomes possible to draw the first distinction and in this way bring the dualities of the creatura into existence.

The first act of the observer is to make a mark. This mark

could take the form of a circle on an infinite sheet of blank paper. The circle delimits the first duality, for it divides the infinite two-dimensional plane into the dualities of inside and outside. With this first distinction it is possible for a movement to begin. For in the absence of this distinction, movement and stillness are one, since all points in space are equivalent and there is no way of distinguishing the transition from one point to the next, from the staying at one point without movement. So the first distinction allows a movement to begin, and from that movement will flow a universe of logic that embraces, according to Spenser-Brown, the foundations of mathematics, linguistics, the physical and biological sciences, and even the generation of time.

To start this movement, cross from the inside to the outside of the circle. This is the basic movement, a transition from one aspect of a duality to the other, and is denoted by the symbol ⌐. Clearly it is the beginning of the congress of dualities that is present in the mating of Geb and Nut or in the unfolding and enfolding of dualities out of the pleroma and into the creatura. This movement can be repeated; the crossing from inside to outside can take place again. But clearly each repetition of this transition of dualities is identical and ⌐⌐ = ⌐. Each time the boundary between inside and outside is crossed, the act is equivalent, no matter how many times it is performed. However, it is also possible to cross from the outside into the inside. Clearly, however, if the movement is made from inside to outside and then from outside to inside, it appears, in one sense, as if nothing had happened. Hence this double movement is equated to nonmovement.

$$\overline{\neg}$$

The congress of the dualities is represented by these two expressions:

$$\neg\neg = \neg \ . \ , \ \overline{\neg} \ .$$

And by gathering them together in strings and concatenations, it becomes possible to generate theorems and a variety of logical expressions. In addition, it is also possible to derive rules of substitution and elimination which enable expressions of greater and greater complexity to be formed and, conversely, for complex expressions to be reduced and simplified. The details of this movement of ever-increasing complexity are of course beyond the scope of this book. However, Spenser-Brown claims that the various logical forms that can be generated in this way reflect something of the structure of thought. In addition they can also describe the sorts of material processes that take place in, for example, electrical circuits and biological systems. Indeed Spenser-Brown has the curious distinction of actually having patented part of his logical system, in respect to its application to railway switching systems.

A particularly interesting feature of this logic is that it is capable of generating expressions that begin to refer to themselves. The general problem of self-referential forms also crops up in a variety of philosophical problems, such as Russell's paradox, which involves the set of all sets that do not belong to themselves. Does this set belong to itself? If it does not, then clearly it does not include *every* set that does not belong to itself, for it excludes itself. In other words, if it does not belong to itself, then it must in fact belong to itself. The paradox is generally stated in the form of a barber who is in the special position of shaving all men who do not shave themselves. Who shaves the barber?

Self-referential forms appear to play a particularly significant role in the evolution of complex systems, such as life. They play an essential role in the relationship of thought to language and in the design of "intelligent" computers. Indeed, all higher forms of thought are able to refer to themselves and to "know" their own content, and in this way, their internal structure can be represented in what could be called "re-entrant" forms. Indeed, a recent theory of consciousness proposed by G. M. Edelman and V. B. Mountcastle employs a mathematical scheme of "re-entrant signaling" to explain the brain's essential working.[11]

Spenser-Brown's re-entrant forms are in fact self-generating expressions that are capable of perpetuating themselves indefinitely, as they constantly enter and leave a distinction. In this sense, they are reminiscent of the congress of dualities in Jung's creatura and in the early origin myths. The whole process, in logical terms, could be compared with that of a computer that gets caught in the self-referential paradox of the Cretan. The Cretan says that "All Cretans are liars." Clearly the Cretan must also be referring to himself when he speaks of liars. But does he happen to be speaking the truth in this case? If so then the statement itself, "All Cretans are liars," is in fact true, and therefore the statements that each individual Cretan makes are false. But if this statement is indeed false, then all Cretans are not in fact liars but speak the truth. But in this case the statement must be true, and therefore the Cretan is a liar, in which case . . . Clearly the best the computer can do is to continue in this endless loop, generating the answers Truth, Liar, Truth, Liar, Truth, Liar . . . or Yes, No, Yes, No, Yes, No . . . or 0,1,0,1,0,1,0. . . . Spenser-Brown argues that such a stable oscillation, in the face of a self-generating form, occurs both in computers and biological systems and represents the generation of time, as the cyclic repetition and the continuous unfolding are set in opposition to each other.

This then is the logic of distinctions and dualities which is supposed to underlie the structure of the world. On first meeting this proposal, the whole idea appears both curious and suspect since logic is normally thought of as being a static, *descriptive* system, rather than an actual independent activity. With Aristotle, the study of logic involved the investigation of particular *forms* of arguments, rather than being concerned with their contents. The Greek philosophers were therefore interested in the actual structure of sentences and with establishing the various rules for constructing "logical" arguments, in terms of successions of particular sentence structures. For example:

> All men are mortal. (Major Premise)
> Socrates is a man. (Minor Premise)
> Therefore: Socrates is mortal. (Conclusion)

is one of the syllogisms called Barbara, which can be thought of as a structural form needed to arrive at a logically correct inference. Clearly such syllogisms work *despite* their contents. For example, in place of "Socrates" the name "Albert Einstein" could be substituted and in place of "mortal" could be "biped." Provided that the major and the minor premises are true, then their actual structure determines what inference will follow. In this sense, logic is a purely formal affair that deals with fixed, rigid structures in thought and appears to be remote from the activity of creation of forms out of a void. Indeed, a line, taken at random from a book on symbolic logic, reads:

$$\forall z \left(Fz \rightarrow Gz\right) \rightarrow \forall y \left[\exists x (Fx \cdot Hy\,z) \rightarrow \exists w (Gw \cdot Hyw)\right]$$

and shows the whole system to be totally abstract. Clearly this is simply a pattern of marks and symbols whose significance lies in its relationship to other patterns. In this sense the meaning of the logical expression is a kind of dance of abstract symbols that some logicians believe mirrors the dance of thought itself. Indeed strong arguments have been given as to why the new programming languages that are being developed for fifth-generation (artificial intelligence) computers should reflect this symbolic dance if they are to capture the workings of the human intellect.[12]

Conventional logic generally takes its meaning as external to itself, for the symbols w, xy, y, z all *stand for* something. That is, they are like algebraic symbols, but instead of standing for numbers they stand for phrases, thoughts, and concepts, and the logical expressions are ways of relating these concepts together. Hence the real meaning of symbolic logic therefore depends upon a whole *context* in which the particular meaning of each symbol is embedded. Therefore, while symbolic logic may appear to be straightforward at first sight, a deeper examination shows that the *meaning* of its expressions depends, in particularly subtle ways, upon a series of contexts.

Take, for example, the simple operation of dividing the world into categories. In logic these various categories can then be related through various symbolic operations in order to obtain new deductions. But while the symbolic relationships are straightforward enough, the act of dividing the world into categories requires a form of perception that is totally context-dependent and this context clearly extends beyond the particular system of logic. Hence the whole meaning belongs to the entire system and not to the particular logical expression. But how then can Spenser-Brown's logic structure a contextless void?

All things in nature are both related and unrelated; they are different in some ways and similar in others and the whole process of discrimination depends very sensitively on the notion of categories. For two things to be compared, it is clear that there must be certain points of similarity between them, but equally they must also be sufficiently distinct for the act of comparison to have any meaning at all. For example, there is no point in comparing a thing with itself. In this way, all things display sets of similarities and differences which can be used to establish categories. But these do not so much exist in the objects themselves as in the act of observation, which always takes place within some particular context. Hence the discrimination that is involved in determining similarities and differences depends critically on a given context. And in turn, this context may be sensitive to a wider context which is, itself, embedded in an ever-changing world. Clearly the meaning in logic is never absolutely fixed but is constantly changing. A man may go into a pet shop to buy a dog for his children. This establishes a particular context in which certain categories are generated—in this case color and breed may be important. However, the man may also want the dog to stand guard when his apartment is empty and here the dog's size will be important. And when it comes to training, the age will be a key factor in determining how fast the dog learns.

So depending upon which contexts are most important, the differences and similarities of price, size, age, breed, color, attitude and so on, will play a greater or lesser part in determining the category of dog. The meaning of a logical form is therefore determined by the overall context and this involves acts of perception and discrimination which lie outside the logical system itself. Hence logic, without a context, has no more meaning than a dance of symbols. How then can logic be said to structure the universe out of nothing? What are the meanings of Spenser-Brown's distinctions, Jung's dualities, and the various polarities and gods that are separated out of the void of the ground?

Clearly the term "logic" is being used in a radically different way than in a purely formal study of the relationships between strings of symbols. Nevertheless Spenser-Brown believes that a universe of thought can be built out of the basic movements of logic, just as the archetypes that structure the mind are grounded in the movements of dualities. Indeed the physicist John Wheeler has also speculated that the world is created out of logic. At first sight this may appear to look as if he is simply saying that the universe is constructed "along logical lines" or that it can be described by logic, for how can a material world have its ground in the contextless dance of logical forms? However, when pressed on this topic, Wheeler is clear that he does not mean logic in the sense of propositions that are *about* something:

> No, it's not in that sense that I'm talking about logic. I'm talking about logic in the sense of the nuts and bolts, if you will, out of which the world is made, just as Einstein and Clifford were talking about geometry as the magic building material out of which the world was made.[13]

Clearly the generation of form out of distinction, or the emergence of dualities out of the pleroma, involves something very different from a context-dependent logic. The emergence of the first distinction out of the void is beyond all context, and therefore, it is very clearly a creative act or a perception of distinction which, in its very action, creates its own context. In a sense, this recalls the philosopher Hegel's notion of the *dialectic*, which is a movement in which the word arises and creates context. For Hegel, this logic is a creative power that generates the universe out of the pure, contextless ground of *being*. Being, as with the pleroma, contains no distinctions and no object for thought to grasp. Indeed, in being, there can be no thought or movement, only a pure perception, for in the physicist's vacuum state, being is in fact *nothing*. So as thesis becomes antithesis, so being becomes nothing. Out of this movement of duality flows *becoming*, which is the synthesis. In the dialectic movement, being and nothing enter into each other and give rise to becoming, which is the name of their movement, and out of which thought and time arise. This is clearly the mirror of the movement of Geb and Nut, the transition back and forth across the first distinction of the circle, or the emerging and dissolution of the dualities between pleroma and creatura.

For Hegel, the world emerges out of the ground of being and nothing, through the movement of the dialectic, and then becomes a self-generating content in which all forms and distinctions are contained. Clearly the first step, however, of all these systems of generation involves a pure creative perception, an action that lies outside all context, all qualification and all movement. It is like God's cry of "Let there be light" in the Old Testament, in which the division of light from dark establishes the first duality out of a pure creative act.

The logic of Spenser-Brown, of Jung, or of the creation myths is not therefore a static form but is the image of a creative act of perception within an empty, contextless void. The distinction that is created then begins to generate its own context, which in turn, acts back to transform the dualities themselves. In this way the first act of perception begins a whole movement of forms and complex levels.

This sense of emergence can also be found in the writings of the mystics. The formless ground in which perception acts are, for the Tibetans, the Bardo state, in which cosmic forces find their perfect balance. At the moment of death, a Tibetan's face must be set before the Clear Light:

> and not thou Art about to experience it in its Reality in the Bardo state, wherein all things are like the void and cloudless sky, and the naked and spotless intellect is like unto a transparent vacuum, without circumference or centre.[14]

The Bardo state is the void within which the first distinction is drawn, the circumference of the circle which is crossed and recrossed as distinctions are formed and dissolved. In the fifteenth century, the mathematician and mystic Nicholas de Cusa pictured the emergence of the world as the movement of dualities or opposites:

> Whence I begin, Lord to behold Thee in the door of the coincidence of opposites, which the angel guardeth that is set over the entrance into Paradise. For thou are there where speech, sight, hearing, taste, touch, reason, knowledge, and understanding are the same, and where seeing is one with being seen and hearing with being heard, and tasting with being tasted, and touching with being touched, and speaking with hearing and creating with speaking.[15]

Here, the dissolution of coincidences or dualities, back into their ground, is equated with the unity of observer and the observed, the seeing and the being seen, the distinguisher and the distinction. Within this ground all activities and structures of the mind become as one, so that creativity alone can act. De Cusa also indicates how the creative act will dissolve forms and structures back again so that they retreat from time into eternity, only to unfold again into new forms. The act of creative perception takes place within the timeless moment in which all distinctions vanish, so that out of a moment in time, the universe is born afresh. But this is not simply a single, historical moment, a unique act of creation that gives rise to consciousness and to the world, but rather it is the eternal and continuous creation in which the world is reborn from moment to moment. Or in another sense, the one unique moment is forever present and constantly manifest in the creative renewal of the universe.[16]

For Meister Eckhart in the thirteenth century, this activity is God, which flows from the Godhead that is the source of all potentiality and the resolution of all distinctions:

> Everything in the Godhead is one, and of that there is nothing to be said. God and the Godhead are as different as active and inactive. . . . God in the Godhead is spiritual substance, so elemental that we can say nothing about it except that it is naught. To say it is aught were more lying than true.[17]

This creative source, which is found beneath the levels of increasing subtlety from which orders of mind and matter emerge, is therefore a clear and unconditioned perception. It is a perception without context that lies beyond all distinction. It exists before the sequential orders of time and is not bound by the domains of thought and language. It is a perception without necessity or goal and acts purely of itself.

This creative perception draws distinctions within the void and sustains the various enfolded and subtle levels which support the orders of matter and mind. But its first activity is the creation of a distinction which exists in the absence of any context. But as further distinctions are generated, a context begins to grow and then to act back upon the distinctions and so produces a dynamic movement of forms. In the pleroma, therefore, creativity is unconditioned and unlimited, but within the creatura it becomes *informed* as the growth of meaning unfolds within the universe of mind and matter.

This creation through the evolution of distinctions, categories, and contexts is also to be found in those myths of creation which equate the appearance of order with the act of naming. Names could be thought of as the first categories but they are not simply passive, descriptive sounds, or referential symbols for, according to these myths, they have an active quality that is able to produce order out of chaos. Indeed the act of naming creates distinctions so that the named stands out against its background and thereby establishes a movement of distinction. In the world's various religious and mystical traditions, the name has an active, magical quality. In early religions, for example, it was necessary to name the spirit or elemental in order to invoke its presence and bind it to the magician or priest's will. Similarly the mantram, which involves the repetition of a word, is supposed to play an active role in transforming consciousness and reality. Indeed the specific vibrations that are associated with the pattern of names in the mantram, as they resonate within the mind in thought, as well as physically through the resonances of the chest and nasal cavities, are believed to be particularly potent. The name is not therefore chosen by accident but its vibrations must be in harmony with the body, thought, and the universe. This active and magical nature of the name is also found in fairy tales, where to know someone's name is to obtain power over him or her, while in Egyptian times, to erase the name from a tomb was to remove a person from eternal life. So the naming of names establishes the first categories which then lead to the whole structure of thought.

It is through the ordering of categories that rational thought is born. So these myths of naming deal not only with the creation of the explicate world of life and matter but also with the activities of thought and consciousness. The creative perception which acts within the contextless void is therefore equated with the name or word whose resonances exist prior to all form and structure. Just as the congress of dualities releases energy from the pleroma into the creatura, so is this energy symbolized in the physical and mental vibrations of the name.

CONTEXTS AND STRUCTURES

The formation of distinctions, dualities, and categories is the first step in ordering the world. Indeed categories exist prior to language and reason, for it is through the ordering of categories that structures of thought are able to emerge and the mind is able to respond to the explicate world in a rational fashion. The first distinctions that are created through an act of pure perception require no context. But in their emergence out of the void, a context also begins to form, which in turn is able to act back on these categories. It is through this two-way movement between contexts and categories, or dualities, that meaning is established.

In the earlier chapters of this book it was indicated how important meaning can be in creating our whole relationship with the world. Meanings are what integrates the body into a whole; they are, for example, the key to the immune system and lie at the heart of synchronicities. These meanings emerge out of the relationships of categories and distinctions to their context within a whole dynamic and ever-changing movement.

Indeed it is this movement of meaning which pervades the universe of mind and matter, of consciousness and the body, and of the individual and society.

A flow of meaning can be clearly sensed while listening to music, which the composer Edgar Varese has called the "corporealization of thought." To take a particularly well-known composition as an example, the first four notes of Beethoven's Fifth Symphony, when they are first heard, occur out of the ground of perfect silence, which is without meaning or context. The first four notes sound out in this void, establish their resonances within the mind, and produce a variety of dispositions and expectations within the listener. This is, in effect, the generation of their first context. But now, as the music continues to play, this context starts to grow. The initial pattern of notes is played over and over again, but this perception takes place in an ever-changing context which acts to transform the way they are heard. The context is created out of this pattern of notes and, in turn, acts back on them to change their meaning. Indeed, the composer Arnold Schönberg argued that all the themes in this symphony, and indeed its whole structure, follow from its first bars. So as the music unfolds, the tension between theme and context gives rise to a particularly powerful movement of meaning.

But, of course, no music is heard in a vacuum, and each time the Fifth Symphony is played, it accretes new musical, social, and historical resonances. For example, a listener may have read that the opening theme is "fate knocking at the door," which will color the context in which the music is heard and change its whole meaning. But as the meaning changes, it acts back on the theme in an active way and changes the listener's perception. Indeed these four notes were eventually broadcast by the BBC during the Second World War, as a symbol of freedom. And in this way, the whole symphony was placed in a much wider historical, social, and moral context. In this fashion, the first "distinction" within the music generates an ever-expanding and changing context, which moves out into the whole society and then acts back on the original theme. In a similar way, a distinction or duality first appears in an empty void to create a context. As distinction and context grow together, they create an ever-changing world of order and meaning, which can never be fixed but is constantly acting back on itself.

CONCLUSIONS AND SUMMARY

The universe springs from a creative source whose primary action is one of unconditioned perception in the void which gives rise to the first, contextless distinctions and dualities. These dualities, which flow from the source, create an ever-changing context which then acts back on them to produce a continuing discrimination and differentiation. All this movement folds into a series of orders and levels out of which the orders of consciousness and the material world unfold. The heart of this movement and hierarchy of levels is meaning, which emerges out of an inseparable exchange between dualities or categories within their ever-changing context. Out of this process, orders and structures are born which then unfold outward into explicate forms. In turn, these explicate forms and relationships, which are the basis of the universe we perceive and interact with and of our conscious awareness as well, form information the content of super-implicate orders. This information is used in an active way to "inform" the activities of higher enfolded orders which are responsible for unfolding the explicate structures of the world. In this way the whole universe of mind and matter has an ever-changing meaning, like the movement of a great symphony, which constantly acts back on itself in creative ways.

Synchronicity flows from this basic movement, which gives its subject a sense of the deeper meaning to the universe and an intuition of the movements that flow from its creative source. But this raises an important question: Why should this process that gives rise to and sustains the whole universe of mind and matter appear to be so unique and unusual that it is experienced only during a synchronicity or a spiritual epiphany? Surely the same sense of meaning and creativity should pervade all of nature and life? However, many people feel that their lives are empty and mechanical and when they contemplate the world they find very little evidence of creativity. While a form of creativity may operate occasionally in such specialized areas as art, mathematics, poetry, music, and the like, it is clearly not in evidence in the way many people lead their lives or engage in relationships. Moreover, it does not appear to operate to any great extent in society itself. The whole world is embroiled in wars, repressions, and revolutions. Vast numbers of people are on the verge of starvation and live in ignorance or under severe repression. Even in the more "advanced," democratic countries there is increasing evidence of violence and unrest, and technological societies do not seem able to use their powers without damaging and polluting the environment. A visitor from another planet might be excused for believing that the human race is quite clever but lacks wisdom and creativity. How could a species which had any sense of the meaning of the universe still perpetuate such misery? Why should synchronicity be considered as some isolated coincidence of mind and matter when the one underlying source is constantly giving birth to the universe at every eternal moment? An answer to these questions is given in the final chapter, where it is suggested that a fragmentation in the way the mind has come to perceive the orders of time, and the growth of the self with all its attachments, has blinded our perceptions to the basic creativity in the universe.

NOTES

1. Lao-tzu, *Tao Te Ching*. There are very many translations and editions of the *Tao Te Ching*, all subtly different. The reader is advised to enjoy and compare several translations.
2. Plotinus, *Enneads*. Editions of the *Enneads* are to be found as volumes 17 of the *Encyclopedia Britannica*'s *Great Books of the Western World* (Chicago, 1952) as well as in editions published by Oxford University Press and Harvard University Press. The complete works, with a concordance, are edited by K. S. Guthrie (Jackson, Miss.: Gordy Press, 1977).
3. John Wheeler in Paul Buckley and F. David Peat, *A Question of Physics* (London: Routledge & Kegan Paul, 1979).
4. *Reports of Progress in Science* 47 (1984): 925–986.

5. "The Inflationary Universe," *Scientific American* 20:5 (May 1984): 116–128.

6. C. G. Jung, *VII Sermones ad Mortuos,* trans. H. G. Baynes (London: Stuart & Watkins, 1967).

7. Ibid.

8. *The Autobiography of Bertrand Russell,* vol. III (London: Allen and Unwin, 1969).

9. Ibid.

10. New York: Julian Press, 1972.

11. G. M. Edelman and V. B. Mountcastle, *The Mindful Brain* (Cambridge: MIT Press, 1978).

12. Not everyone, however, holds this view, and Marvin Minsky, one of the "fathers" of artificial intelligence, has given strong and persuasive arguments to show that formal logic does not play a significant role in the mind's structure, but rather strings of empirical rules, exceptions, and counterrules move together in a more complex ensemble of "nonlogical" thought processes.

13. John Wheeler in Paul Buckley and F. David Peat, *A Question of Physics* (London: Routledge & Kegan Paul, 1979).

14. *The Tibetan Book of the Dead,* ed. W. Y. Evans-Wentz (Oxford University Press, 1960).

15. Nicholas de Cusa, *On Learned Ignorance,* trans. Fr. G. Heron (London: Routledge & Kegan Paul, 1954).

16. These issues are also discussed in A. Huxley, *The Perennial Philosophy* (London: Triad Grafton Books, 1985) and in F. C. Happold, *Mysticism* (Harmondsworth, Eng.: Penguin, 1971).

17. Meister Eckhart, *Tractates,* trans. C. de B. Evans (Watkins Publishers, n.d.).

8 TIME AND TRANSFORMATION

A synchronicity acts as a mirror, a mirror in which the constant folding and unfolding of the universe out of its ground is reflected. In earlier chapters, images and metaphors were developed which point to the ways in which reality is sustained from its creative source. This creativity acts as a pure, unconditioned perception in the void, a perception that brings the first dualities into existence. This basic generation was equated, for example, with the emergence of the creatura out of the pleroma and with the congress of gods, in which potential and formative energy is released out of its infinite ground. It is these various processes and movements which find their symbolic expression in a synchronicity.

As the first dualities emerge out of the void, they give rise to a context which then acts back on them. In this way the first categories and structures come into existence which ultimately give rise to the various movements of matter and consciousness. The universe is therefore pictured as emerging out of a series of highly subtle and enfolded levels in which process and active information can be thought of as two sides of a single order. The end result is the emergence of explicate orders of mind and matter out of their underlying enfolded forms. According to this account, therefore, mind and matter are not distinct substances but two sides of one reality, orders which emerge out of a common spectrum that contains additional subtle, and as yet unexplored, orders that may be found to play significant roles in events on the subquantum level, the evolution of life, and the operation of society.

Clearly this whole account should be taken in the spirit of a metaphor, for the complexity and subtlety of the universe lie beyond all attempts to capture it in language and images. However, the essential point of this image is that it involves a central creativity that pervades everything, from its continuous origin in an unconditioned act of perception, to the constant, subtle movement of its various orders, levels, and structures. The spectrum of orders out of which mind and matter emerge is extremely subtle and fast-moving, for its ground is never fixed but is always involved in a constant, creative renewal. Even the relatively fixed, explicate, and mechanical aspects of the universe also emerge in a continuous fashion out of their underlying, implicate order. In this way the elementary particle, for example, is constantly being born, sustained, and dying back into its ground or vacuum state.

The universe is sustained through an act of creative unfoldment in which no order is absolutely fixed but is able to respond to an ever-changing context. Clearly creativity pervades every element of nature. But if this is indeed the case, then why is creativity not more evident in our own lives? For unlimited creativity is generally taken to be a special gift, something that is unique and associated with those occasional geniuses who emerge in the arts and sciences. Most people, by contrast, feel that their capacity for creativity is seriously limited, for they are caught up in the day-to-day activities of work, relationships, and family that allow them little energy or latitude for change. So whatever creativity does take place in a person's life is generally channeled into rather narrow limits that are established by circumstances and the various customs, beliefs, and restrictions of society.

Many people, when they attempt an overview of their lives, sense that they are trapped by time and history. Thus they feel the victim of childhood traumas, the failures of the school system, their parents' economic and social standing, bad judgments made at work, and trapped in the neighborhood or city and the country they happen to live in. Even society, and the nation itself, appears to be a victim of its past mistakes, which make present conflicts inevitable, so that truly creative solutions seem out of the question.

To take a specific example, people living in Northern Ireland feel trapped by the violence that surrounds them. But they also see this as inevitably following from social conditions that grew out of a variety of political decisions which can be traced back for several centuries. The result is the present "Northern Ireland problem," in which any solution seems doomed to generate yet more problems and conflict, and the individual is swept up in an endless series of violent reactions. The same could, of course, be said for the Middle East, and for many other areas of the globe. In each case, society, governments, and the individual feel trapped within an intolerable and insoluble situation, in which any possibility of creative transformation appears to be out of the question, for each person holds on to what they feel are last-ditch positions that involve absolute necessities, unbargainable rights, and self-evident beliefs. What is true on the national scale is also true within the family, between husband and wife or parents and children. In all cases, creativity seems to be ruled out by all manner of rigid and inflexible structures and attitudes which are inherited along with the problem itself.

Even the ways in which the human race deals with the planet itself have led to such intolerable difficulties as denudement of the forests, energy crises, pollution, disruption of the atmosphere and weather, extinction of whole species, and the decay of lakes. If the world truly arises out of a source of infinite subtlety and creativity, then has this origin now become polluted, like a once mighty river that supported all manner of wildlife at its banks and innumerable species of fish in its waters, but is now dead and stinking?

How could this have come about? Why is creativity not able to animate society and the individual so that nations are able to approach change in free and open ways, for the good of all, and the life of each individual becomes pervaded with meaning? Synchronicity has been singled out in this book as expressing the "meaningful relationships between inner and outer events."

In a similar way, the epiphanies within a poet's and artist's life offer illumination into the inner workings and meaning of nature. But why should such events appear exceptional or unique, when meaning is essential to the unfolding of the universe?

While the source of all reality is an unconditioned creativity, it does appear that human society, and the individuals within it, often operate in a fairly mechanical way so that they respond to new situations from relatively fixed positions and in uncreative ways. In other words, they appear to be trapped in structures and forms of their own making, such as the beliefs, goals, and values that have become so rigid that they are unable to move in the flexible and subtle ways that characterize the general order of the universe.

Does this mean that the creative source has become inherently limited, or diminished by the consciousness that it created? This does not seem credible, since even those material structures which appear to be eternal and enduring must, in fact, be constantly created and sustained out of a wider context which may itself change in unexpected ways. In fact no structures or orders in the universe can be considered to be totally permanent, for they are always subject to change. What is present in matter must be even more pervasive in consciousness, which is, in its essence, mobile and open to creation. The problem, therefore, cannot lie within the general nature of consciousness itself but must be some special feature or "error" that has crept in during the evolution of the human race.

Some thinkers have argued that the mind is indeed limited, for it became trapped through the very speed of its own evolution. H. G. Wells, for example, made a comparison with those first sea creatures to emerge onto land. At first they were not fully fitted for a land-based existence and were therefore forced to return periodically to the water. In a similar way he argued that the human mind had evolved so rapidly that it was not yet fitted to exist exclusively in a world of higher consciousness. Others have pointed out that the human brain contains fixed structures from its reptilian past which manifest themselves as aggressions and irrational responses that overwhelm the "higher" areas of the brain.

But here the question arises, to what extent is consciousness dominated by these fixed structures, and are they forever static, or like other material structures, are they sustained by a deeper unfolding and therefore are open to creative transformation and change? In other words, is the human race doomed to change only by the slow processes of evolution and natural selection of the physical brain? Is it limited by the static mental structures and social orders that have evolved over the past thousands and tens of thousands of years, or is consciousness fundamentally unlimited in its potential for change, so that a total transformation in the human mind can take place outside evolutionary time?

All these questions spring from the consideration of the nature and meaning of synchronicity that began in the first chapter. But clearly their significance goes far beyond this particular field and into the whole question of the future of the human race and, considering the threat of nuclear war, to the very survival of life on this planet. In order to explore these questions, and to arrive at a new understanding of the nature of synchronicity, it is necessary to investigate the nature of time, which is also a key aspect of synchronicity, and to explore the whole question of the evolution of the self. In this way an answer will be found for why the human mind is limited in its creativity when it arises from the unbounded order of creativity.

CONSCIOUSNESS AND THE INDIVIDUAL

Consciousness is a subtle order with a delicate, sensitive, and intangible movement that is quite different from the order of explicate matter, yet is inseparable from it within the common spectrum of orders. Consciousness cannot be reduced in any absolute way to the physical operations of the brain, neither can these material processes be described as totally conditioned by mind. Rather, mind and brain arise as two indivisible aspects of the one underlying source.

Up to now, however, consciousness has been discussed in a

rather abstract sense, in terms of the "mental" side of the universe, rather than the specific consciousness of particular individuals. In the first chapter, it was argued that synchronicity requires a bridge to be forged between matter and mind, and in the chapters that followed, it was demonstrated that the processes of nature have a mental aspect, which was also referred to as an "objective intelligence." For example, the collective motion of electrons in a plasma or superconductor, and the unity of cells in the slime mold, all behave in ways that are similar to the cooperative behavior of a group of human beings. This suggests that some form of "intelligence" may be operating within matter. Indeed, in Chapter 6, a new interpretation of the quantum theory was introduced in which "active information" plays a significant role in "informing" the quantum field that gives rise to various quantum processes. Likewise, the super-implicate order could be said to have a "mindlike" side in that it acts to structure the unfolding of the implicate order into various explicate forms. Moreover, these implicate, explicate, and super-implicate orders may extend indefinitely into ever more subtle levels which include aspects that can be considered as "mental." Clearly, in the previous chapters, the terms "mental," "intelligence," and "consciousness" have been used in novel and changing ways, in an attempt to reach some sense of the unity between mind and matter.

However, the word "consciousness" is generally used to denote that light of awareness and attention which illuminates the mind of the particular individual, rather than the whole universe. Just as the elementary particle unfolds out of the quantum field, the soliton appears in the nonlinear field, and the vortex emerges from the river, so may an individual consciousness emerge out of the complex background order of consciousness that extends into the whole universe. The individual mind is therefore a sort of localization or concentration of consciousness that unfolds into the brain and body of the individual. But just as the electron will fold into other elementary particles and back into its ground of the quantum field, and just as the vortex has no absolute independence from the ripples and vortexes of the river, so too an individual mind cannot be separated, in any absolute way, from the consciousness of society as a whole. In this way the individual mind unfolds out of the consciousness of all humanity and then folds back again, in a continuous process.

Indeed it is only relatively recently, historically speaking, that an individual consciousness separated from that of the "group mind" of the tribe or social group. Many passages in the Old Testament, for example, move in a fluid way between speaking of the tribe and its individual representative without making any marked distinction between them. This suggests that such a differentiation was not yet firm. This essential unity between individual and tribe has been referred to as the "corporate personality." And it is possible that in even earlier, prehistoric times, mind moved beyond the tribe into surrounding animal life and pervaded the whole of nature. Even today, the few surviving hunter-gatherer groups do appear to have a strong sense of unity with the animals they hunt. The Naskapi, for example, appear to communicate with the animals during dreams and drumming, and Manitu, which inhabits humans, also resides in the weather, life, and other aspects of nature.

In its origins, the content of consciousness is the whole world, but in the individual it becomes focused and concentrated, bound up with the individual's body and drawing upon various memories, habits, life experiences, and dispositions to result in a personal consciousness. Indeed this individual mind may have grown out of the society as a sort of reflection. Just as a person comes to know his or her own face not by looking inward but by looking in a mirror, so will society reflect back something of an individual's persona. The self, in this sense, is projected outward into society and then reflected back and taken for some actual, persistent substance or entity.

In this way consciousness unfolds into the individual mind and so becomes associated with a particular person, who then interacts, with others and with the world in general. Through the long process of evolution of the human and society, the mind developed its powers to discriminate, calculate, play, reflect, develop strategies and solve problems, and generally to develop an increasing technical power and an increasing knowledge. But the price of all this appears to have been the development of a self which is increasingly isolated from a more direct contact with nature or society. This sense of loss and of being divorced from the inner harmonies of nature has often been explored by the poets, and is illustrated in the quotations from Wordsworth and T. E. Lawrence in Chapter 1.

Even the individual consciousness is divided from itself, for a large part of the mind is said to be "unconscious" and to contain a wide content that is not normally available to the self. However, various mystics claim that the separation of the individual self from the unconscious and the rest of the world is not absolute and that a deep sense of unity with the whole universe can be achieved, so that even the ground of consciousness can begin to be explored. In this way the mystic feels that life is pervaded by meaning and a sense of "oneness" with the whole of nature.

Something similar, but on a much smaller scale, appears to happen during a synchronicity in which a person experiences a strong sense of meaning which unites inner thoughts, dreams, and feelings with patterns of events in the outer world. If such epiphanies of meaning were to be sustained throughout the whole of life then clearly the human mind would operate on a different level. While preserving its powers to plan, predict, and solve problems, it would also be able to reach out and share the corporate meanings of society and maintain a greater sensitivity to the rhythms of nature. In this way rigid structures of thought would be dissolved and creativity would operate through the whole field of consciousness.

THE TIGER AND THE FOREST

In order to understand why a strong sense of meaning occurs only in isolated synchronicities, or with unique individuals called mystics, it is necessary to discover why the individual mind has divided itself from the whole field of consciousness and the creative source. A good starting point is to consider the image of a tiger in the forest. The tiger has sensed danger and merges into the background, watching the forest with great intensity. The animal vibrates in its sensitivity. Its whole body expresses its absolute attention and watchfulness. In an almost timeless sense, the tiger becomes one with the forest and responds to every nuance of its environment.

The tiger, through its whole body, is a pure act of perception and total awareness; its consciousness extends outward into the whole forest. How sharply this contrasts with the way most people live their lives, with the senses deadened and a feeling of being cut off from the environment and even from their own bodies. Indeed, it is only in childhood that people feel a sense of total involvement with the world, in which the mind is not trapped by the self and life is lived with the intensity of the tiger.

But suppose now that someone is transported from in front of the television set or office desk and set down in the tiger's forest. Immediately the whole body is stirred into an intense awareness of the environment, as the senses strain to pick up the slightest sound or movement. Within such awareness, there is very little room for the "self" with all its memories and concerns; rather the whole organism is in an undivided state of extreme sensitivity, as if the mind were located right on the surface of the skin and responsive to every aspect of the forest.

As the hunter stalks the tiger, the forms of the forest are registered at the limits of the senses. A sudden flash of color or rustle in the undergrowth is detected with a "sixth sense"; for example, a darting movement is picked up in the corner of the eye so rapidly that it is gone before the mind has time to analyze or compare it. The flash of movement is pure, unfiltered perception that is registered in a fleeting fraction of a second. Within such heightened awareness there is no division between mind and body, for perception is a function of the organism as a whole.

This "sixth sense" can be illustrated by comparison with the way a frog's brain works. In neurobiological terms, the visual receptor cells in the frog's brain that respond to movement are linked directly to its motor system. The frog's tongue therefore darts out to the fly even before "seeing" has had time to fully unfold within the frog's brain. Indeed the frog must act so quickly to respond to the ever-changing forms of nature that it does not have time to reflect on what it sees. Perception and action operate without division or reflection. It is almost as if the frog's awareness operates on the implicate level, never having time to unfold into explicate visual forms, but constantly responding to the environment so that observer and observed are inherently inseparable. The frog's perception is totally direct; it "sees" without seeing. But while this may be of considerable advantage in catching flies, it also means that the frog occasionally eats a scrap of paper wagged in front of its eye by an experimenter, for its visual knowledge of the world is considerably impoverished.

In the human mind, out of this first direct sensitivity and rapid awareness now grows the focusing movement of attention. When a sudden movement is detected by the sixth sense, it is picked up by the periphery of the body's senses. If there is sufficient time, the mind may then decide to focus its attention on this transient sensation and attempt to isolate it from the constantly changing stimuli of the forest and so learn more about it. In terms of the physiology of the human vision system, the first stimulus is detected in the peripheries of the retina, where it is registered in the brain in an implicate way, as a pure sensation of movement without the unfolding of any recognizable object. But this awareness now activates attention, in the form of a rapid scanning movement of the eyes which brings the object into focus on the more sensitive central region of the retina. As this sensitive spot, rich in receptor cells, scans back and forth over the object, the brain receives a wealth of new data, which includes specific details of the object's size, shape, colors, movement, edges, surfaces, texture, orientation, highlights and shadows. Gradually these visual clues are unfolded within the brain, while additional information is provided from the memory of similar objects seen in the past, and deductions as to its scale, speed, structure, and so on, are made. Finally the object itself is integrated out of all these processes and unfolds into a final state of recognition. This complex action of attention therefore involves a simultaneous inward and outward scanning as the mind begins to unfold an explicit picture of the object, distinct from its background in the forest.

The meaning and recognition of the object therefore unfold out of a very complex movement that begins in the implicate order with a very rapid undifferentiated *awareness*, in which there is no separation between the observer and the thing observed, which then unfolds into *attention* as a form of focusing and directed scanning, whereby an explicate object is more gradually unfolded out of the background. While the implicate awareness is fast enough to keep in harmony with the ever-changing and fluid impressions produced during a walk through the forest, the explicate attention is a more reflective process, which requires an act of scanning in time the internal and external contents of consciousness and the retrieval of memories and experiences. Clearly if the hunter is to survive in the forest, both forms of response to the environment are needed, so that there can be a constant movement between implicate and explicate orders, awareness and attention, and back again. While awareness without attention gives rise to an overall sense of meaning it cannot provide a differentiated understanding of the details of particular explicate objects and their behavior. On the other hand, attention without awareness would consist of isolated, explicate forms without any sense of their overall context or meaning.

During the hunt, awareness and attention operate in perfect harmony and there is no sense of a passage of time, for the hunter lives in an eternal now. Something similar happens when a person listens very intently to a piece of music or engages in creative work. There seems to be no "self" present, for the awareness and attention of the whole mind and body are fully absorbed so that when the music, or the task, ends there may be a sudden shock of falling back into the "real world" and discovering that a considerable amount of time has passed. Within the forest, therefore, the hunter and the hunted are one, and time only exists as a dance of the hunt itself.

While there may be no sense of self during the hunt, or while working creatively, there will certainly be an awareness of *inner* processes that arise within the mind and body. These are first detected by the "sixth sense" as fleeting sensations coming from within. Indeed, in the midst of the hunt, there may be no strong differentiation between inner and outer awareness. Consciousness is undivided, and awareness of the movements of inner feelings and outer sensations is far too fast to be focused upon and differentiated. However, at times it is important for the mind to direct its attention on certain of these inner sensations and to differentiate them from those produced in the external environment. It is obviously important, for example, to differentiate a sudden external movement in the undergrowth from an internal movement produced by a swing of the head.

In the case of vision, hearing, and other senses, the human mind is well able to make such differentiations at the automatic level. But when it comes to inner thoughts, feelings, memories, and emotions, this is more difficult to do. While listening to a piece of music, for example, a rich variety of feelings and sensations are all one with the total listening. It is only when attention is directed and focused inward in a more deliberate movement that it becomes possible to differentiate the fleeting feelings and memories that are being generated internally from those evoked in response to the music, and at the best of times, this discrimination is imprecise and it is very easy to confuse what is happening inside with what is happening outside.

THE HUNTER IN THE ARMCHAIR

While the hunter is in the forest, there appears to be no limit to consciousness, no "unconscious" area that is closed to awareness. In the midst of the hunt, awareness and attention move in harmony with the rhythms of the "eternal present" of nature. However, when the modern hunter sinks back into his or her armchair, there are times when the mind detaches itself from the immediacy of the outside world and turns its attention inward, and it is in this movement that the "self" may assume supreme attention.

Within the earliest tribes there was a strong sense of communion in which consciousness was engaged in a collective way. But with the rise of the first cities, civilization grew more complex, specialized, and fragmentary, so that individuals began to function as entities apart from society and with an increasing sense of their own independence. Within this new milieu, attention became more directed toward the inner awareness, so that thoughts, feelings, and emotions began to be unfolded into the explicate form we now call the self. Provided that this attention to the inner environment took place in a harmonious way, within the ever-changing context of society and nature, then it was still possible for the individual and society to operate creatively. However, there developed the real danger of treating these unfolded inner feelings as being more important, real, and vital than the movements of the external world. As the mind looked ever inward and attempted to focus and fix its inner movements, it began to develop a more fixed notion of the self. In place of a fluid center, which ultimately merged into the ever-changing awareness of the whole of consciousness, grew the historical self with fixed memories and attitudes that remain constant within the flux of the world and separate in a rigid sense from society and nature.

Clearly, at this stage the self began to separate itself from the source of meaning in the universe and likewise the flow of creativity became blocked by the rigid attachments of the self to its interior structures. As this process continued, the self rigidified and became the supreme focus of attention, so that its survival, in a paradoxical way, was even more important than that of the body. In time of war, for example, the self is motivated to preserve its various abstract ideas without regard for life itself, as if the self were immortal and ultimately untouched by injury to the body.

The self holds on to what is comfortable and secure, and avoids all that is painful or disturbing or threatens the survival of its own existence. In turn, these inner mental images, which are sustained at the cost of great energy, are projected outward into society where they become shared as collective beliefs. The end result is that the consciousness of society is no longer a fluid, sensitive order but something relatively fixed that flows from the abstractions of the self. In this way, the more subtle ground of consciousness becomes dominated by fixed forms. Soon the whole self is in danger of being trapped in a deadly confusion of its own making, which began by giving supreme authority to its own thoughts and of acting toward them as if they were more real than the tiger in the forest! The end result is a whole new order of life in which absolute necessities, goals, beliefs, and aspirations stand in a dominant position and overrule the fast and subtle awareness of the body and the external world. These more subte elements begin to fade and, with this fading, is lost the sense of deeper meaning of nature.

In place of the hunter whose whole body is alive with sensitive awareness stands twentieth century humanity—self-divided, confused, out of touch with the body, and robbed of any meaning of the universe. Only on extremely rare occasions can a person write, as did T. E. Lawrence:

> We started off on one of those clear dawns that wake up the senses with the sun. For an hour or so, on such a morning, the sounds, scents and colors of the world struck man individually and directly, not filtered through or made typical by thought.

For many people the response to life has become mechanical so that there is little opportunity for creativity to act, and in its attachments, the self is trapped in a sequential order of time in which it constantly strives to escape from its limitations. It is in this very effort to change that creativity becomes blocked and the self becomes attached to its sense of constant becoming rather than being.

Is it possible therefore for the creative source to permeate the life of the individual? By no longer sustaining the mechanical order of time and attachment can the division between mind and body, individual and society, and society and nature be healed and the whole order of consciousness transformed in a creative way. Is it possible that the balance of life on this planet may be restored and a deeper sense of meaning function within the individual and society?

TIME AND ETERNITY

The major barriers to a creative transformation of consciousness are the attachments of the self, which give rise to a
mechanical order of becoming in which the more subtle and
faster movements of nature are lost. In order to understand how
the individual mind can change in a creative way, it is necessary, therefore, to explore the nature of orders of time and
whether the current mechanical and sequential order can come
to an end.

Time, for Newton, "of itself, and from its own nature, flows
without relation to anything external." Time, in the eighteenth
century, owed nothing to consciousness; moreover it was not
conditioned in any way by the universe itself or the bodies in
it. Everywhere, from earth to the most distant stars, time
flowed equally and at the same rate. On the first day of
creation, God had set a gigantic clock in motion whose ticks
permeated the whole of nature. Bodies therefore existed *in*
time, which swept them along in its inexorable movement of
change. As the Victorian hymn put it: "Time, like an ever
rolling stream, bears all its sons away."

Of course, Albert Einstein put a stop to all that when he
showed that time does not flow equally at all parts of the
universe, since its rate is affected by the presence of matter
and energy. Indeed time can no longer be thought of as
absolute, for the rate of any clock must now be referred to
within a particular frame of reference.

While Einstein had done away with the idea of absolute
time, in favor of a measure that is relative to each particular
observer, nevertheless the overall order of time still retained
many of its Newtonian aspects. For example time is still a
stream which unfolds through a series of successions, although
in Einstein's case this rate of unfolding depends on the state of
the observer. In this chapter, however, it is suggested that the
time order of nature is in fact wider than suggested by Newton
or Einstein. Time does not consist of a single order of succession but of a whole spectrum of orders of which eternity and
the mathematical order of succession, or flowing stream, are just

two particular aspects. Consciousness itself is not bound within any single one of these orders and is therefore extremely sensitive to the movements of time. The self and modern society, however, appear to have become attached to a mechanical, sequential order of time that is essentially the same as Newton's and this acts as a significant barrier to the more subtle movements involved in the unfolding of creativity.

By acknowledging the operation of different orders of time, it may be possible to understand consciousness and the operation of the self without becoming trapped in the various paradoxes that haunt any attempt to think about time and mind. To begin, it is important to realize that the perception of time itself is never a direct sensation. A person is not so much aware of time as of movement, change, and process. It can even be argued, from the scientific perspective, that time (and space) is in fact a derived concept that springs from the more primitive notions of process and change. In a similar fashion, people once measured space, for example the distance between two villages, by the amount of walking that had to be done to reach one from the other. In this way the amount of walking, or the measure of a particular process, can be taken to define a distance or time.

Likewise, atomic time is the measure of the amount of process that takes place in the quantum domain. In other words, the sequential order, shown on the clock, that is so ubiquitous in our modern world is not so much "given," but emerges out of the prior sensations of process and change. In this sense, primitive tribes are said to live in an "eternal now." While they are engaged in hunting, the group operates as a single consciousness which is in harmony with the ever-changing order of the hunt, the movement of the forest, and the activities of game. Hence the time order of the hunt is an extremely complex dance which could be thought as operating upon an implicate level. The consciousness that corresponds to this highly subtle time order is able to stretch out into the fast and fluid movements of the forest.

Even in its daily life, when not engaged in hunting, the tribe operates within time orders that are structured through customs and rituals that are in harmony with the transformations of nature such as the gradual, or rapid, transformation of the dawn, hunger and eating, day and night, waxing and waning of the moon, coming of the rains and drought, progression of the seasons. Such a time order is of the nature of an eternal rhythm in which change is set against eternal recurrence. Indeed some anthropologists suggest that these time orders, as celebrated in ritual and custom, act to bind together the whole society into its collective consciousness.

The essence of this tribal structuring of time is both eternal and moving. For each dawn is both new and yet the same. In the act of waking to the dawn, the mind is alert to new movements and sensations of a subtle and rapid nature, yet this dawn has a deep unity with every other dawn that is experienced by the tribe. So the birth of the day is both fluid in its movement, and yet part of an eternal order of the tribe. That a moment can be both timeful and timeless appears paradoxical to our own conception of what time should be. However, it should not be forgotten that this timeful order was able to bind human societies together in an effective and meaningful way, for within this order of change and return, each action has its place and meaning. Clearly this order has something in common with that of synchronicity, which grows out of the eternal timeless instant that is pregnant with the potential for change.

This eternal order still persists in the Catholic mass, where the act of consecration brings the congregation into contact with a timeless moment in which every historical act of consecration is united with its origin in Christ. The fourth-century philosopher, St. Augustine, offered some particularly interesting reflections on time order when he argued that time has no absolute, independent nature but exists only in its passing. The past, he said, is gone and the future is yet to be; only the present exists. In this sense, therefore, the past and the future can exist only in the present. This leads to a time order in which there is "a present of things past, a present of things present, and a present of things future." Indeed St. Augustine appears to be suggesting that the most immediate perception, out of which time arises, is the direct perception of change, for "the present of things present is sight."

But paradoxically, the Christian notion of time was itself responsible for destroying the notion of an eternal order, for this is clearly at odds with the belief that "Christ died for our sins." In other words, across Christian Europe there spread the notion of time with a beginning, and a linear, sequential order that moves into the future. This sequential order obtained its most precise treatment with Newton.

But in fact this transformation in the order of time was probably the result of a much deeper and far earlier movement within the whole order of the consciousness of society and the individual. As the consciousness of society broke away from direct contact with the harmonies of nature, and planning, control, and the first technologies began to develop, a new time order began to evolve in which the notion of "becoming" dominated over that of "being." In this way society became identified with a linear time of successions from past to future.

As societies became more sophisticated, they were able to plan for the future, store grain against bad seasons, organize long-term building projects, direct large numbers of citizens, and involve themselves in an increasing control over nature. Such societies clearly felt themselves involved in a form of progress, growth, improvement, and accumulation of wealth and knowledge. In the movement from past to future, the society did not remain with itself in an eternal "now" but constantly moved away from itself in an attempt to become "better." Likewise the individual's life was stretched out on a linear scale in time, and as it moved into the future, it strove to accumulate power, riches, and knowledge.

But in adopting this new time order, society was no longer determined internally through meaning, but externally in terms of an absolute order of time. Within this order, tasks are assigned to a priority and a value within time. Indeed there is often not "enough time," so that many important events must be relegated until "tomorrow." Every important process is assumed to take place within time. Individuals are no longer related according to the complex cycles, rituals, and movements of nature, society, and consciousness, but are tied to a rather mechanical order of time, the "ever-flowing stream" which sweeps everything along in its path.

Within Western society, this time order, and the notion of progress that goes along with it, is considered to be self-evident so that the earlier eternal and timeful orders are taken to be illusions, or religious fictions for the weak-minded. At all events there is not sufficient time to think about eternity. Such things are best left to the old or to one's death, in which all movement has its end in eternity.

This rigid time order of succession has begun to dominate the order of the individual and, in turn, has been projected back onto society and nature. Within this order, considerable division and fragmentation exists, for life is no longer pervaded by meaning but is determined by the mechanical order of succession. In this way, mind is divorced from body, the individual from society, and society from nature. It is only by putting this sequential order in its proper place that the self will free itself of its constant movement toward progress, and its awareness will stretch out into the whole of consciousness with all its subtle orders.

In its origins, the self had only a relative independence within the ground of the consciousness of society that moved out into the wider orders of life in general and possibly beyond. It may well have been in this way that the Shang people lived their lives and carried out their tortoise shell divinations. The Shang society, while preserving a direct contact with the whole of nature, was also able to distinguish itself from the world, and to give the individual a relative independence. The order of the society therefore included the very subtle orders of nature and the eternal and timeful orders. But in addition to the eternal order of time, such a society was also able to make use of a sequential time order, which it used in planning for the future, reflecting on particular tasks, and separating the actions of the society from those of the individual. In this way the Shang may well have been able to develop the hierarchies of command and control that they needed in order to engage in long-range building projects. But while the Shang could structure their society in a more explicit and fixed way than, say, the Naskapi, they were also able to return to the global order of consciousness through the daily ritual of the oracle. In this fashion, the differentiated and relatively fixed orders of the society were constantly pervaded with meaning, through the act of synchronicity practiced by the emperor.

But as societies became ever more complex and sought to gain increasing control over nature and their own internal organization, the ideas of progress and "becoming" gained in importance. Indeed this notion of progress became increasingly identified not so much with the society itself but as emanating from the individual. In this way the self began to reign supreme, and as early societies moved toward the culmination of the Renaissance, the highest value was given to the self.

Within each part is enfolded the whole, so that each element becomes a microcosm of the macrocosm. In this sense the individual truly stands as an image of a wider reality, with all its complex orders. Provided that the self is a fluid element within this microcosm, sustained by the creative source and merging with the whole of consciousness and nature, then its identification with the origin of things is not totally false. However, as this self becomes more rigidly identified with set structures and with the sequential order of becoming, it believes itself to be the only and true source of all progress and creativity. Out of its fixed limited order this self constructs an image of the eternal which it then strives to attain. The self becomes absolute and uses all the energies available within the unfolding of the individual, to sustain the image it has produced. It is attached to this image, which it believes to be eternal and of the same essence as the creative source.

In operating from its fixed forms and relatively limited order, the self assumes itself to be the origin and sustainer of all things. It has confused the inward and outward reality and overwhelms any awareness of more subtle areas and orders of consciousness. It is in this way that the meaning and time orders of nature are dimmed. It is as if a person were to organize a picnic beside a thruway. The noise of the traffic would simply block the more delicate sounds of nature, the birds, the insects, and the wind in the trees. In a similar way the noise of the self blocks out the movement of the more flexible orders of consciousness and the interconnections of the individual to society and nature. Or to use another image, the self is like a television set that has been left on in a room. While the occupant of the room is engaged in an important task, his or her attention keeps wandering back to the flashing, insistent images on the screen. These images are quite trivial in their content, compared with the task in hand; however, it is their very seductiveness of color and movement that tends to attract attention away from the more subtle and vital movements of the task.

In this way the self has fragmented itself from the general field of consciousness and has become blocked from creativity so that a synchronicity now appears to be a rare and isolated incident, rather than one aspect of the general order of time and unfoldment. Similarly, society is wedded to an almost static vision of time in which the present is inherited from the past and the future is relatively determined. In seeking the eternal, the self and society have limited themselves. While all around them nature moves in fast and subtle ways, people have become blocked from the wide arena of their consciousness and are free only to operate from limited, fixed positions. In this way whole areas of consciousness are lost to direct awareness and are now believed to be "unconscious," or as with society and nature, are assumed to be external to the individual mind.

But in fact, no area of consciousness is truly closed to awareness. It is possible for the mind to move out into society and nature, and for it to reach down into its deeper and more subtle areas, which Jung called the "collective unconscious." Despite the dominant role played by the self, and the mechanical orders of society and the successive movements of time, creativity still operates in limited domains and there is available to each one of us an unfocused sense of a deeper awareness. While listening to music, looking at a work of art, being overwhelmed by nature, or engaging in a new relationship, a person may be deeply moved and have a sense of touching something that lies outside the self. At such times there may even be a sense of the dissolution of fixed orders, the temporary ending of time and a loss of the self. This can also happen when the insistence of the mechanical orders of inner and outer worlds is weakened during sleep, hallucination, or intense creative work. In such cases awareness becomes much wider and deeper and it is possible for creativity to operate from a more flexible and energetic order.

Synchronicities are clearly of this very nature, for they open the floodgates of the deeper levels of consciousness and matter, which, for a creative instant, sweep over the mind and heal the division between the internal and the external. Something similar may be involved in what the psychologist Abraham Maslow calls "peak experiences," sudden ecstatic moments of great happiness, awe, and of a feeling of unity that gives way to serenity and contemplation.[1] Synchronicities, epiphanies, peak, and mystical experiences are all cases in which creativity breaks through the barriers of the self and allows awareness to flood through the whole domain of consciousness. It is the human mind operating, for a moment, in its true order and extending throughout society and nature, moving through orders of increasing subtlety, reaching past the source of mind and matter into creativity itself.

Such experiences release considerable meaning, energy, and creativity and give an intimation of the total transformation that is possible for both the individual and society. However, in so many cases people return to their lives unchanged, or with just the memory of an extraordinary experience. Only in exceptional cases does this opening of the floodgates of consciousness produce a true and lasting transformation in which the self is freed from the limited order of time. In his autobiography, Bertrand Russell describes his early life as being rather puritanical and concerned with abstraction rather than the more human feelings. One day he came upon the wife of his colleague, A. N. Whitehead, in severe pain. As he tells in his autobiography:

> She seemed cut off from everyone and everything by walls of agony, and the sense of the solitude of each human soul suddenly overwhelmed me.[2]

Russell went on to describe a feeling of the ground giving way beneath him and of finding himself in quite another region so that

> . . . at the end of those five minutes, I had become a completely different person. For a time a sort of mystic illumination possessed me. . . . I found myself filled with semi-mystical feelings about beauty and with an intense interest in children, and with a desire almost as profound as that of the Buddah to find some philosophy which should make human life endurable.[3]

Russell records that this vision faded but that

> Something of what I saw in that moment has remained always with me, causing my attitude during the first war, my interest in children, my indifference to minor misfortunes and a certain emotional tone in all my human relations.[4]

If Russell is to be believed, then this experience of a deeper awareness acted to transform his whole life. But in most cases, however, such a change is strictly limited, for our mechanical selves are never subtle enough to capture and dissolve into the deeper and faster movements of consciousness. Instead, the self is pervaded by reactive feelings and relatively mechanical thoughts. While the operation of thought is far more subtle in its movement than the orders of gross matter, it is nevertheless limited in comparison with the deeper movements that are potential in our consciousness. Clearly, it is only through the ending of the restricted orders of the self, which operate through its attachments to its own image, that the individual will be transformed. Even in the case of Bertrand Russell, the nature of his transformation was probably rather limited and operated on restricted areas of his life and personality. But is a deeper transformation possible in which creativity flows into all areas of consciousness?

According to the traditions of the Far East, and the writings of certain Western mystics, it is possible for there to be an "ending of time," which suggests that the attachment to a limited order of becoming may itself cease. This is also referred to as "the death of the self," a death in which the absolute image of eternity, which the self has created for itself, dies away and with it all the rigid, mechanical, and limited orders that block the flowering of creativity. In such a transformation the division between mind and body, individual and society, will end and consciousness will stretch out to embrace the global order of all nature and beyond. Clearly such a transformation is not confined to the mind of the individual but involves the whole of society. While the sequential order of time will remain, for the solution of certain practical problems, it will now have its proper place within a spectrum of time orders. Likewise the self will also continue to play its role within the life of the individual and society.

THE INDIVIDUAL AND WHOLENESS

Synchronicity gives us an image of what such a transformation may be like, for within the operation of its meaningful coincidences, time has its end and creativity dissolves and transcends all structures and distinctions. Synchronicity is an image of the creative source, for within its timeless moment, awareness floods over the whole of consciousness and matter to produce a profound sense of identity. Out of this timeless moment flow the events and patterns of the synchronicity. These extend across the artificial distinctions of mind and matter, self and body, individual and society, society and nature. Synchronicity is therefore an intimation of a much greater transformation. An intimation of a more creative life in which the self takes its proper place within consciousness.

In many contemporary writings, this notion of wholeness and the breaking down of rigid distinctions into the fluid cycle of birth and death is, however, portrayed in a rather loose and nebulous fashion. Indeed, the notion of "holism" has become rather fashionable so that it suggests a self that becomes immersed in a warm bath of mindless gravy. Clearly this notion of holism is alien to the approach of this book. A better image is that of an intense and vibrant stillness. This experience of stillness is sometimes achieved during creative work, in close contact with nature, or in some forms of meditation. It can be described as both an emptiness and a fullness. It is empty because the constant movement of becoming and the sequential order of thought slows down and there is a sense of being released from attachments to fixed positions. That constant activity of thought that has been called "the monkey" begins to operate with less intensity as the whole body and mind become quiet so that a much more subtle movement may be sensed. It is full because the intense watchfulness and awareness that has always been present is now experienced more directly.

In this stillness, mind and body are no longer experienced as being divided and a great energy floods the whole system. A person may no longer feel bound and restricted by time and is alert, almost vibrating with awareness. This stillness can then lead to more effective forms of action in which mind and body, attention and awareness, self and consciousness are no longer divided. It is the stillness not of sleep or boredom but of the tiger in the forest or a mind that is totally focused on a creative task.

To merge with the whole is not, therefore, to drown in the bath of indistinctness but is to awake into a state of considerable awareness and activity. For the whole is richly structured and contains many orders of great dynamism and subtlety. Reality emerges out of the source of unconditioned creativity and, through its operation, unfolds orders and distinctions of higher and higher degrees. The world of matter, for example, unfolds through its implicate orders into explicate form which then feeds back into its underlying levels.

Clearly such a whole is far from being structureless, for it is particularly rich in its internal, dynamic operation. Within it, the material universe can by no means be considered as an "illusion," since both the explicate and the implicate have their roles to play in creating reality.

Therefore in healing the division between the self and the whole, individuality is not lost, nor is the world treated as an illusion and time as unreal. Rather the self, matter, and time all have their place within the more subtle orders of movement that unfold from the source. Eternity does not exist outside the self; rather, eternity and time are equally real and have their origin within a common source. Likewise "to die to the self" does not mean to sacrifice all identity or freedom of action within the explicate world. Rather it suggests a dying of attachments to rigid, fixed forms and an unfolding of sequential time into its wider order. The self lives on but as one aspect of the more subtle movement that involves the order of the whole of consciousness.

This movement, which operates from the creative source, also acts to dissolve fragmentation, which could be defined as the splitting of things that belong together and the drawing together of things that belong apart. So the dissolution of fragmentation does not imply the abandonment of all distinctions and categories; rather, it suggests that distinctions are constantly being created, modified, and ended in harmony with the general movement of reality.

At the origin of civilization the desires to wonder, worship, and understand may well have been all of a piece. At least this is the impression that comes down to us from the earliest myths, rituals, and works of art. The knowledge that came from this understanding, and the social structures that flowed out of the religious and social sense, albeit rather limited and undifferentiated were, nonetheless, deeply pervaded with meaning. It is this sense of meaning, and oneness, that is so lacking in our lives, our relationships, and our institutions today. Wherever the need for creative change and transformation is perceived, it generally soon degenerates into a limited set of reactions and into fairly rigid structures. Somewhere along the way the human race lost the spice and excitement of simply being alive.

In the time of the ancient Greeks there was a great thirst for understanding. The birth of philosophy made no distinction between religion and science; all sprang from the same source of wonder and awe. Philosophy concerned itself with the origin, source, and nature of all things, with how certain knowledge is to be obtained, with the operations of reason and language, with the good conduct of the individual, and the proper operation of society. Philosophy was a whole in which all things and all questions could be explored. Its intentions were to enrich the human mind and give it even greater freedom.

However, over the centuries, science began to separate itself from philosophy to the point where, today, many scientists have little time for philosophical speculations. Likewise science fragmented itself into a host of different subjects and specialties and philosophy divided itself into a number of restricted academic concerns. Understanding today has given way to the accumulation of knowledge, and knowledge itself is divided into a myriad of specializations. In this way, as our knowledge of the universe, and of ourselves, becomes more and more detailed and differentiated, it begins to lose all sense of its wider context. It becomes knowledge without meaning and without understanding. But very clearly, all the different areas of modern knowledge must, at a deeper level, have significant interrelationships. The way in which we view the material universe, for example, has a profound effect on the way we behave in our daily lives. Our "psychology" cannot be differentiated from the whole order and nature of the society we live in. Philosophy, psychology, science, art, and religion all spring from a deep human response to the universe and cannot be pursued in isolation but must always be carried out from within a much wider context.

What is being advocated here is not a return to the approach of, for example, the ancient Greeks, but a movement forward toward a greater sensitivity and awareness of the limitless possibilities and potentialities of the whole universe. This book began with a discussion of synchronicities, of meaningful coincidences that appeared to defy the normal laws of causality that operate within our universe. At first, the particular incidents of synchronicity may have appeared to be rather superficial and not particularly moving. However, they were intended simply as clues, as tiny cracks in the surface of our rationality that hint at a much deeper world that may lie beyond. Now we have seen that world, or at least taken a first glimpse at it. It suggests that we have built our lives and our civilizations on an illusion. An illusion of the supreme reality of the self, of becoming over being, of temporal progress over infinitely more subtle time orders that merge into eternity of the surface reality of things over their deeper, hidden orders. Synchronicities have opened a window onto a creative source of infinite potential, the well-spring of the universe itself. They have shown how mind and matter are not distinct, separate aspects of nature but arise in a deeper order of reality. Synchronicities suggest that we can renew our contact with that creative and unconditioned source which is the origin not only of ourselves but of all reality. By dying to the self and its mechanical, reactive responses to nature, it becomes possible to engage in an active transformation and gain access to unlimited ranges of energy. In this way, body and consciousness, individual and society, mind and matter may come to achieve their unlimited potential.

Synchronicities have therefore served as the starting point on a journey that has led us to the limits of human imagination. Once we realize that our consciousness is without limit, then it becomes possible for us to engage in a creative transformation of our own lives and of the society we live in. From this perspective, we will have no more need for tortoise shells and milfoil stalks for we will have learned to live with the wisdom and understanding that has been present in us since the dawn of humanity.

NOTES

1. *The Farther Reaches of Human Nature* (Harmondsworth, Eng.: Penguin, 1971).
2. *The Autobiography of Bertrand Russell*, vol. I (London: Allen and Unwin, 1967).
3. Ibid.
4. Ibid.

INDEX

Active information, 166–179, 186, 194
Air resistance, 43–44, 47
Alchemy, 14, 19, 21
Archetypes, 198
Aristotle, 53, 154, 155, 202
Art, 31–32
Astronomy, 29, 154–155
Atoms, 191, 192
Attention, 222–226
Awareness, 222–226, 234–236

Babylon, 190
Bardo state, 206
Bateson, Gregory, 83, 199
Baum, L. Frank, 120
Bayeux Tapestry, 3
Bernard instability, 78–79
Big bang theory, 194–195
Binary code, 135
Biology, 4, 5
Bohm, David, 142, 168–171, 172–173, 176, 183, 186, 192, 194
Bohr, Neils, 4, 15, 185
Bone oracles, 124–126, 129–133, 141, 143, 144, 145
Book of Changes. See I Ching
Brain, 106–111, 151–153, 178, 201, 217–218, 222
Buckley, Paul, 87
Burghölzi Clinic, 10
Byers-Brown, W., 20

Cabinet of Dr. Caligari, The, 30
Calculus, 31
Carbon atom, 156
Casimir, H. B. G., 21, 121
Catholic church, 230

Causality, 35–47, 52, 56–57
Cells, 59–60, 63, 66, 80, 159–161
Chemistry, 4, 5, 39, 80, 155, 156
China, 3, 14, 30, 65, 66, 125–146
Christianity, 230–231
Clusterings of events, 7–10, 25, 26, 65–66
Coincidence, 1, 7–10, 23, 25, 32, 61
Collective unconscious, 99–112, 148, 166, 234
Confucius, 134, 138
Consciousness. *See* Mind
Contexts, 209–211
Coriolis forces, 44
Creation myths, 190, 196, 202, 206
Creativity, 185–212, 215–218, 226
Crystals, 162–165

Darwin, Charles, 31
De Cusa, Nicholas, 207
Democritus, 191, 192
Descartes, René, 149–150, 153, 171–172, 187
Dialectic, 205–206
Dickens, Charles, 28–29
Dissipative structures, 77–80
DNA, 160–162, 166
Dreams, 18–20, 28–29, 100–102, 106–107, 123–125, 174, 220

Eccles, Sir John, 151
Eckhart, Meister, 207
Edelman, G. M., 201
Egypt, 190, 191, 197, 209
Einstein, Albert, 155
    anticipation of solitons, 76
    gravity, 43

Einstein, Albert *(continued)*
  and Kammerer's work, 9
  and Pauli's work, 15
  quantum theory, 32
  relativity, 54
  time, 228
Electromagnetism, 31
Electrons, 16, 68–70, 93, 192
Embryo, human, 159–160
Energy, 155, 192–195
Eternity, 228–237, 239
Evolution, 30–31
Experiences, 85–88

Ferenczi, Sandor, 100
Fibonnaci series, 89
Field phenomena, 55, 56
Fine structure constant, 22
Ford, Alan, 123
Franck, J., 21
Freud, Sigmund, 10–12, 98–102, 111
Frogs, 222–223
Fu Hsi, 134

Galileo, 47–48, 53
Genetics, 160–162
Gnostics, 20, 196
Gravity, 3, 43, 48, 49–50, 154–155
Ground state. *See* Vacuum state
Gulliver's Travels, 29
Guth, Alan, 194

Hamilton-Jacobi theory, 55–56, 155,
  169
Han dynasty, 135
Hanna, Barbara, 25
Hawking, Stephen, 194
Hegel, Georg, 205–206
Heisenberg, Werner, 4, 14–15, 26, 40,
  64, 94, 103, 195
Heraclitus, 191, 192
Hero of Alexandria, 53
Hexagrams, 134–138, 140, 143, 144,
  182
Holography, 172–173
Hsü, J., 137
Hume, David, 40–41

I Ching, 133–141, 143–146, 181–183
Immune system, 61–62, 186
Implicate order, 166–179, 189, 192
Indeterminism, 37–38
*Individual Dream Symbolism in Relation
  to Alchemy*, 18

Inflationary universe theory, 194–195
*Interpretation and Nature of the Psyche,
  The*, 22–23
Interpretation of Dreams, 10
Ireland, Northern, 216

James, William, 173
Jung, Carl, 10–14, 17–29, 57, 106
  classic synchronicity, 6–7
  collective unconscious, 99–103, 108,
    148, 166, 234
  creatura, 197, 202
  definition of synchronicity, 35
  dualities, 205
  ESP experiments, 199
  I Ching, 133, 138–139, 141, 143
  logic, 206
  objective unconscious, 105
  origin of synchronicity, 188
  pleroma, 191, 196–197
  psychoid, 187–188, 198

Kammerer, Paul, 7–10, 14, 25
Kandel, Eric, 108–109, 152, 178
Kelvin, Lord, 3–4
Koestler, Arthur, 9, 65
Kuhn, Thomas, 120

Laing, R. D., 199
Lake, B. M., 74
Lakes, 45
Language, 141–142, 144
Lao Nai-hsuan, 138
Lao-tzu, 188
Lasers, 70
Lawrence, T. E., 1, 221, 227
Laws of Form, 199
Leibnitz, Gottfried Wilhelm von, 31,
  135
Leonardo da Vinci, 53
Leucippus, 191, 192
Lewis, G. H., 28
Life, organization of, 59–63, 155–156
Light, 31, 186, 187–188
Linde, A. D., 194
Linear systems, 71, 81, 83
Logic, 199–206
Longshang people, 126, 129
Lorenz, Edward, 44
Lyell, Sir Charles, 31

Malebranch, Nicholas, 54
Mansfield, M. F., 29
Maslow, Abraham, 235

Matter, 103, 148–183
  elementary particles, 93–96
  inanimate, 162
  internal structure of, 167
  and mind, 103–111, 148–154, 165, 169, 174, 182, 185–187, 214–215
  origins of, 194
  patterns of, 88–90, 196
  subtle orders of, 154–157
Maxwell, James Clerk, 31, 155
Mechanics, 193
  mechanical universe, 35–58
  Newtonian, 3, 4–5, 36–37, 53, 54
  quantum, 15, 151, 168
Medicine, 3
Memory, 162–164, 166, 173, 174
Metals, 68–70, 71, 73
Middle Ages, 3, 14, 65, 66, 154
Middle East, 190, 197, 216
Mind, 148–183
  collective, 99–112
  conscious, 217–221, 225–229, 235
  and matter, 103–111, 148–154, 165, 169, 174, 182, 185–187, 214–215
  mechanical order of, 157–159, 174–175
  unconscious, 11–14, 97–112
Mindel, Arnold, 27–29, 32
Molecules, gas, 50–51, 162–163, 192
Morphic fields, 159–168
Morphogenesis, 59–61
Motion, 45, 47–48, 50, 53–56, 149, 154–155
Mountcastle, V. B., 201
Murnau, F. W., 29

Naskapi Indians, 122–126, 143, 145, 148, 220, 233
Nature
  field theories of, 55
  interconnections in, 47
  patterns of, 2, 9, 21, 96
  realities of, 3–5
  transformations of, 230
Nervous system, 151, 152, 153, 177, 186
Newton, Isaac, 83, 86, 171
  calculus, 31
  causality, 36, 38, 52
  gravity, 3, 43, 48, 49, 154–155
  laws of motion, 45, 48, 50, 56, 149, 154–155
  light, 31
  mechanics, 3, 4–5, 36–37, 53, 54
  time, 228–229, 231
Nonlinearity, 71–74, 76, 77, 81
Nosferatu, 29
Number 137, 22

Objective unconscious, 105

Paradigms, 119–122, 141, 179
Particles, 93–96, 168–170, 192, 195
Pauli, Wolfgang, 10, 14–26, 40, 57, 94, 102, 103, 121, 148
Pauli effect, 21–22
Pauli principle, 15–17, 93
Peters, R. H., 45–46
Philosophy, 239–240
Phonons, 73, 93
Phosphorus, 45
Physics, 4–5, 17, 24, 25–26, 37, 47, 88
Planck, Max, 32, 54
Pleroma, 191, 196–209
Plotinus, 188
Pool (billiards), 39–40, 41, 50, 52, 56
Popper, Karl, 179
Pribram, Karl, 173
Prigogine, Ilya, 64, 78–80, 140, 181, 183
Probability, 10, 38, 199
Progoff, Ira, 25
Psycho-Analytic Congress, 11, 12
Psychoid, 187–188, 198
Psychology, 25–26, 97–104

Quantum theory, 4, 15, 32, 37, 54, 64, 94, 151–152, 155, 163, 168–170, 185, 186, 192

Reductionism, 39, 60, 63–65, 75, 83, 104, 179–181
Relativity, 4, 15, 54
Russell, Bertrand, 198, 201, 235–236
Russell, J. Scott, 74

St. Augustine, 230
Schönberg, Arnold, 210
Science, 154, 179–180
  fragmentation, 113–114
  laws of, 87
  power of, 37
  rise of, 47
  scientific approach, 3
Science, Order and Creativity, 142

Sea slug, 152, 178
Self, 224–229, 232, 233–239, 241
Seriality, 7–10, 25
Seven Sermons to the Dead, 13
Shang people, 126–133, 141, 145, 148, 232
Sheep, 165
Sheldrake, Robert, 162–167, 183
Slime mold, 66–68
Snow, C. P., 77
Snyder, S. J., 160
Solitons, 74–77
Space-time, 193–194
Speck, Frank, 124
Spenser-Brown, G., 198–202, 204, 205, 206
Steinhart, P. J., 194
Stillness, 237–238
Storr, Anthony, 28
Structures, 209–211
Superconductivity, 70, 75
Superfluids, 70, 75
Swift, Jonathan, 29
Symmetries, 89–90, 94, 103
    abstract, 93–97, 195
    broken, 90–93, 196
    constitutive, 90, 92
    descriptive, 90
Synchronicity, 1–2, 5–7, 22–32
    development of idea of, 12
    and *I Ching*, 181–183
    as intimation of transformation, 237
    Jung-Pauli concept of, 10, 16, 21, 22–26, 61, 121
    of living organisms, 61–62
    and meaningful patterns, 114–119
    metaphors for, 81–82
    Mindel's work, 27–29, 32
    natural history of, 26–32

and structure, 81–83
Tantric texts, 14
Taoism, 21, 22, 136, 138, 188
Tennis, 43–45, 50, 52
Thermodynamics, 77–80, 87
Thought. *See* Mind
Tibet, 206
Tigers, 221–222
Time, 41, 42, 174, 175, 228–237
    See also Space-time
Titanic, 29
Trigrams, 134, 136–137
Turner, Joseph, 31

Uncertainty principle, 4
Unconscious mind, 11–14, 97–112

Vacuum state, 191–196
Varese, Edgar, 210
Variation principle, 54, 55
Vermeer, Jan, 31
Von Franz, Marie-Louise, 25–26, 139

Waddington, C. H., 161–162
Weather, 44–45
Weine, Robert, 30
Wells, H. G., 217
Wheeler, John, 4, 37, 87, 193, 205
Wholeness, 237–240
Whorf, Benjamin Lee, 142
Wigner, Eugene, 151–152
Wilhelm, Helmut, 65, 82, 140
Wilhelm, Richard, 22, 30, 138, 141
Wizard of Oz, The, 120
Wordsworth, William, 2, 221
Worldview. *See* Paradigms

Yuan, H.C., 74

ABOUT THE AUTHOR

David Peat was born in Liverpool, England, in 1938. After obtaining a Ph.D. at Liverpool University he moved to Canada, first to teach at Queen's University and then to carry out research at the National Research Council of Canada. His investigations into quantum mechanical structure and the foundations of relativity and quantum theories led him to question the whole nature of the scientific worldview. In 1971, while working with David Bohm in London, he began to develop an interest in Carl Jung and the ideas of the collective unconscious, but he found them difficult, at first, to reconcile with the current approaches of science.

Over the last ten years Peat has devoted himself to pursuing this interest, and to writing a number of books, including *The Looking Glass Universe*, with John Briggs. He is currently working on a new book, *Science, Order and Creativity*, with David Bohm. His investigation into the underlying, subtle orders of consciousness and the universe have led him not only into science and psychology but also into writing for the stage and radio. Internal order and symmetry have also encouraged him to take up painting and sculpture in stone and bronze.